Hidden Treasures

Asia/Pacific/Perspectives
Series Editor: Mark Selden

Identity and Resistance in Okinawa
by Matthew Allen

Woman, Man, Bangkok: Love, Sex, and Popular Culture in Thailand
by Scot Barmé

*Making the Foreign Serve China: Managing Foreigners in the People's
Republic*
by Anne-Marie Brady

The Mongols at China's Edge: History and the Politics of National Unity
by Uradyn E. Bulag

Transforming Asian Socialism: China and Vietnam Compared
edited by Anita Chan, Benedict J. Tria Kerkvliet, and Jonathan Unger

*China's Great Proletarian Cultural Revolution: Master Narratives and Post-
Mao Counternarratives*
edited by Woei Lien Chong

North China at War: The Social Ecology of Revolution, 1937–1945
edited by Feng Chongyi and David S. G. Goodman

*Social and Political Change in Revolutionary China: The Taihang Base Area in
the War of Resistance to Japan, 1937–1945*
by David S. G. Goodman

*Local Democracy and Development: The Kerala People's Campaign for
Decentralized Planning*
by T. M. Thomas Isaac with Richard W. Franke

Islands of Discontent: Okinawan Responses to Japanese and American Power
edited by Laura Hein and Mark Selden

Women in Early Imperial China
by Bret Hinsch

Postwar Vietnam: Dynamics of a Transforming Society
edited by Hy V. Luong

Wife or Worker? Asian Women and Migration
edited by Nicola Piper and Mina Roces

Biology and Revolution in Twentieth-Century China
by Laurence Schneider

Contentious Kwangju: The May 18th Uprising in Korea's Past and Present
edited by Gi-Wook Shin and Kyong Moon Hwang

Hidden Treasures

Lives of First-Generation Korean Women in Japan

JACKIE J. KIM

With an introduction by Sonia Ryang

ROWMAN & LITTLEFIELD PUBLISHERS, INC.
Lanham • Boulder • New York • Toronto • Oxford

ROWMAN & LITTLEFIELD PUBLISHERS, INC.

Published in the United States of America
by Rowman & Littlefield Publishers, Inc.
A wholly owned subsidiary of The Rowman & Littlefield Publishing Group, Inc.
4501 Forbes Boulevard, Suite 200, Lanham, MD 20706
www.rowmanlittlefield.com

P.O. Box 317, Oxford OX2 9RU, UK

British Library Cataloguing in Publication Information Available

Library of Congress Cataloging-in-Publication Data

Kim, Jackie J., 1969–
    Hidden treasures : lives of first-generation Korean women in Japan / Jackie J. Kim.
        p.   cm. — (Asia/Pacific/Perspectives)
    Includes bibliographical references and index.
    ISBN 0-7425-3594-0 (cloth : alk. paper) — ISBN 0-7425-3595-9 (pbk. : alk. paper)
    1. Koreans—Japan—History. 2. Women—Japan—History. 3. Japan—Ethnic relations. I. Title. II. Series.

DS832.7.K6K5525   2005
305.48'8957052'0922—dc22

                                                                                      2004024108
Printed in the United States of America

To my Halmŏni
(1917–1992)

Contents

Part II
Journey of a New Bride

Part III
Solitary Sojourn

Part IV
Growing Up in Japan

Preface

Hidden Treasures presents life histories of first-generation Korean immigrant women in Japan as a contribution toward understanding the roots of Japan's largest minority population.

The ten women whose voices are arrayed in this book range in age from seventy-two to eighty-nine years at the time of interviewing, conducted between 1994 and 2000. They were born between the years 1910 and 1926, just as the Yi dynasty (1392-1910) came to an end with the start of Japanese colonial rule. They were among the nearly two million Koreans who came to Japan during Korea's colonial period.

Their feelings and inner thoughts told in everyday life settings bring forth important dimensions of lives at the margins of Japanese society. Their voices enrich the understanding of social conditions and political dynamics concerning Koreans in Japan by interweaving personal experiences with historical events. Each woman's narrative—spanning almost a century between two cultures, languages, and traditions—offers insight into the experiences and outcome of a colonial era.

The narratives reveal how, in the midst of the challenges of immigrant life, along with the hardships of World War II, first-generation Korean immigrant women through myriad strategies were able to survive. Their lives illuminate suffering and accomplishment, isolation, the breaking and forging of familial and communal solidarities, clashing traditions, and persistence in the face of social, political, and cultural challenges. The lives depicted in these pages have been chosen for their variety and depth.

All of the women interviewed spoke in a mixture of two languages—their Korean mother tongue and Japanese. Their narratives have been organized into subsections and repetitions have been minimized. However, the structure and language are entirely their own. I have attempted to preserve many of their pauses, sighs, exclamations of grievance, and laughs in order to maintain their varied voices and intonations.

A number of Korean and Japanese words and phrases that were used have been included followed by a translation or description to convey the nuances of the speaker. Throughout the text, endnotes clarify cultural elements as well as phrases, sentences, situations, or incidents, or briefly identify important historical events, topics, or issues. Korean and Japanese terms are defined in the glossary. For Korean, the McCune-Reischauer system of romanization has been used, and for Japanese, the modified Hepburn system.

The final culmination of this project is the fruit of labor by many who faithfully believed in its importance. My utmost love, respect, and applause go to all the women who invited me into their lives, and especially the ten stars who shine through these pages.

This book would have never come to form without the editorial and layout expertise and unending dedication of Michael Wachutka, my personal managing editor for life. Deep and sincere gratitude goes out to Mark Selden who guided this work to the finishing line, with patience, faith, and support. Many thanks to Yumi Selden for her encouraging words and keen editing skills, and a heartfelt appreciation to Sonia Ryang for her detailed and comprehensive introduction.

The present-day portrait photos of the women were taken by Gotō Yoshiya, one of the most talented young photographers I know. Chikako Kashiwazaki diligently read through the manuscript and contributed invaluable comments. Warm thanks to Pastor Kim Seung-Jae and family, John Stephan, Fukuoka Yasunori, Frank Baldwin, Linda Grove, John Clammer, James Farrer, David Slater, Ueno Chizuko, and Christine Yano whose faith in this project gave me strength in discouraging times.

Lastly, the love, prayers, and devotion of my mother Bok-Sun Kang and sister Christina E. Kim have been the wind beneath my wings. They are the pillars that support me and the anchor that steadies me. Finally, every inch of my heart goes to my life-mentor and inspiration who led me every step of the way. I am merely a pen in His hand.

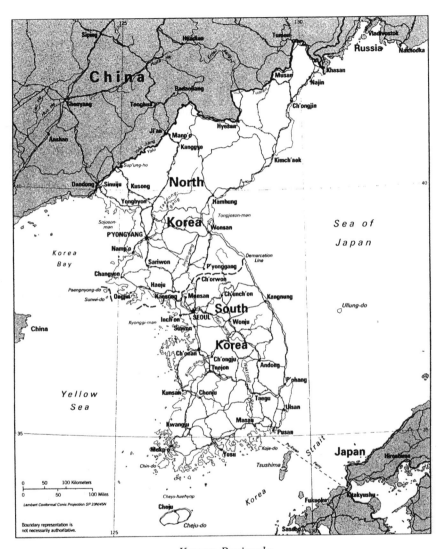

Korean Peninsula

Scale ca. 1:5,800,000; SP 23N/45N (E 124°-E 132° / N 44°-N 33°); Lambert conformal conic proj., Washington, D.C.: Central Intelligence Agency, 1993.

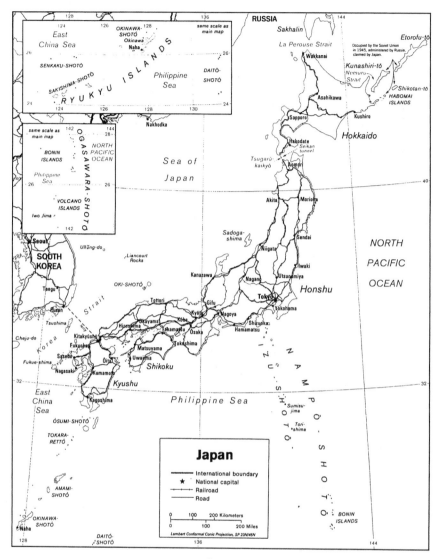

Japan

Scale ca. 1:11,600,000; SP 23N/45N (E 130°-E 150°/ N 50°-N 20°); Lambert conformal conic proj., Washington, D.C.: Central Intelligence Agency, 1996.

Introduction

On Korean Women in Japan: Past and Present

Sonia Ryang

In introducing Jackie J. Kim's unprecedented life histories of Korean-born women who have spent the last half century or more living in Japan, I face this predicament: how to render what is unique to these women intelligible to Western readers and also how to convey the fact that what first appears different and remote is in fact not so alien to our daily lives. This is because the intricacies of life are invariably subsumed within the most mundane yet at times the most unexpected ways. Often it is only in retrospect that those in the throes of life's turmoil recognize how difficult and complicated the situation has been. Life histories that the reader will encounter in the following pages are eloquent exemplars of such reflections.

What is unique to these women is their participation in tumultuous times in the modern history of Korea and Japan, involving multiple displacements physically and psychologically, geographically and culturally. From colonial subject to diasporic subject, from a young and naïve virgin bride to self-made matriarch, these women transformed themselves in multiple ways. Each transformation involved risk, determination, and pain, as the women grappled with multilayered structures of gendered, colonial, ethnic, and socioeconomic relations of power. Many of these transformations also, however, entailed self-enhancement, fulfillment, accomplishment, at times, triumph and joy. In order, then, for readers to visualize the cultural and historic complexity and specificity of the lives of these women, I first present an overview of the historical background in which they were born and grew to adulthood. This will be followed by a more specific discussion of the Korean community in Japan, the changing position of women within the community, and the generational gap pertaining to such matters as understanding of self, ethnicity, and the nation.

Historical Background

After decades of pressuring the Korean court, Japan formally colonized Korea in 1910. From then until Japan's defeat in World War II, Koreans experienced far-reaching historical change. Colonial rule transformed all aspects of the lives of the colonized. Together with efforts by the colonizer to pressure Koreans to become more Japanese, Koreans were introduced to new realms of science, knowledge, economy, society, and above all, social relations including kinship and personhood, or more concretely, what it meant to be a Korean under colonial rule (see Shin and Robinson 1999).

One immediate result of colonial rule was that large numbers of uprooted Korean farmers formed a free-floating labor pool: many in the northern part of Korea moved to Manchuria, Sakhalin, and Siberia, and many in southern Korea gravitated to Japan, in a desperate search for jobs. The stories of the women introduced here began in the southern part of Korea in the initial years of colonialism. While postwar Korean scholarship emphasizes the deep resistance to Japanese rule and generally ignores colonial migration with the exception of forced labor (or *kyōseirenkō;* see below), a large number of southerners chose migration to Japan as the best hope for overcoming poverty and finding economic opportunity: between 1919 and 1929, the number of Koreans in Japan increased from 26,605 to 275,206 in 1929 and by 1941 there were 1,190,444 (Morita 1996: 71).

Like immigrants throughout the world, many encountered arduous and underpaid work, living in shanty-town-like ghettos and facing ethnic discrimination and cultural disdain (see Weiner 1989). The majority of Korean migrants came as single male workers, creating a highly skewed male-female sex ratio as in the case of early Chinese migrants to the United States. In 1920, there were 11,543 Korean men and 917 Korean women between ages twenty and twenty-four. In 1930, 62,208 men compared with 19,555 women in the same age group and as late as 1940, there were 99,406 men as opposed to 54,387 women in this age group, a narrowing yet substantial gender gap (Morita 1996: 41).

After the invasion of China in 1937, Japan's Asian policy took a radical turn that profoundly affected Korea. Koreans were to be more fully integrated throughout the Empire not as Koreans but as new Japanese, newly born subjects of the Japanese emperor. A series of reforms was implemented to that effect. In 1939, the reform of household registers was carried out in the colony, making Korean household registry identical with its Japanese counterpart. This paved the way to making Korean males eligible for conscription as the emperor's soldiers. In 1941, Korean conscription began. In the same year, the Japanese government began drafting labor from the colony as Japan faced an increasingly acute shortage of industrial labor. With the outbreak of the Pacific War in 1941, securing labor became an absolute imperative for the empire. With millions of Japanese males drafted and sent abroad, and with many other Japanese emigrating to the new frontier in Manchuria, Korea's colonial rulers targeted Korean men as a crucial workforce. Koreans were brought to Japan as forced labor or *kyōseirenkō* to work in military industry, in mines, and construction; some were lured by false advertisements, some came as a result of government deception, and some were kidnapped or hoodwinked by Korean local leaders or profiteers. In short, Koreans came to the imperial metropolis by the hundreds of thousands.

When the Pacific War ended in August 1945, there were 2.4 million Koreans in Japan. With the destruction of Japan's cities and industry by U.S. bombing in the final months of the war and the return of Japanese troops, large numbers of Koreans faced unemployment. By 1948, following the repatriation of many to Korea, the total population of Koreans in Japan had been reduced to 588,000 (Wagner 1951: 95). This population would form the core of the so-called *zainichi* Koreans today.

Zainichi means "being in Japan." It is a relatively recent coinage. During the U.S. occupation of 1945 to 1952, Koreans in Japan were designated *zairyū chōsenjin* or Koreans "remaining" in Japan. In other words, in the minds of U.S. and Japanese authorities, despite the fact that they were Japanese citizens, Koreans remained in Japan as temporary sojourners. Their permanent settlement in Japan was unthinkable to the authorities. This migrant population, so avidly sought by Japanese authorities under prewar and wartime conditions of acute labor shortage, had become an unwelcome burden in the wake of military defeat and the return to Japan of millions of Japanese soldiers and settlers in Korea, Manchuria, and other parts of Asia. Presuming that all Koreans in Japan would eventually repatriate to Korea, the Japanese government showed no interest in providing assistance to integrate former colonial subjects who remained in the metropolis. Indeed, it marginalized Koreans by excluding them from the ranks of Japanese nationals, by canceling Japanese citizenship that Koreans had held under colonial rule (see below).

For their part, facing unemployment, loss of citizenship, and discrimination, most Koreans in Japan generally saw little reason to remain in Japan. Following the first wave of repatriation, however, news about the situation in their home towns and villages in southern Korea under U.S. military government began to filter back to Japan: severe inflation, political turmoil, social instability, cholera epidemics, violent clashes between the authorities and residents, and the installation of a U.S.-appointed regime with no significant indigenous support base. By comparison, northern Korea under the Soviet Union appeared to be led by Korean leaders with a record of anti-Japanese struggle. With uncertainty about a divided, unsettled, and occupied Korea, the remaining Koreans in Japan also divided along lines of allegiance to the northern and southern regimes with both sides looking to the eventual reunification of Korea. Many looked forward to return to their hometown following Korean reunification. Within a few years, however, the situation drastically changed with the devastation of the Korean War (1950-1953), the subsequent tension surrounding a divided Korea, and the prospect that Korea's partition might become permanent.

As Jackie J. Kim documents from diverse perspectives in this book, life in Japan for Koreans in general and women in particular was demanding. Under colonial rule and wartime conditions, many of the jobs available to them were arduous and poorly paid, and Koreans suffered numerous forms of discrimination. During the subsequent occupation, U.S. forces treated Koreans with suspicion, often suppressing their nationalistic demands by force (Koshiro 1999 and Inokuchi 2000). The nationality of Koreans who remained in postwar Japan was ambiguous and the 1947 legal reform required Koreans to register as aliens. The 1952 San Francisco Treaty signed between the United States and Japan, and excluding the Soviet Union and China among others, formally removed Koreans from membership in the Japanese nation. In other words, the treaty rendered them stateless. This was an unusual solution: in the cases of the independence of many African states in the early 1960s, measures were taken to prevent the production of stateless people. In 1952, however, Koreans simply lost Japanese citizenship without acquiring the citizenship of either of the two Koreas. Thus, by the handshake between the former colonial ruler (Japan) and the new dominant power in Asia (United States), Koreans in Japan became unwelcome elements in Japanese society who had no civil status (including nationality) and very few legal rights (including voting entitlements).

In 1965, Japan established diplomatic relations with South Korea. The Japan-ROK treaty guaranteed Koreans in Japan who opted for South Korean nationality permanent residence in Japan. This further divided the *zainichi* community. Those who did not apply for South Korean nationality were left as stateless persons in Japan.

Despite the fact that fully 98 percent of first-generation Koreans in Japan came from the southern provinces, at least initially large numbers of *zainichi* Koreans refused to accept South Korean nationality. In order to grasp this situation, it is necessary to examine the postwar emergence of rival politics within the Korean expatriate community in Japan. The complexity of Korean expatriate politics is revealed in the background of some of the women's lives introduced here, as directly or indirectly they experienced the tumultuous waves of postwar national partition and the subsequent fierce and bloody confrontation between the divided Koreas. Numerically, as well as in terms of organizational strength, supporters of the northern regime among the *zainichi* Koreans were more powerful. This was in no small part because of the positive image of the northern regime represented by the young anti-Japanese fighter Kim Il Sung (thirty-three years old in 1945), as opposed to that of the southern regime headed by the aging Syngman Rhee who returned from decades of living in the United States with his American wife. In the early years of the occupation, Korean communist leaders were released from jail in Japan. This also had an impact on expatriate politics: the majority of *zainichi* Koreans were not communists, but fiercely anti-

Japanese, and the communists' record of staunch resistance to the colonial authorities, therefore, appealed to many. The League of Koreans, formed in October 1945, came under communist influence and quickly won substantial support in the *zainichi* community, while the south-supporting organization, *Mindan* in its Korean abbreviation, failed to attract comparable mass support.

After the emergence of separate governments in Korea in 1948, and with the reverse course or right turn in U.S. occupation policy and growing support of the League for North Korea, in 1949 the occupation authorities banned the League, purged its leaders, and confiscated all of its properties and savings. Following the purge, supporters of North Korea joined the Japanese Communist Party and with the outbreak of the Korean War in June 1950, formed their own underground organization, *Minjŏn* in its Korean abbreviation. The Korean War sharply intensified the confrontation between *Minjŏn* and *Mindan*: *Mindan* sent volunteers to fight in support of the South in the Korean War, while *Minjŏn* waged an aggressive anti-*Mindan* campaign in Japan. By the time the Korean War ended in 1953, their divide was irreparable.

In the meantime, internal divisions between internationalists and nationalists split the Korean left. Internationalists held that Koreans in Japan needed to join efforts with the Japanese Communist Party in its goal of igniting simultaneous revolution throughout East Asia. In this thinking, Korea's revolutionary reunification would be achieved at the same time as Japan's revolution. Consequently, the first task for Koreans in Japan would be to cooperate in the Japanese revolution, much as Korean communists had supported the Chinese revolution in the course of the anti-Japanese resistance in the years 1931-1945. The nationalist group, by contrast, opposed this stance and insisted that Koreans in Japan needed to be part of the *Korean* revolution. Their first task was, therefore, to assist North Korea in its war against the United States. After the 1953 Korean armistice, in 1955, following a protracted debate, the Korean left, with nationalists in the ascendancy, reorganized their forces under the General Association of Korean Residents in Japan or *Chongryun* in its Korean abbreviation.

Chongryun declared itself an overseas organization affiliated with North Korea. Defining its task as working to improve North Korea's image in Japan, including the encouragement of repatriation to the north, it proclaimed that it would not interfere with Japan's internal politics. In this way, *Chongryun* sought to protect itself from another purge by the authorities. From the outset, the North Korean government supported *Chongryun*. Beginning in 1957, it contributed educational funds to help *Chongryun* to provide Korean language education for *zainichi* Koreans (on *Chongryun*, see Ryang 1997). From 1959, it also welcomed Koreans who wished to repatriate to North Korea. Between 1959 and 1984, 93,339 Koreans moved from Japan to North Korea. It was a one-way traffic, reflecting the lack of diplomatic connection between the two countries. Niigata, the northern Japanese city where Jackie's interviews began, became the port for Koreans' exodus to North Korea. Repatriation became an emblem of *Chongryun*'s political victory over *Mindan* (see Ryang 2000a for repatriation).

Seen this way, one can appreciate that the 1965 option to choose South Korean nationality came in the middle of the heightened tension in the deeply divided Korean community in Japan. Those who did not opt for South Korean nationality remained stateless, retaining the name *Chōsen* (Korea) in their alien registration certificate. *Chōsen*, however, does not connote any nationality. According to the interpretation of the Japanese alien registration law, it means that the carrier of this certificate or his or her ancestors originated in the Korean peninsula. As such, *Chōsen* represents no nation, not even North Korea, unlike *Kankoku*, which is the abbreviation for *Daikanminkoku* or the Republic of Korea. Only when one had acquired the permanent residence, one was eligible for social welfare and other benefits. By contrast, those who did not opt for *Kankoku* nationality had no national status, overseas travel document, or citizenship. Although not everyone who was affiliated with *Chongryun* had *Chōsen* registration, the great majority of *Chongryun* affiliates were bereft of civil rights in Japan and placed under tighter police surveillance than those who opted for the nationality of South Korea, Japan's Cold War ally in Asia. The effects of this "divide and rule" policy adopted by the Japanese authorities can be glimpsed in the words of many of the women Jackie J. Kim interviewed.

In 1979, the Japanese government ratified an international human rights covenant and in 1982 it joined the United Nations refugee convention. These treaties obliged it to change certain existing practice vis-à-vis Koreans and other minorities. Thus, in 1982, permanent residence became available for *zainichi* Koreans who did not accept South Korean nationality and for the first time in thirty-seven years since the end of the war, they became able to travel abroad with a reentry permit to Japan. In the early 1990s, the permanent residence for all *zainichi* Koreans was upgraded with wider access to benefits and social security.

The Korean Community in Japan

Throughout the Cold War, the politics internally dividing the Korean community touched all aspects of *zainichi* lives, encompassing what language to speak, how to call Korea "Korea"—either *Kankoku* or *Chōsen*, for example—questions of citizenship and education, and whom one's children should marry. Divided into *Chongryun* and *Mindan*, rival Korean expatriate leaders fought over the mass base for their organizations. For a long time, that is, until the 1980s, *Chongryun* held the upper hand in terms of number, organizational network, mobilization capacity, and material wealth. At its peak, *Chongryun* administered close to 180 Korean schools from elementary school to graduate school, closely supervised by its local headquarters and extending to each prefecture of Japan. *Chongryun* schools presented North Korea as "the genuine homeland of all Koreans including overseas Koreans" and North Korean leaders were revered as "Great Leader" and "Dear Leader" just as they were in schools in North Korea. Reflecting the long-lasting political turmoil and persecution under the military dictatorship in South Korea, and in the absence of independent information about life in North Korea, North Korea's popularity was strong among Koreans in Japan.

From the mid-1980s, many little-known aspects of North Korean society were disclosed to the world. Koreans in Japan faced the reality of North Korea's deteriorating economy, unequal distribution of power and wealth between leaders and the people, the leadership cult, and increasing isolation following the collapse of the Soviet Union, the development of strong Chinese ties to the United States and South Korea, and continued nuclear weapons development while ordinary people starved. News of North Korea had a special channel to reach Koreans in Japan. Following issuance of reentry permits to Japan to *Chongryun*-affiliated Koreans in the early 1980s, *Chongryun* organized regular trips to North Korea, facilitating family reunions with those who repatriated. This unprecedented contact eventually revealed to the families in Japan the deep suspicions with which repatriated Koreans were viewed in North Korea and the discrimination faced by those who had supposedly returned to the "motherly bosom of our fatherland." More serious allegations included deaths and missing among repatriated family members. It was against this background that the news of abduction of Japanese civilians by North Korean agents during the 1980s was disclosed to media in Japan and beyond, after the Japanese prime minister Koizumi's visit to North Korea in 2002. This was the last straw for the confidence and trust that Koreans in Japan had placed in North Korea (see Ryang 2003).

The decline of North Korea's popularity, however, did not necessarily mean the rise of South Korea's popularity among Koreans in Japan. By the 1980s, the major protagonist in diasporic nationalism, the first generation, was reduced to a handful of elders among the overall population of Koreans in Japan. Japan-born younger generations, though sympathetic with their parents' and grandparents' cause, grew up more and more immersed in Japanese popular and youth cultures, fully exposed to Japanese media, advertising, and fashion, as well as books and film. The younger generations are fluent in Japanese; even those who studied in *Chongryun*'s Korean schools where the instructional language is Korean and they are taught Korean in all levels speak Japanese at home and among their Korean friends and neighbors, dividing the use of Korean and Japanese between school and all other spheres of life (Ryang 1997: chaps. 1 and 2). As soon as they graduate from Korean high school, except for a minority that attends *Chongryun*'s college (Korea University), they are absorbed in Japanese society in terms of job and recreation.[1] Even those who are employed by Korean enterprises conduct business as well as their social lives in Japanese. Furthermore, even *Chongryun*'s cadres and officers speak Japanese outside the office and formal occasions, among themselves, their friends, and their family. Today, unlike the 1960s and 1970s, although the majority of Koreans in Japan hold South Korean nationality, this is not translated into stronger political commitment to South Korea or hostility toward North Korea. Korea's reunification and the repatriation of all *zainichi* Koreans, the ideal that the first generation strenuously upheld, have since become insignificant and irrelevant to the lives of younger generations, who see their future to be existing in Japan, not in Korea.

As early as the 1970s, the number of marriages involving Korean and Japanese partners exceeded those in which both partners were Korean (Kim 1996: 179). At the end of the last century, less than 20 percent of all registered marriages involving Koreans consisted of Korean-to-Korean marriage. Since the 1980s, moreover, the high hurdles placed as obstacles to naturalization were somewhat reduced, and hundreds of thousands of Koreans have naturalized as Japanese citizens. It is said that in the year 1995 alone, ten thousand Koreans became naturalized Japanese citizens (Kashiwazaki 2000: 29).[2]

Generational differences evident in the life histories introduced in this volume are as important as are gender difference in shaping the Korean community in Japan. Korean literary output in Japan was long dominated by male writers who were either first generation or older second generation. These writers, all deeply engaged in expatriate politics, were committed to the reunification ideal and the eventual repatriation of all *zainichi* Koreans to the homeland (see Lie 2000). Their writings tended to focus on nostalgia for the lost patria, the alien and oppressive qualities of life in Japan, resistance to ethnic discrimination, above all highlighting the temporary or transient nature of the life in Japan for Koreans. These themes were presented from distinctly male-dominant perspectives. Women's images in their writings often highlighted the figure of the suffering, oppressed, abused, yet all-loving mother, sacrificing to support a violent husband's drinking and gambling while raising children as proper and proud Koreans under hostile conditions.

In the 1980s, the Korean literary milieu in Japan was shaken by the award of the Akutagawa Prize, arguably the most prestigious Japanese literary award, to a naturalized Korean woman, Yi Yang-ji. As a naturalized citizen, her Korean pen name "Yi Yang-ji" is not her legal name, yet she presented herself as a Korean woman in Japan, who was struggling to recover her lost ethnic essence. The Akutagawa Prize had been awarded to a Korean author before, but it was a male of the older generation. What was different in Yi's case is that she vividly captured her painful and ultimately abortive journey to recover her Korean origin: her prize winning *Yuhi* is the story of a *zainichi* Korean girl studying in South Korea, a story that doubles with her own, as Yi herself went to South Korea to study, only to be spurned by her fellow Koreans for being too Japanized. Her personal quest for home and authenticity of the self resulted in a number of provocative writings that shed light on the complex intersection of nation and gender.

What does it mean to be a Korean in Japan for a young woman like Yi? What does it mean, furthermore, to be a naturalized Japanese of Korean origin? What, then, does it mean to write about such agony that was personal and at the same time, political, born as a result of a historical past involving Japanese colonial rule, confrontation between the two Koreas, and the turmoil of ethnic politics and discrimination against Koreans in Japan? Can Yi ever simply be a woman with a gendered identity alone, and not a Korean woman or a naturalized Japanese woman when ethnic and national identities impose themselves heavily on her? These questions infuse her literary creation. Her writings were criticized by some for being insufficiently nationalist or nationally conscious, that is, for failing to explicate themes of expatriate politics, and even for insisting that ultimately the search for identity for *zainichi* Koreans must be centered in Japan, not necessarily in Korea. But others have seen in Yi's writings the dawn of a new era—one in which Korean women unapologetically expressed their own gendered identity and in which women, by their very marginalization in both the *zainichi* community and in Japanese society, discovered and embraced their own ambivalence (see Hayes 2000 and Wender 2000).

A similar shift is evident in the everyday lives of Korean women in Japan. Researchers have noted that the homeland-oriented expatriate movement silenced women's personal realm. My past ethnographic fieldwork involving life histories of Korean women in Japan revealed that the orthodox nationalist discourse of colonial displacement of Koreans in Japan, which characterizes the forced labor mobilization or *kyōseirenkō* as the totalizing and authentic past of *zainichi* Koreans, effectively undermines other experiences of the colonial past. Specifically, women's past is ignored within this framing of colonial oppression: women may have experienced a more direct and brutal violence from their husband or in-laws in the strictly patriarchal and patrilineal kinship system of traditional Korea, and in its transplanted version in Japan. Yet, representation of such experiences was suppressed by the women themselves who internalized the dominant expatriate discourse that constructed and shaped the representation of colonial history (see Ryang 1998a, 1998b). Jackie's life histories open a new horizon making it possible to explore this unexcavated theme, bringing to light women's words that touch the hitherto unclaimed past that existed outside the public, political, and male-dominated expatriate sphere of Koreans in Japan. These include stories of domestic violence by both husband and sons, and of betrayal and exploitation outside the orthodox discourse of colonial oppression. But they also highlight personal triumphs and accomplishments in overcoming dehumanizing conditions associated both with Japanese society and familial life, conditions that each of these migrant women faced. Each woman's history and story illustrate the complex intertwining of the personal and the political, the national and the diasporic experience.

What is important to register, in introducing Jackie J. Kim's valuable work, is her methodology of letting women's words speak for themselves, one that falls within an honored tradition of oral history. Oral history was initially used to record nonliterate people's culture and experience. Anthropologists have long turned to oral history or life history to document lives of people who have not learned to write or read (Shostak 1981 and Mintz 1974, for example). The validity of this method, however, has been subjected to numerous critiques, especially during the 1980s, reflecting a fierce debate within anthropology, literary criticism, history, and other disciplines pivoting on issues of intersubjectivity, translation, and the authority of authorship. In anthropology, the emergence of books such as *Writing Culture* (Clifford and Marcus 1986) was at once reflective and constitutive of ongoing questioning of the way oral data are collected in the course of fieldwork. Diverse questions were raised, touching upon the politi-

cal and epistemological premise of ethnographic practice. How can the ethnographer claim the text as his or hers when it is a product of intersubjective
exchange with informants and interviewees in the field, mostly relying on their
words and representations? How can the author explicate the situation and
subjecthood of the informants, while not asserting his or her own authority and
authorial intervention? How else, then, other than by collecting oral data in the
voice of the interviewees, can an author bring to life the voices of the oppressed
as well as their silence? Moreover, even when the reader or listener sees or hears
only the words of the informant, to what extent is the product mediated by the
presence or interventions of the ethnographer? Is there any plausible method that
scholars can deploy to authenticate the voices of the oppressed, or is oral history
inevitably distorted as a result of the author's role in filtering or mediating the
so-called "raw" voices of the interviewees?

A recent case in point is that of Rigoberta Menchú. Rigoberta's stories in *I,
Rigoberta Menchú, an Indian Woman in Guatemala* (Burgos-Debray 1984) offered a shocking revelation of the oppression of the indigenous population and
the state of deprivation, suppression, and international indifference to which indigenous people have long been subjected. Rigoberta Menchú received the Nobel Peace Prize in 1992. Seven years later, David Stoll published a book charging that there were serious factual misrepresentations in the stories (Stoll 1999).
To be sure, Rigoberta Menchú may not have represented the story of "all poor
Guatemalans," just as the discourse of *kyōseirenkō* or forced labor does not represent the colonial past of "all Koreans in Japan." Indeed, the way Korean
women in Japan have been universally subsumed within orthodox (male-dominant) discourse on the colonial past disconcertingly reflects intracommunity relations of power, as suggested earlier. Nevertheless, the story of forced labor
needs to be continuously told, side by side with nonorthodox representations of
the colonial past. This is important especially given the lack of recognition of
the violations committed under forced labor and the refusal of the Japanese government to provide compensation to former colonial victims including the "comfort women." Likewise, the story of Rigoberta and her family as told by
Rigoberta herself needs to be heard in order for the world to have a firsthand
(even partial) account of indigenous people's lives in Guatemala.[3]

Practitioners of oral history have long recognized that stories told by one
who experienced the events give us one significant version of the events (see,
for example, Tonkin 1992). But even first-person accounts are mediated. To put
what has been narrated into text involves a number of transformations and metamorphoses. First, copies of words (even those that were tape-recorded) need to
be put into a written system of a given language, often a language different from
the original. We repeat ourselves, make corrections, ask the listener to wait
while we think about the right word, recall that what we said was not accurate,
and think as we speak. In other words, the practice of speaking or storytelling is
never as coherent or as seamless as it frequently appears in the text (see Crapanzano 1986). The oral historian/ethnographer typically seeks to put incoherent
words into a coherent and structured framework. This involves the application of

conventions of a writing system to the unconventional, unique, unsystematic, and above all unpredictable ways in which individuals speak. Even when the author deliberately tries to preserve laughter, pause, and other contingencies accompanying speech, they nevertheless are "written about" in the final analysis. Nevertheless, giving voice to the voiceless, that is, the oppressed, persecuted, victimized people whose history is marginalized, excluded, and erased by the "official" history is itself a project worth pursuing despite textual limitations and inevitable metamorphosis of the spoken to the written. The dilemma of translating spoken words into written language is not something that the oral historian/ethnographer should deny or avoid, in my view; rather, conscious use should be made of the discrepancy between spoken and written language, externalizing and analyzing it, and making the reader aware of the limitations as well as potential of such a project.[4]

Japanese historians, folklorists, linguists, journalists, and reporters have a long history of using oral history as a primary method to collect data. The work of Yanagita Kunio, whom one might call the founding father of Japanese folklore studies, consists of detailed recording of oral data. A more recent case is the corpus of Honda Katsuichi. His skillful use of oral history, interviews, and conversations with the survivors of the Nanjing massacre of 1937, with the anti-U.S. Vietnamese guerilla soldiers during the Vietnam War, and with ethnic and other minorities such as the Ainu of northern Japan, who struggle to preserve and create their cultural heritage in resistance to the dominant culture, have been as effective in recording the voices of the voiceless as the work has been controversial (Honda 1981, 1993, 1999, for example). Oral history has been widely used by critical sociologists in Japan to document the reality of oppression and discrimination that Japan's minorities and outcasts face. Researchers sympathetic with residents of *Buraku* or "special hamlets," who have been subjected to discrimination over the centuries, consciously use the method of *kikitori* or "listening and taking" records.

The history of *zainichi* Koreans is another important branch in which the *kikitori* method has proved to be effective. In light of the lack of proper compensation, reparation, and apology on the part of the Japanese government with regard to colonial and wartime atrocities as well as slave labor, *zainichi* Korean scholars and writers in Japan have used the *kikitori* method in order to record the words of people without history, that is, those whose experiences have been largely excluded from history books. The words of Korean survivors of the forced labor recruitment or *kyōseirenkō*, for example, have been primarily responsible for bringing the attention of postwar Japanese society to the slave labor that Koreans and Chinese were subjected to in the mines and factories during the war (see Pak 1965, 1992, for example). Numerous researchers and individuals, both Korean and Japanese, participate in this project (see, for example, Pak, Yamada, and Yang 1993 and Hayashi 1989, 1994).[5] More recently, in English, voices of younger generations of Koreans have appeared in eclectic collections of interviews (see, for example, Fukuoka 2000). The uses of oral history are particularly essential where official records do not exist, are silent on the issues, or, as in the case of many sensitive issues of war and colonialism, have been deliberately destroyed by the Japanese authorities.

Compared to the documentation of forced labor, in which the victims are mainly men, Korean women's oral history lagged. While oral history projects on forced labor took place as early as the 1960s, it was only in the late 1980s that Korean women told the story of their experiences as "comfort women," eventually providing a rich documentary record. The major rectification of this situation rose from among the former "comfort women" themselves who had been forced to work as prostitutes for the Japanese military during wartime, frequently under slave labor conditions. The telling of their stories had to wait for the friction and adjustment in nation-to-nation relations between the Japanese and South Korean states and, especially, for the end of the Cold War. In other words, prior to the "elevating" of the comfort women issue into governmental discourse between Japan and the Republic of Korea, women who had been forced to work as prostitutes for the Japanese military were ostracized, humiliated, and silenced as a national shame for Koreans and as a story that could not be told internationally. With recent interventions by feminist and human rights groups in South Korea, assisted by Korean and Japanese feminists in Japan, former comfort women were given a legitimate venue to convey their personal histories.[6] As former comfort women began to speak about their experiences, revealing multiple oppressions to which they had been subjected—first, by the Japanese military and imperialism, and second, by postwar Korean society that adhered to the logic of maleownership of the nation's women, rendering their past of military sexual workers an unspeakable shame and therefore forcing them to maintain silence—testimonials were recorded and the role of oral history of this generation of Korean women became an extremely important site of historical memory and political intervention.

Important dimensions of the problem of documenting women's lives persist, however. For example, the ways in which Korean women, as daughters, wives, and mothers, suffered at the hands of their own fathers, husbands, and sons still largely remain an unrecorded part of the history of the colonial era in Korea, in Japan, and in Manchuria. Similarly, the numerous ways in which women resourcefully worked in order to feed their children by accepting jobs as trash collectors or home-brewers are scarcely mentioned in the history of expatriate life, because such activities are generally seen by the writers of official histories of the Korean diaspora as part of an illegitimate or embarrassing past. In this light, I wish to draw the reader's attention to the concept of home in the diaspora. More often than not, in our language the woman of a household is referred to as a "homemaker." This seemingly innocent term could not be more controversial when applied to the cases of the elderly Korean women in Japan whose stories are told here. Under both the male-dominant kinship system of Korea and the sexist structure of Japanese society, these women had no entitlement to the resources of the family and lineage, and hardly any claim on inheritance. Often it is said that until a Korean bride bore a son, she had no place in her husband's family. But, even this is not the full story. Sometimes, as at least one example in

Jackie J. Kim's interviews shows, sons internalize male-dominant norms and inflict violence on their mothers.

If, in the words of *zainichi* critic Suh Kyungsik, Koreans in Japan are "quasi-refugees" in the contemporary nation-state system (Suh 2003), Korean women in Japan of the generation of Jackie's interviewees were frequently refugees in their own homes and families, in the sense that as young brides they typically did not have a place in the domestic hierarchy; living with chronic instability due either to poverty or domestic violence, many gave birth to multiple children alone and without assistance, and experienced painful relations with their husbands. Scholars have paid some attention to the ways in which the diaspora experience differentially affects women and men, but in the case of Korean women in Japan, diaspora is embedded in their statelessness inside the home. As such, the ways in which the kinship system marginalizes even their domestic position needs to be closely connected to the ways in which the earlier colonial system and contemporary ethnic discriminations against Koreans in Japanese society condition their ontological insecurity after five or more decades of diasporic living. For example, born in 1910 in southeast Korea, my grandmother never learned to read or write Japanese, living most of her life in Japan, therefore, as an illiterate, giving birth to eleven children, yet having no place in my grandfather's house except as handywoman, and died as a foreigner in Japan. She was buried in South Korea, near my grandfather's family grave, which for her would mean a double alienation—she was Korean but spent most of her life in Japan, she was a daughter-in-law, but never knew her in-laws well enough due to her diasporic life. She had no place either in Korea or Japan, inside or outside the home, alive or dead (Ryang, in preparation). I see my grandmother's life overlapping in the lives of many of Jackie's interviewees.

Jackie J. Kim's project needs to be located against the background of Korean women's history. These women are not only victims of, but also witnesses to, the domestic oppression of the female and the young in twentieth-century Korean and Korean diaspora society. However, they also display impressive commitments to raise their children as best they can in the face of societal and familial adversity. Many of the women testify to the matrimonial system in which they as young girls were married to mostly unknown men and in which they experienced the subsequent sexual relationship with the husband as a burden, both psychologically and physically. Conjugal love was rare in such unions, yet women had no alternative but to put up with what they were told to do. Inevitably, women remained strangers to their married-in lineages, especially because of the colonial migration and subsequent diasporic existence. The reality of diaspora severed them from traditional bonds among women in the extended family, and few had the good fortune to keep in touch with their natal family after marriage in their teenage years. Jackie's women's voices introduce multiple dimensions of this situation, at times taking the form of bitter denunciation, at other times through deep sighs of renunciation, at others in the quiet pride of women who overcame adversity under trying familial circumstances.

Every one of Jackie J. Kim's interviewees tried to create a home for her husband and children, whether by relying on religious faith, reinforced by a political vision, or through incessant personal struggle, financially, socially, and domestically. This valuable collection introduces us not only to the personal realms of elderly Korean women in Japan, but also to the ways that Korean women, excluded from legitimate membership in the household, and subjected to enormous task at work and in the home, found ways to cope, and frequently, to overcome the adversity that was their lot. There are diverse themes in the words of the women Jackie interviewed, many of them unrelated to the grand narratives of nation, colonialism, and ethnic identity.

Beyond the boundaries of the household, these women's lives speak to us about colonial immigration, ethnic discriminations, and power relations inside an ethnic community, seen through their eyes. Precisely because these women stood at the margins of many spheres—nationalist politics, domestic hierarchy, colonial rule, and gender relations—their words can convey stories that go beyond the quotidian. Precisely because these women lived through a tumultuous and painful period of multiple transitions—first from colonial subject to stateless person or "*zainichi*" in occupied and postoccupation Japan, and secondly, in the post-1945 years, as adherents of expatriate politics following national partition, and as living witness to the rapidly changing gender relations inside Korean homes—their lives can teach us much about the legacies of the past that the new generation of Korean women in Japan must face and overcome. Their voices will also speak to readers about fundamentals of individual lives intricately intertwined with history and cultural tradition, which are relevant beyond the confines of Korea or Japan and illuminate our understanding of the emergence of modernity, legacies of colonial rule, and diasporic form of life.

Notes

1. This does not mean that first generation Koreans speak only Korean, either. As can be seen in Jackie's interviewees' usage of Korean and Japanese languages, the use of Japanese language is widespread among the older generation as well. Japan is not a society that tolerates or encourages bilingualism. Survival for the first generation required that they learn Japanese and use it as their daily language.

2. It needs to be added, however, that while it is true that more Koreans now become Japanese citizens, difficulties of naturalization remain in terms of obstacles, obscurity, and the lack of information or explanation for many Korean applicants. I am aware of a few cases where after years, some close to ten years, of marriage to a Japanese person and even after the birth of children, applicants are still waiting to hear from the Ministry of Justice.

3. I have written elsewhere about this controversy and with a broader theme of writing "from within," that is, with the insider's perspective, which is never free from relations of power and never a zone free of moral dilemma. See Ryang (2001).

4. Such a project can involve not simply the recording of the spoken word, but also asking the interviewee (where literate) to write a short piece or, in the case where the interviewee and the interviewer do not speak the same mother tongue, using a third lan-

guage that is shared by both. An example of the former can be found in Mintz (1974) and of the latter in the way Elisabeth Burgos-Debray and Rigoberta Menchú used Spanish, which Rigoberta learned as an adult, rather than Quiche Indian, Rigoberta's native tongue, in order to share a common language.

5. Similarly important was the recording of the oral history of the Korean survivors of Hiroshima and Nagasaki atomic bombings. Since the Japanese government systematically excluded non-Japanese survivors from receiving any social and medical benefit from the government, Korean survivors were neglected and denied the admittance of their suffering. Historians, again both Japanese and Koreans, have made a great contribution in drawing this unjustifiable treatment (for example, Pak 1982, Yoshitome 1980, Takagi 1987, Hayashi 1991). See also Weiner (1997).

6. Numerous records, writings, and artistic creations appeared with regard to the history of comfort women. Many of them are based on the firsthand account of the former comfort women, which are at times painful to read. Only to cite a few, the list will look like: Nishino (1992), Suzuki (1993, 1996), Yamada (1991), Yun et al. (1992), Kurahashi (1994), Kim et al. (1995). See also Yang (1998) and a special issue of *Positions* entitled "The Comfort Women: Colonialism, War, and Sex" (Choi 1997).

Prologue

In Search of Hidden Treasures

In Niigata in the northern part of Japan, where I lived for three years, an unexpected meeting set me on a course to tell the stories of these women. Longing for a taste of spice after my first few months in Japan, I walked into "Seoul" *yakiniku* restaurant on a sticky August evening. I checked out the surroundings and took in the atmosphere. Housed in a dusty glass box covered in oil specks, a small Korean doll dressed in the colorful traditional *chŏgori* watched from the corner of the counter. A Korean calendar hung on the side of the room, its brightly made up models in traditional clothes kneeling to greet the guests. Next to it, there was a large poster of a model wearing a bright yellow bikini and holding a frosty mug of Asahi beer. Toward the back of the restaurant where the customers could sit in a room covered with tatami mats to grill their barbecue meat and various intestines hung two smiling wooden masks. On the other side of the counter on a shelf made especially to enshrine a small TV blared the monotonous cheering of the high school baseball playoffs.

I sat in the center, in front of the refrigerated glass counter, uneasily wiping my hands with the yellow *shibori* (handtowel) as I stared at the menu on the wall. Having been in Japan for only three months at that time, I could neither speak nor read Japanese and was quite anxious. I wasn't sure how to order let alone what to order, because the style of the food and the servings were different from what I was used to. I continued to wipe my hands and stalled for some time until I saw an old woman behind the counter. She was mixing the raw meat with garlic, soy sauce, and ginger with her bare hands. She periodically lifted her spice-stained hands with small pieces of meat dangling on the tip of her forefinger to slide up her glasses that hung on the ball of her small, flat nose. She was laughing and speaking Japanese in a loud smoke-stained voice to a customer, but her face looked like a "typical" Korean grandmother's. Finally, I said in Korean, "Do you speak Korean?" She chuckled and said, *Sure, what do you want to eat?* in a heavily accented dialect of the southern provinces of Korea. Our lively conversations that began there led me to record the voices of women like her.

To search out more prospects, I went to a Korean Association in Niigata City[1] to speak to the person in charge. When I described to Mr. Song what I wanted to do and asked him to introduce some of these women to me, he just smiled, shook his head, and whispered in a very low voice. *These women are as ignorant as they can get. They don't know how to express themselves intelligently. They don't even know what school is. They don't even know how to write their own names. Don't waste your time interviewing them. You ask them questions but they can't understand what you want them to say. Why don't you do something like the political relationship of the North and South Koreans in Japan and how we can better it? That would be much more interesting and worth your time.* Mr. Song then wrote a name and a phone number on a small piece of paper and slid it in front of my teacup. He said that if I wanted to interview someone about the history of Koreans in Japan, I should talk to experts like the man whose name was on the paper.

Two days later, I met with an older man named Mr. Sŏ. It seems that he was once a supporter of North Korea and used to be an activist for the *Chongryun* organization. He said he had passionately advocated repatriating Koreans to their "Fatherland" of North Korea in the mid-1960s to 1970s as a humanitarian act for this minority group that was the target of overwhelming prejudice in Japan. He said that he had believed that Koreans who have aligned with the North should be allowed to leave Japan and go to North Korea if they wished. But this passion began to fade into disappointment and later disgust after he took a number of his comrades back and he saw the poor living conditions of their "homeland." He realized that all that was being said about North Korea being a paradise was nothing but false propaganda.

We talked a bit about my project. I asked Mr. Sŏ if he knew any women that I could interview; he frowned and waved his hand in front of him. *No, I don't know any of those noisy women. Every time they open their mouths, all they do is complain about their husbands. They don't know anything—ignorant, all of them. All they know how to do is talk badly about their husbands, saying this and that about how they drank and beat them—all useless talk.* He paused. *There's that old woman who runs that* kimch'i *store on the main street.* He let out a loud laugh. *When she sees me, she runs the other way. I guess they are all scared of me, because I tell them what I think of their complaining.*

Contrary to such warnings, the women's stories were a historical journey, traveling across time and depicting lives that have hurdled unimaginable obstacles and barriers. In the beginning, many of the women whom I approached expressed doubts that they could tell a story that would be of any interest. But almost always, their reluctance slowly began to vanish as I told them of my own story, that of my family, and what led us to make our journey to "far-away America." I revealed to them many aspects of my life and those of my family that I had never spoken about until I began to talk with them. As they sat with me one by one recalling, remembering, and reliving—they spoke as though experiencing a resurrection of a life that up to that moment was stored away in a dusty web of memory.

Sharing Lives

Our conversation usually took place in the women's homes, where they live alone or with extended families. We would usually sit around the dining table, and during wintertime around the Japanese heated table called a *kotatsu*. All of our talks started with a rundown on the state of their health. Then the women would ask me about life in America, my age, and whether I was married. Upon hearing my age and the fact that I have not yet been betrothed, they let out a shocked gasp. *Hey, you have to get married! Studying is great and admirable, but you really should think about getting married soon. What about children?* One woman warned, *If a woman is too smart, the man won't stay. That was the problem for me. I was too capable, and so my husband, I guess didn't feel like sticking around.*

Then they always asked about my family, my parents, what province they are from, what their occupation is, how many brother and sisters I have, and how long we have been in America. I told them that my parents divorced when my mother was barely thirty-five and pregnant with me, because my father had a lover who was expecting a child too. Upon hearing this, the women would shake their heads and click their teeth. I told them that my father took my brother to raise, because he was the first-born son and left me and my sister with my mother. They nodded their heads in understanding. I told them that my mother, with her independent spirit, most likely too ashamed to go back to her mother's house, carried a huge jug on top of her head going door-to-door selling sesame seed oil. They would sigh an *"Aigu,"* a Korean expression showing grief, sadness, and sympathy. I told them that finally failing to make ends meet, eating off of one relative's table after another with one eye watching our mouths and the other eye on the faces of our sometimes ungracious hosts, my mother decided America was the only way out, the only future that she could see for herself—but especially for her children. They would shake their heads side to side and sometimes look down at the palms of their hands.

Grandma, how about you? How did you come to Japan? I would ask. Many laughed and shook their heads, or some let out a raspy sigh. But almost all said in their accented dialect, *There aren't enough words to describe it. . . .* I would then assure them that all I wanted to do was hear the stories of their childhood in their homeland, what had brought them to Japan, and the kind of life that they have led until now. As soon as I said this, almost all of them smiled and let out a quiet laugh, looked down at their rough, wrinkled hands, rubbing one on top of the other with an expression that says, *"How do I begin . . . ?"* Some tightly shut their eyes, let out a deep breath, and rubbed their lids with chapped hands, almost too tired to travel back in time to a place they had left behind buried in the farthest corners of their thoughts. They then slowly opened their lids, some dabbing at the moisture gathered at the corner of their eyes, and others taking a gulp of the lukewarm tea sitting before them. It was then that we embarked on our journey.

In Pursuit of Meaning

What is this world, a place called "past" for these women? What does the past represent? When I first began conducting interviews, I met a woman who worked at *Mindan*,[2] a South Korean organization with a small branch in Niigata, which organized a monthly gathering of a few of the women and their Japan-born children. I visited the organization—by chance passing by and finding the place tucked away behind a small alleyway of clustered drinking establishments in front of the main train station. There I met Kim-*san*, a second-generation Korean woman who worked there as a secretary. I introduced myself and asked if it were possible for her to introduce me to some women. She said she was not sure if she could introduce anyone, but if I liked I could meet her mother.

Happily I agreed, and the very next day I sat in front of a tall heavyset woman with a slightly hunched back and bent knees. To break the ice, I told her in Korean where I was from, what I was doing in Japan, and what province my parents were from. She listened carefully, nodding her head. She proceeded to ask me questions about life in America, whether there were many Koreans there and how they make their living. I answered all of her questions and when I asked where she was from, she answered *Kyŏngsangnam-do*. I asked her how old she was when she came to Japan. She sat quietly, reached for her "Caster" soft pack cigarettes, lit one, and inhaled deeply. Her dried lower lip stuck to the cigarette butt as she quietly intoned, *I was thirteen years old.* Her expression darkened as she continued to inhale deeply on her second cigarette, lit before she even finished the first. *I shouldn't have gotten on that boat. My mother begged me not to go. My family, everyone told me I was crazy. Something must have gotten inside me.* I asked her why she had had such a great desire to come to Japan, all by herself. *It was my p'alcha[3] that I separate from my parents.* She continued to chain-smoke, one after another, not responding to my questions, just shaking her head and repeating again and again, *I shouldn't have gotten on that boat. It was my* p'alcha *to separate from my parents at such an early age.*

She did not say much about her childhood or her life in Japan. She did not lament in detail the various *kosaeng*[4] that she said had been her whole life. However, it was etched deeply in her face, her expression, in the way she stooped low, bracing one elbow as she brought her cigarette up to her mouth rhythmically. Perhaps it was pain that she remembered, or maybe it was relief that those times had finally passed, but as she exhaled the smoke synchronized with the heaviness of the sighs that escaped her determined jawline, her face exuded an expression tired with age but relentless in spirit. She sat with me for nearly four hours. At some points during the interview she looked as if she wanted to say something, and yet, each time she held back, not daring to give voice to parts of her life, which perhaps passed through her mind like a movie in slow motion. What I thought then was a failed interview in fact served as an invaluable source. It shed insight into the ways these women rationalized their hardships and struggles according to their cultural definition of fate and destiny. The past that they reconstructed was not about lives merely lived but lives suffered and survived by women whose very strength stemmed from a belief that hardships were meant to be overcome. The ability to endure enabled them to experience a sense of power as survivors who in the name of sacrifice could overcome all obstacles, imbuing their lives with meaning and validating their existence.

The ten voices in this book resonate stories of work, strength, willpower, steadfast spirit, and sacrifices that echo the essence of lives that have been lived to its very depth. As these women discovered voice through their narratives, talking casually about the particularities of their past and the difficulties overcome, they experienced an awakening of an inner strength.

"A Woman's Life"[5]

Even though my heart feels pain
To a point where I think I can no longer endure it
Because I am a woman, I can't say a word
I bear alone an inseparable sorrow
I continue to walk this tiring life's journey
Ahhh . . . I am told I have to endure it
So I spend it in tears, a woman's life

Notes

1. In Niigata in 1998, 189 first-generation Koreans were registered with the South Korean organization *Mindan*, and approximately an equal number were registered with the North Korean organization *Chongryun*. The port of Niigata has long played an important role as a bridge to North Korea. At present, ships transport goods and people at least once a month. Although the Koreans are scattered throughout the prefecture and there is no cohesive residential community, *Chongryun* maintains a very tight-knit organization through its branch office and school.

2. The political division in Korea was reflected in the Korean community in Japan as well in the establishment of the anticommunist organization *Mindan* in 1946 and the pro-North *Chongryun* in 1955. *Mindan* is the organization of Koreans who officially registered as nationals of South Korea and were permitted to obtain permanent resident status in Japan following the normalization of diplomatic relations between the two countries in 1965. It provides numerous services such as language studies and maintenance of

tradition through various cultural activities, social support as well as aid in coping with discrimination.

3. One's destiny or fate. For further explanations of this term see Tieszen (1977: 51). Many of the women viewed their life of hardship as fate inscribed in their cosmology for being born female. They believed that leaving their homeland was also charted by destiny. The women expressed their situation as *Tako-nan p'alcha*—fate that has been "received" or "granted" as they came into this world.

4. The common discourse shared by the women throughout the narratives was one of *kosaeng*, which the women contextualized as an ensemble of various physical, emotional, as well as mental experiences. The term describes a hard (tough) life and suffering.

5. A Korean folksong often sung by a group of women at a field site in Kawasaki.

Photos I:
Remembering Their Younger Days

Pak Sam-Yang, in her early thirties, with her husband

Tanaka Kimiko and her husband
before going to Japan

Kimiko's parents in Korea

Kimiko's (center, back row) first picture ever taken, at the age of fifteen

Sixtieth birthday party of Kimiko's (kneeling at the right) mother-in-law

Kimiko and fellow Korean laborers picking rocks (center, face half covered, hiding from her husband)

Yasuda Kimiko, first picture ever taken with her husband,
on the day of renewing their alien registration

Sŏ Meng-Sun (sitting) and her eldest daughter

All of Meng-Sun's children

Meng-Sun's eldest daughter in North Korea (sitting)

Pak Hui-Sun (farthest right) with friends from the night school that was closed after the teacher was taken away for reading communist literature

Hui-Sun (center) and friends from the cookie factory, before they were almost sent off to Manchuria during the war

Hui-Sun's wedding (age 19); the makeshift ritual was performed in a rush due to the B-29s jetting overhead; the cock laid on the table was startled by the noise and pecked at the ceremonial rice, spraying it all over

Pak Sun-Hui, before going to America to study

Part I

To Join My Husband

Chapter 1

I Love to Study

Tokumoto Hiroko (Jung Bun-Ki)

I met Tokumoto Hiroko through a reporter for Niigata Shinpō, *a small local newspaper. The reporter had interviewed Hiroko when she was awarded an honorary graduation diploma from the neighborhood elementary school, for attaining sixth-grade-level reading and writing skills in Japanese. When I contacted the reporter, he said that he would gladly provide me with her address, but warned me that her memory was a bit shaky since she was still recovering from a small stroke she had had a few years ago. I nevertheless gave her a call and spoke to her daughter-in-law, who gave me directions to their home.*

Hiroko came out to greet me. I was pleasantly taken aback by her youthful appearance. She extended a manicured hand, nails polished in light pink, to shake mine. Her jet-black hair was pulled back in a neat hairdo, and her manner was elegant. She spoke in a soft and gentle voice, and although her words were a bit slurred from the stroke, her memory of the distant past was impressive.

Hiroko informed me that because she could not clearly hear voices over the phone, she usually asks people to fax rather than to call. In her living/bedroom, a small lamp next to the front door lights up to show that the phone is ringing. On the wall hung a calendar, marked with brief notes written in big letters to remind her of her cram school lessons, doctors' appointments, and the schedule of the helper who made biweekly visits.

On her kitchen table, her textbooks and practice workbooks were stacked next to her neatly kept pencil case and fluorescent reading lamp. A pair of black knee-high boots was kept next to the kitchen table for her to use on chilly days since the kitchen has no heating. She said that the boots keep her legs warm as she sits at the table to practice writing Chinese characters.

Now that all of her children are grown, Hiroko feels that she can dedicate her time to her own pleasure, which consists of study. Although her son and his family live in a house right behind her own, she is usually alone, except during mealtimes when her daughter-in-law comes to cook for her. Hiroko said that spending time with family and friends makes her happy, but her greatest joy is having time to herself to read her textbooks and to complete her often difficult homework assignments.

Hiroko is proud that her children have all completed upper-level education, allowing them to take up professions such as teaching and medicine. One of her children works as a top member of the Chongryun[1] *branch office, another owns a preparatory cram school, and a third is a doctor at the university hospital in the city. She feels that her children's and grandchildren's accomplishments are her successes. She believes that by teaching them to develop themselves through education, she has compensated for her own lack of education. She insists that even at her age a person has the power to pursue an independent life through learning.*

I think the age I was born into was bad. If my mother had talked to me about things, then I might have known how to deal with them. But I was born and raised deep in the countryside where the aristocratic system was strict. As a result, my parents raised me to be dumb throughout my life—with all this foolish talk about *yangban* upper-class behavior, not allowing girls to ever leave the house without being carried in a sedan even to go a short distance, and not allowing us to know how to walk with our own two feet. Whatever happens, there is nothing to fear when you have an education. Once you do, there is nothing that you can't do. I used to tell my children that being illiterate is the same as being dead. . . .

I can try to tell you the history of what I have lived through, but I wonder whether young people these days would understand it . . . *Ha, ha, ha.* . . . (She laughs quietly.) I was living in Kyŏngsangbuk-do. . . .

My name is Jung Bun-Ki. My Japanese name is Tokumoto Hiroko. I was born on April 14, Taishō 7 (1918). I am seventy-nine years old. The reason why we started using this Japanese name was because when we started this business, the company signboard had the name "Tokumoto." We thought Japanese people wouldn't understand our Korean name, so we used the name that was already there. Soon I also started using the name "Hiroko" for myself. When I was growing up in Kyŏngsangbuk-do, I was never called by my own name. When you are a child, they call you not by your name but *agi* (baby), and when you grow a bit older, they call you *akasshi* (young miss). And when you get married, you are never called by your name, and that is why you grow up not even knowing your own name, let alone knowing how to write it. You grow up in darkness, not knowing anything. . . .

When I think of the past and the days that have gone by . . . when I try to tell you everything . . . words can't describe those days. Before, I remembered a lot, but recently I am forgetting more and more. You know, I started studying Chinese characters recently, and maybe if I was to have started even two or three years earlier, I think that it would have been good. These days, I keep forgetting the same characters that I have learned again and again. Maybe my ability to remember is gone forever. But I still remember certain things vividly. . . . When I was a little girl in my village, all the women would get together—all the grandmothers and their grandchildren. My grandmother would dress me up and take me to the gathering. I would play with one of my grandmother's friend's granddaughters who was about my age. . . .

Father's Death

When I was a child, I never forgot a thing—no matter what. When my father passed away, I remember my grandmother and my aunts—all feeling so sad—ran up after my mother to the top of a nearby hill. When I think about it now, I realize that she was trying to commit suicide. She was crying so much, saying that she wanted to die together with my father. I see it so clearly still. . . . Times like that, I haven't forgotten. . . . Even now I can't forget it. . . . *Ha, ha, ha.* . . . (She laughs quietly.) Later, whenever something was bothering me—I would think about that time. You know, you live your whole life and there can't only be good things, and there are so many regrets. . . . I guess nothing good comes out of regret. But when there were bad times, and I thought I couldn't take it anymore . . . I would think of my mother and how she must have felt. Then I would feel a little bit better. . . .

Originally, my family owned a lot of farmland.[2] My father took care of all of the properties, until he was taken away by the Japanese and put in prison for four years and eight months. Finally he was released, but soon afterward he passed away. My grandfather was also captured, but he was soon released without being beaten as much. At that time, Korea was a Japanese colony. I remember my father looking quite old and sick when he came back from prison. He passed away a few months later in the first week of June. He was thirty-three years old. The weather was getting warmer, but the body had to be placed inside the house throughout the mourning period until his burial. And so, in order to mask the smell of the body, a big pot of beans was roasted slowly over the fire. At that time I was only six years old and I didn't know anything. . . . *Ahh.* . . . (She sighs.) Can you believe it? Not knowing that the aroma of the beans was supposed to cover up the smell of my father's badly beaten corpse—I tried to eat the beans. *Ha, ha.* . . . (She laughs quietly.) I tried so hard to pick up every little bean to eat. . . . *Ha, ha.* . . . When my father stopped breathing . . . my mother said she wanted to die together with him. Everyone gathered around him and was crying so much. . . . My father and mother were said to have been very close. . . . At that time I didn't know what was happening, I just remember holding on to my mother and crying as she kept saying that she wanted to die, too.

When I was growing up, I didn't know anything about "*shokuminchi*" (colony). We were under Japanese rule, but we didn't refer to it as *shokuminchi*. After I came to Japan, I often heard the word *shokuminchi, shokuminchi,* but when I was in Korea—I heard a little bit here and there, but I didn't know anything in detail. Later I thought back and connected this incident to that, and finally came to understand those things that I heard as a little girl about the Japanese. But back then, I had absolutely no idea what was going on.

I didn't even know the word for *shokuminchi* in Korean. You know, in Korea, we wear white *chŏgori* (traditional linen dress), and my grandfather and grandmother always wore this white dress. In order to discourage the Korean people from wearing their traditional white dress, the Japanese police used to take a water gun filled with blue ink and shoot it at people. My grandfather got hit several times, and I remember him coming home from the market with blue ink all over his clothes.

Growing Up as a *Yangban*

I can't say that my parents or my grandparents were particularly strict with us when I was growing up. But I guess in the old days there was a strict tradition. So it wasn't that they themselves were strict, but rather it was the customs of the time. My house was of the *yangban* class, and my mother was from a *yangban* family. She was a "Nam." This was a very prominent name. When I went back to Korea, I was quite surprised to find out that we were the twelfth-generation descendent of the royal family. Anyway, in my house when relatives visited, men and women never sat together in one room. The men used the big room, and the women used the little room. Meals were always taken in separate quarters. Respect for parents and elders was of utmost importance. In the morning, everyone would first greet the elders—my grandfather and grandmother—by lining up from the eldest daughter-in-law on down. If a gift came to our home, my mother would never, ever, touch it first. She would tell me to carry the gift nicely to my grandmother and hand it to her. And after my grandmother opened the gift to see what it was, she would return it to me. I would then take it to my mother, and my mother would arrange the goods very nicely in a container, then hand it to me to take back to my grandmother.

Education

When I was little, I was lucky enough to know the Korean *han'gŭl*, and I read many novels.[3] That is the reason why I was able to understand more about our language and our customs. My aunt, my father's sister, taught me *han'gŭl*. She knew her letters and she taught me how to read and write. I loved learning, and I had my aunt teach me as often as possible. In my neighborhood, there were hardly any women who could read and write. It was my dream to learn Chinese characters. But most of the scholars who used to teach in our town's schools were taken away by the Japanese. For those who were quite wealthy and could afford to pay, there were night schools. But those schools were so far away. Back then, we had no bicycles, so the only way to get to school would be to walk for hours past at least three villages. The boys were able to learn their Chinese characters through a Korean book called *Ch'ŏnja moji*. If you were to learn everything in that book, then I think by today's standards you would know enough for junior high school.

In my household, everyone was a scholar. But they said that because I was a girl, I didn't have to learn. Not only that, I wasn't allowed to step out of the house. The custom in Kyŏngsangbuk-do was much stricter than in Kyŏngsangnam-do. In the old days, it was thought that if girls were allowed to learn to write, when they married, they might write letters back to their parents saying that life in their husband's household was too hard to bear. There were many people who, for that reason, didn't want to educate their girls. But my family at least allowed me to study the Korean *han'gŭl*. In the home, we used to help with different chores, and because I loved to read so much, I spent my free time reading novels. After coming to Japan, I was able to go out of the house by myself freely and even to ride the bus for the first time in my life. When I came to Japan, I came alone—without my parents or siblings. I came without being able to read, write, or speak anything in Japanese. . . .

Marriage

I was sixteen years old when I married. It was on March 12. . . . I didn't know what my husband-to-be looked like. That was the custom. I didn't want to marry into his family, so I cried for a month . . . a whole month. Today, the girl would simply run away. Anyway, even if I had wanted to run away, I wouldn't have known how. . . . *Ha, ha.* . . . My mother simply said that because I was of marriageable age, I was going to be betrothed. My husband was seven years older than me—he was twenty-three years old. I couldn't believe that they were going to marry me off to a person that much older. Nowadays, you can say you like this person or you don't like that person and decide for yourself. I don't know why, but just having to hear anything about getting married, I hated it. But regardless, proposal letters went back and forth between my mother and his, and then the engagement gifts started to arrive at our home.[4]

My husband's family held the highest position in his village. His family and relatives were all said to be scholars. They studied and taught the Chinese classics. But my father-in-law was having great financial difficulties and was thinking about moving to Manchuria, taking the whole family. But my mother-in-law's brother refused to have his only sister go as far off as Manchuria, where he would never be able to see her again. My mother-in-law's family was quite wealthy and prominent. So her brother paid for her and her family to move back to the village near her *ch'inchŏng* (natal household). Through the introduction of a matchmaker, I married into my husband's family.

After I married, for one year I stayed in my *ch'inchŏng* and my husband came once during the spring, and then for *o-bon* (summer Buddhist festival for ancestor worship). During the first year, you stay in your *ch'inchŏng*. Then you go and formally greet the elders in your husband's household, and afterward you come back to your *ch'inchŏng* again. A few months later, you go to your husband's home and you stay there for two or three months, and then you come back home to your *ch'inchŏng*. If you go for example during spring then you stay until fall. Then comes the final time when you go to your husband's home, you can no longer come and go, but must stay in your husband's household forever. That was the custom for the *yangban* class. I went to my husband's household the following year on March 2 according to the lunar calendar. On my way back to my *ch'inchŏng*, on March 11, I had to take three sedans filled with laundry. I was the new daughter-in-law, and I was to do the laundry of his family and even of their distant relatives within the neighborhood—adults, children, and everyone, all brought their laundry. Back then of course there were no machines, so you had to do all the washing by hand. At my *ch'inchŏng,* I wasn't allowed to go out of the home to do the washing, so, everyone else washed the laundry for me. On April 1, I went back to my husband's home again. From then I was to stay in my husband's household forever. Before I left, my mother said that once I arrive at my husband's household, from that moment my mother-in-law would be my new mother. No matter what, I was now *mukō no hito*—a part of the other family. Even if my husband were to die right after I went to his home, I would have to stay there throughout my life.

In the Korean custom, the father-in-law and father-in-law's older brother were thought to be quite strict, and therefore much to be feared. Well, I grew up without a father, and I think I really missed having one. Luckily, my father-in-law and my father-in-law's older brother showered me with kindness and affection. Did I tell you that a few years before my father-in-law passed away, while my husband was in Japan, I cured his illness. While climbing the mountain one day, my father-in-law was stung by a wasp on the foot. That night he fell ill with an infection. Day by day, his heel became more and more swollen. He would turn this way and that, moaning *"It hurts, it hurts. . . ."* We lived deep in the countryside and there was no doctor in the area. One day the pain in his foot seemed unbearable, so I took a small knife and made a cut in the infected area. As expected, yellow pus gorged out, and since it had to be removed in order for the infection to heal, I put my mouth on the infected area and sucked out the pus. I continued to suck out the yellow mucus until there was nothing but blood left in my spit. I did this for several days. Afterward, no matter how much I washed out my mouth, I couldn't get rid of that taste for a long while. I can still smell that awful taste in my mouth as I tell you this now. At that time, I didn't look upon my act as anything special. We were taught that for a parent one should be ready to give up one's own life at any time.

Husband

My husband was a generous man. Whenever someone was in need, he would give everything he had. So he wasn't very good in business. But when he used to work in companies, he was well liked and trusted. Everyone liked him. Well, once you marry, it doesn't matter whether you have a good relationship or not, you have to stay no matter what. Until he died, almost every day early in the morning I would go to the nearby market and buy the freshest fish and serve it to him for dinner to eat with the brew that I made at home. *Ha, ha, ha. . . .* You say love, but what is love? This is what was expected of people in the old days. Anyway, when we were young, there was no way we could have a deep conversation. In front of our parents-in-law or siblings-in-law—we couldn't talk to each other directly. When we were first married, we never even slept together in one room. We women had to do all the housework and the kitchen work, and we would all sleep together in the women's quarters—daughters in one room, and the daughters-in-law in a separate room. My husband slept in the men's quarters.

Of course, not everyone had this kind of arrangement. I think that it was particular for the *yangban* class. Back then, the parents-in-law decided which day the couple would be able to share one room especially for that night. The mother would tell the son to do so. If there was an elder, for example a grandmother, she herself would tell the grandson and give him permission. There was a saying often repeated by the elders, that when a child is made in the mother's stomach, even a father who is as far away as Seoul would cry of joy. I guess just because you sleep together in one room, it doesn't mean that you will bear a child, and because you sleep separately doesn't mean that there will never be any children. So it seems it is the ancestors and the gods who decide and make a child.

I had my eldest daughter when I was twenty years old, and soon after that I had my second child. My husband and I were together for about five or six years. Then he came to Japan, and we were separated for six years. When my father-in-law passed away, I had to observe the three-year mourning period. I had to pay my respects to the dead spirit by serving rice and soup to the altar morning and night. For three years you have to wear white, and until the mourning period is over you can't go anywhere. Even after it was finished, I continued to live with my mother-in-law, two children, and my younger sister-in-law, and continued to farm until my husband was able to get a permit for my children and me to enter Japan.

Coming to Japan

Back then, some people came to Japan hoping to earn a lot of money, but others came as drafted laborers. My husband and his brother were both drafted as laborers.[5] He received a letter ordering him to work for a *gunji kōjō* (war plant). My husband earned a reputation as a good worker and so he was transferred to work for a power plant. He then worked in Itami near Ōsaka for a government-run iron manufacturing company called *Nihon Seitetsu*. He was able to receive a permit to invite his family. So that is how we ended up coming to Japan. It was Shōwa 19 (1944), and Japan was in quite a mess, so such permits were difficult to come by, but because he was so well liked by his boss, he was able to obtain the permit. That was the reason why our children and I were able to come to join him. Otherwise, we probably would have been apart forever.

I remember getting off the boat with one child on my back, holding the other in one hand, and my other hand balancing a big sack filled with all of our belongings on my head. The things were getting so heavy and I was just about to ask for help when someone called to me. It was a family friend who was living in Shimonoseki. He had come to meet us at the port, having received a letter that we would be arriving. We stayed in Shimonoseki for three nights. From there, my friend put me on a train to Nanba in Ōsaka. My children and I got on the train headed for Umeda station, but I didn't know exactly where to get off, and got off at Kōbe. When I got off in Kōbe, it was morning and it was quite cold, because it was the middle of April. My children, who were six and eight years old at the time, were shivering because of the cold. I was carrying the younger one on my back, and I was in such a panic—looking here and there—because I had absolutely no idea what I was to do or where to go. All I had in my hand was my husband's letter with the address written on it. I held on to that paper . . . I held on to it tight. . . .

My husband had written in his letter that if I hang on to this one slip of paper and show it at each station, they would let me pass. It must have worked, because I was allowed to get on and off the train. Well, I walked a bit along the platform at Kōbe station and I saw a stationmaster. I rushed over to him and I couldn't speak any Japanese of course, so I started to speak in Korean, "*I need to go to where my husband is. . .*" I showed him the address. Then, he gestured for me to go somewhere. . . . Now of course I know it was a police box. The sack on my head was so heavy and with the two kids, I had no idea where to go. I put down the huge sack and I told my eldest daughter to stand in front of it, and I warned her not to move or go anywhere. I said, "*If you move from here, I won't know how to find you and you wouldn't know how to find me. So if you move, we may be separated and never find each other.*" I went the way that the stationmaster gestured, and had to go all the way up to the third floor. When I got there, I was lucky. There was a Japanese policeman who spoke such wonderful Korean. He came downstairs with me to where my daughter was waiting, and he told me which train to take and after how many stops to get off. I was so desperate and afraid I was going to get off at the wrong stop again, so I asked him to take me and my children all the way. But he said because the police station was very busy, he couldn't do that. When I think about it now, I guess they must have been in a terrible frenzy, because it was April of Shōwa 19 (1944), when Japan was still in the middle of war. When I got off at Itami station, I showed the address to the stationmaster there and he told me to wait at the ticket booth. Then I was lucky once again, because the stationmaster came back with a Korean man, and he took me all the way to Nanba where my husband was living. When I finally got there, my husband said that he and his friend had waited for a long time at Umeda station, and when we didn't show up, he was so worried that we might have ended up somewhere else far away. I only had the envelope with my husband's address on it. When I think about it now, I have to laugh. I thought to myself, no matter what, I couldn't lose that piece of paper—I had to hold it firmly in my hand. Sometimes, I really wonder how I came all the way here with two small children to find one man in this entire Japan with that one little piece of paper.

Wartime

Soon after coming to Japan, I had a son. It was Shōwa 20 (1945), January, and it was still wartime. We were able to receive help from the factory, *Nihon Seitetsu* (Japan Ironworks), where my husband was working. The factory manager said my husband was a good man, so they made sure that we at least had decent housing. The company also gave us extra food. We were busy running from this bombing and that bombing. It's something that I can't put into words. . . . *Ah.* . . . (She lets out a tired sigh.) My son was born in January, and in March there was a big bombing in Osaka near where we lived, near Tsuruhashi. . . . It was a huge bombing. There was a factory truck available to help us escape, and we went all the way up to a mountain in Tottori. We began living there, making coal and selling it. At first we didn't even know how to make coal. It was way, way far up in the mountains. We somehow spent months there and soon it became autumn. We were so deep in the mountains; we didn't even know that the war had ended.

The war ended in August, right? In autumn we came down to the town area, back again to Ōsaka, near Tennōji. All the Koreans were saying that they were going back to Korea. I very much wanted to go back, too, but we didn't have any money for all of our train fares to Shimonoseki.[6] We had just come down from the mountains—we didn't know anyone, and there was no one we could borrow that kind of money from. At that time in Japan, there was nothing to eat. There was only corn, crushed barley, and rice bran. We would take the rice bran and make it into a small round ball. My children were so hungry. . . . My daughter said she heard that if people ate too much of this "*nuka*" (rice bran), then all of their hair will "*nukeru*" (fall out). *Ha, ha.* . . . I asked her if she didn't want to eat it then. But she said she didn't care if all of her hair fell out, she was so hungry. *Ha, ha.* . . . (She laughs quietly.) There was no food—only whatever we received in rations. The rations wouldn't last our family for a week, and the situation was the same for everyone. We would go and buy some things from the black market here and there, but then, sometimes, we would get caught and have it all taken away, and there would be nothing. So as soon as I received the rations, I would start preparing to make them last. Once they were gone, nothing could be done. So I would start to save bit by bit from the first day I received it, to somehow make it last until the next distribution. We received rations twice a week.

I had no other relatives or family around me. If there had been someone, a relative or someone, then I don't think that I would have had to endure such *ko-saeng* (suffering). My husband was the first son, and because my mother-in-law was still living in Korea, I had to try to send as much money as possible to her, because I was the first son's wife. I asked my mother-in-law to come with the children and me to Japan, but she said that it would be too hard for me to take care of an old person as well as the children. So she told me to go ahead first, saying that she would come later. At that time, my youngest sister-in-law was not married and she was still living with my mother-in-law. My brother-in-law was already in Japan, stationed up north. So until my mother-in-law passed away, we sent her money—whether or not we ourselves were having a hard time. Every year we sent about ten thousand yen. It's not because we had money that we sent her this big amount every year. It was something that we thought we had to do.

Anyway, we lived for three years in Ōsaka, and then after that we came to Niigata. A friend showed us how to raise pigs, and also we learned to make soap. We opened a soap business, but it didn't do well. Then we moved to this neighborhood. Before, this place was an iron factory. The business was for sale, and we sold our house and bought this iron-making business. We have lived here since. My husband had a friend in Niigata, but mostly we came because Niigata is known for its rice. My husband thought that if we came here, then we could feed our children white rice all the time. . . .

Work

I think when I came to Niigata, I was twenty-eight or twenty-nine years old. I came here before I was thirty. First, we started making soap, but after a few years the business went bankrupt. After that, we had no other way to make a living. We used the leftover supply of soap for almost thirty years. . . . Koreans had a difficult time then, but the Japanese also had a hard time getting food. Well, for a while I brewed illegal alcohol. In the evening I squeezed out alcohol for the customers to come and pick up. One day my neighbor reported us to the police. The neighbor was a Japanese person who thought that we were making a lot of money. Police officers came to my house and took everything as evidence. . . . From one to ten, they took everything. They took my husband in for fifty days. . . . *Ah* . . . (she sighs heavily). That was a long time ago. The children and I . . .

Ah . . . (she sighs deeply). Things like that . . . how I felt then, I can't put it into words. . . . The policemen took everything. . . . I didn't know how to speak, because I hardly knew any Japanese then—I didn't know anything. All I knew was that my husband was being taken away. I had no idea when he would be let out. What were we to do? I told the policeman that the children and I wanted to go with my husband, and that I didn't care if we all went into jail together—but no matter what, we all had to stay together. . . . Of course, the policemen didn't take us with them. Really, at that time, there was nothing left in the house. . . . Nothing. All of our goods, all the money—everything was taken away, there was nothing. Every day, there was barely enough for that day. What I had sold in alcohol was used for what we needed from one day to the next. But everything— everything was taken away. I was left without a thing. . . .

That is the reason why. . . . That is the reason why. . . . *Haaaa* . . . (she sighs deeply). There is no end to my story. . . . At that time the Korean War had just started. My eldest daughter was, I think, just starting junior high school. (She whispers.) *Ah* . . . (she sighs). "*Are ga ne.* . . . That child. . . ." She would go all the way to a town called Aoyama—at that time it was only rice fields and farmland. She would go all the way there by herself, and she would pick up bruised potatoes that had been discarded. She would bring them back home, and we would steam and sell them in order to make a living while my husband was in jail. . . . *Ah* . . . (she sighs). My children really tried so hard. . . . But as for me, I was so embarrassed. Failing in our soap business and my husband in jail. . . . Every time I left the house, our former employees would call me respectfully, "*oku-san, oku-san*, Mrs., Mrs." I was so embarrassed that I couldn't stand it. For me, I really thought countless times of ending it all and dying. . . . *Ahh* . . . (she sighs quietly). It was too hard to take. It was so hard to endure. Often I went to the nearby sea and I thought about walking into it and never turning back. When I considered only myself, then I thought I should just go ahead and end this miserable life. But when I thought about my children and how they would have to try to survive on their own, I would give up such thoughts for a while. . . . *Ahh* . . . (she sighs). Many times, I went down to the sea thinking never to return. I can't really say that there was one particular reason, but it was just so hard—trying to make ends meet and feeling so alone. . . .

Then, one day I thought for a long time. Here was my child trying so hard to make ends meet, and I thought to myself, how ridiculous I was for feeling so embarrassed about our situation. You know it really is a terrible experience when your business is failing. . . . For many years we used the leftover soap, all of us, the family and also all the workers. We had made soap and sold it all over Japan from Hokkaidō on down. Then, this big business failed. . . . I thought to myself that even my children were trying so hard, and as a parent, I couldn't continue to go around feeling embarrassed. I cringed to think what I must have looked like in front of my children—feeling too embarrassed to even go out of the house. . . .

I had to make a living, never mind what people thought. After that, my two daughters and I went around to pick up scraps of metal and iron.[7] At that time there were a lot of scrap pieces here and there. Every day we went out to pick them up. One of my friends went to Aizuwakamatsu in Fukushima prefecture to sell iron scraps, which sold at a fairly good price. I remember that from one sale we received about twelve thousand yen. I paid two thousand yen for a big scale, and then we invested the rest of the money in the scrap business. You know, I still have that scale. When we started the scrap metal business, we didn't know anything about it. In order to buy the scraps to resell, you needed money to invest. At that time, I wasn't even aware of such a thing as borrowing money from a bank. Instead, I went to my neighbors to borrow money, and also I went to the pawnshops for money. That is how we ended up staying here in Niigata all this time doing this business. It is here that my husband passed away, and then my son quit his job as a schoolteacher and he started running the business. My husband had so many friends, both Korean and Japanese. When he passed away, so many people came to the funeral. And there were many Japanese people. Usually for a Korean person's funeral, not so many Japanese come to pay their respects. I think it was because he was such a good person. More than fifty people came to pay their respects.

Children

Although I'm not educated, if something happened concerning my children at their school, I didn't care how I spoke my Japanese, I went to talk to the teachers right away. I was called to my children's school several times because they were called "*Chōsen-jin, Chōsen-jin*" by the other children. From the beginning, when they were going to elementary school, and later when they started junior high school, I went to their teachers to ask them to tell the others that my children were Korean. The reason for that is, when you try to hide it, and when the other kids somehow find out that they are Korean, their bullying is merciless. But if you tell the other children that you are Korean from the beginning, and if you don't act as if you are ashamed of it—trying to hide it all the time—then there is less bullying. So I never had my children use Japanese names in their schools. They all used their Korean last name Pak with its Japanese reading "*Boku.*" When we first moved here, and I went to meet with the teachers, they asked me if I wanted the children to be called Tokumoto in school. Well, I told the teachers that they are not Tokumoto. I told them I wanted them to call my children by their true last name—Boku. So the teachers said if that was what I wanted, they could only go along with it.

When my eldest daughter graduated from junior high school, I went to talk to her homeroom teacher, and he said that it would probably be better to send her to a Korean high school. That was how she started going to a Korean school. But there was no Korean high school in Niigata so she started going to the *Chongryun* school in Ibaraki. That school is bigger than any Japanese school in Niigata. My daughter was quite surprised that Koreans could have such a big school. She used to be so unhappy from being bullied at school in Niigata, but when she went to the Korean school, she changed completely. Whenever she came back home for spring and summer vacation, her face showed such happiness. After she graduated from high school, she wasn't sure if she wanted to go to college. But I told her that she would be the first girl in our family to go to college, so I told her to go, no matter what. So she went to the North Korean University in Tōkyō.[8] After graduating, she worked for three years as a teacher at a Korean school in Tochigi prefecture. Then she got married, and now runs a *juku* (cram school) for both Japanese and Korean students in Kanazawa. All of my children attended the North Korean school.

Reflection

I continue to tell my children and grandchildren that because I am not educated I had to endure such hard times. And so that is the reason why, no matter how much I suffered, I tried to make sure that we could afford to educate our children to the highest level. Of course, if they didn't want to study, then there was nothing that could be done about it. But I really wanted my children to study and learn as much as possible. I used to tell my children that no matter what . . . no matter what, I wanted them to study, so in case something were to happen, they will not suffer. Education is power. . . .

You know, I had six brothers and sisters. There were five of us girls and one boy. I am the fourth child. Now they are all dead. The oldest was my brother and he died when he was eighty-seven years old. When he was eighty-six, I went to Korea and I was able to see him for the last time. Last year he died. Now there is only me and one sister left. And, you know, I'm going to study until the day I die. I can't believe how good it feels to attend school. I really can't believe how wonderful a place called school is. I couldn't have even dreamt that a school would allow me to come and study with the children. I thought, school, at this age? In Ōsaka, there is a large number of Koreans, so there are many classes where old people could learn how to read and write. But here in Niigata, it took two or three years for me to find a place. Then, I was introduced to the principal at an elementary school near my home. When asked if I could join the classes, he didn't call back for about a month. So I thought I wouldn't be able to study, just as I expected. But then a telephone call came and a few months later, I entered a fourth grade reading and writing class. When I went to the school for the first time three years ago, the teacher wanted me to read the Japanese textbook, and I was able to read reasonably well. But when I had to write, I couldn't write the characters. When I don't look at the characters first, then I can't write them, and if I don't write for a few days, I forget them again. I think if I were to have started studying when I was in my thirties or even forties, instead of in my seventies, then I wouldn't have suffered this much. It seems that whatever it is, you need to study. . . . If you can't read and write . . . I can't put into words how frustrating it is.

I love to study . . . so much. After I started studying . . . every night until two or three in the morning I read, and sometimes I don't go to sleep until four o'clock. I think that having to go to sleep is such a waste of time. You know . . . under this bright fluorescent light—to be able to write on a clean white piece of paper—letters all in black . . . I just can't tell you how much fun that is for me. So I read and study until two or three in the morning. . . . Sometimes I write all the characters that I have learned, and sometimes I read the stories in the textbook. Actually, my ability to write Chinese characters with a brush is pretty good, but when I write with a pencil, it is quite different. In the beginning, when I held a pencil and wrote the letters—I had to laugh. *Ha, ha, ha.* . . . I couldn't write very well at all with the pencil. As a child, when I wrote some of the *han'gŭl* with the brush, I wrote pretty well, because the brush is so soft. But my hand stroke felt so harsh with the pencil, and I could hardly write with it. *Ha, ha.* . . .

You know, until now to this age . . . living my life, I have never found anything as pleasurable . . . for the first time in my life, as studying. Up to now, I have tried many, many things, and there hasn't been much that I haven't tried in order to survive. But all my life, I had to work so hard and suffer the way I did, because I didn't have an education. I had to always depend on others. When you come to know people, if they know that you are capable of something, then they think of you as someone worth knowing, but if not, then you end up like this— being cheated, for instance in business, simply because you don't know things. If I were educated, then I think that I could have become a big person—a respectable person.

So now, after going to school and learning to read and write, when I come back home and everyone is out of the house . . . I read. Then the book becomes my companion, my conversation partner. When I read the stories in books, sometimes I laugh with the people in the stories, and sometimes I cry for them, too. I laugh by myself, and when it is sad then I feel sad as I read. Sometimes, I read the stories out loud. I stand up and read in a loud voice just like my little elementary school friends. Then, as I read and if there are some words that I don't know, then I ask anyone, because everyone around me—from my own children to my grandchildren and even the little youngsters at school—they are my teachers. But as much as I can, I try to figure it out by myself. Because, it is this very thing of trying to figure out what the words mean, and finding out on my own, that is the most fun. . . .

Notes

1. Endorsed by the North Korean government, *Chongryun* supported the reunification of the divided country under the communist regime. Those who were aligned with North Korea presented themselves as "overseas nationals of North Korea," although most of them were born in the South. *Chongryun* is a vast organization, operating through its headquarters in Tōkyō as well as local chapters in forty-eight prefectures. There are eighteen affiliated organizations: Youth League, Women's Union, the Young Pioneers,

Teacher's Union, Merchants and Industrialists Union, Artists' Association, to name a few. There is also a theater company and twenty-eight independent commercial companies, which includes an insurance company as well as a bank. One of *Chongryun*'s primary goals was educating Korean children and instilling national pride as citizens of an independent North Korea, and it carried out its ethnic education objectives in accordance with the guidance of the North Korean educational system. *Chongryun* maintains elementary to high-school-level education as well as its own university. However, since the death of Kim Il-Sung and the much-publicized economic hardships of their "homeland," its schools have slowly begun to lessen the emphasis on the North Korean political and ideological rhetoric and instead emphasize the importance of maintaining a "Korean" identity. In addition, as a way to maintain student population and increase enrollment, they have begun to emphasize *"kokusaika"* or "internationalization" and multilingual education. For an extensive work on the vast *Chongryun* organization, see Ryang (1997).

2. In the early years of Japanese rule (1910-1945), Korea experienced far-reaching land reforms through a reorganization of agricultural land. The economic policies implemented by the Japanese brought forth a cadastral survey requiring landowners to identify, codify, and register their lands. Ignorant of the new laws or unable to pay the increasing rent, many tenant farmers were evicted. They resorted to slash-and-burn agriculture in the mountains or worked as low-wage laborers. Numerous landless peasants and impoverished rural laborers were among those who looked to migration as a way of escaping deteriorating conditions. Thus, the majority of migrants to Japan were from the southern provinces of Kyŏngsangnam-do, Kyŏngsangbuk-do, and Chŏlla-do, which were known to have the most fertile land. See Cumings (1981: 41-45).

3. According to Kim (1977: 159), novels written in the Korean alphabet of *han'gŭl* gained much popularity in the latter part of the Yi dynasty with women who were able to read. The themes of the novels acquainted the women with what was going on in the world, along with what Kim refers to as the "three fundamental principles of conduct," concerning plots such as praising loyal subjects, faithful sons, and virtuous wives.

4. The letters are in the form of proposal and acceptance. Deuchler (1977: 18) writes that the proposal letter contained the groom's vital statistics, which included his *p'alcha*—the four pairs of cyclical characters that indicated the hour, day, month, and year of his birth, according to the Chinese calendar. The acceptance letter contained the dates of the betrothal and the wedding. She explains that the groom's household prepared gifts of colored silks or thread, and other special items that were symbols of fertility— millet ears, silkworm cocoons, and red pepper.

5. From 1937, with the expansion of Japan's war on the Chinese mainland, the manpower shortage increased, leading to the extension of the National Manpower Mobilization Act (*Kokumin chōyō rei*) to Korea in 1939. Private companies could take advantage of mass recruitment in areas designated by the colonial government. In 1941, the Ministries of Home Affairs and Welfare and the colonial government set up labor recruiting stations in local provinces, counties, and villages and quotas were assigned. Young Korean women also were a source of cheap labor for a variety of textile and manufacturing jobs. See Lee and DeVos (1981a: 52-53). Starting from 1943, over 350,000 Korean men were drafted into the Japanese army and navy. See Ryang (2000a: 3).

6. Initial repatriation began as early as September 1945. Between September and December, approximately 640,000 Koreans returned through official channels, with Japanese naval and merchant vessels transporting them free of charge. See Lee and DeVos (1981a: 59). However, several factors discouraged Koreans from returning home. The Supreme Command for Allied Powers (SCAP) issued a directive forbidding any repatriate to take more than a thousand yen back to Korea (the yen-dollar parity was fixed

from 1945 to 1971 at ¥360 = $1). The repatriates frequently encountered riots and famine on return home. With stories and rumors flying, many Koreans decided to remain in Japan, at least for the time being.

7. During the Korean War (1950-1953), scraps of metal and iron were in large demand to produce weapons, wartime equipment, and supplies. Many Koreans collected and sold scrap metal for recycling, and worked as junk dealers. See DeVos and Chung (1981: 233).

8. The North Korean University or Chosŏn University was established on June 13, 1959, and is located in Kodaira City in Tōkyō. See Lee (1981f: 170-173) and Ryang (1997: 4).

Chapter 2

I Have Done My Best

Kōda Sumi

The monthly luncheon gathering sponsored by the Niigata Korean Association proved to be a feast of homemade sushi, kimchi, and spicy Korean style baked dried pollack among a mix of Japanese and Korean dishes.

After lunch, a woman who had made a dark blue dress for Sumi showed it to her, and they discussed its material and color. The other women all agreed that it was just the right shade for the occasion. Sumi accepted their compliments as she looked over the sewing on the cuffs and hem. I lightly touched the hem of the sleeves and told her that the color suited her quite well. Sumi smiled and continued to finger the material of the dress while the others chatted about food, families, and trips. She waited a while and quietly said, "Well, I hope it looks nice . . . because it's the last dress I'll wear."

In response to my shock, she smiled and explained softly that she had the dress made especially for her funeral. She said that at least for that last day, she wanted to wear what she thought was best for her. Sumi laughed quietly and said she didn't want to look foolish wearing a silly outfit. She would decide what looked best on her.

Sumi lives alone in a spacious two-story home. She mainly stays in the main room downstairs next to the kitchen. Even when Sumi is by herself and not expecting guests, she maintains her routine of putting on makeup and keeping her short hair neatly combed. On days when she does not have any doctor's appointments, she leans back on her favorite chair in front of her kotatsu *with the blaring TV for company.*

19

Sumi spoke Japanese with a slight Korean accent. Her voice was firm, belying her gentle demeanor. She talked about the hardships of her past, and yet, whenever painful images crossed her mind, she would look down at her hands, and then lift her sliding glasses and smile. She never let out a loud laugh or a leg-slapping cackle like many of the women with whom I talked. Her gentle smile never left her face, regardless of her true mood or feelings.

Throughout the interview, one could sense the strong pride and independence with which she faced every situation. Even in confronting her own funeral, Sumi preferred to take care of every detail, rather than cause trouble or discomfort to her children.

My *kohyang* (hometown) is Chinju. Korea is now called "Han'guk," but before it was called "Chosŏn." Before, Chinju was said to be the best place in Korea. Now there is Seoul and it is the most important city, but before, Chinju was the place of importance in Chosŏn. At that time, because of the *oenom* (derogatory word for Japanese), many people were not able to attend school. All the old people, because of the *oenom*, couldn't study—you know that time when the Japanese tried to take away our country.

I heard this story quite often as a child. . . . There were orders for the Chinju *kisaeng* (entertainment woman) to gather to entertain the Japanese officials. During the summer, the Chinju *kisaeng* met their customers on a large raft in the Nangang River. At the gathering, the *kisaeng* made them drink a lot. Afterward, one of the *kisaeng* strangled the top official, tied herself to him and then drowned the man as well as herself. I heard such stories. . . . There is even an old song about that incident. Even now, that Chinju *kisaeng* is famous, and a beautiful house is dedicated to her name. At that time, I wasn't born yet. This is all talk of the old days. But I remember that when I was about five or six years old, in my town there were only Japanese stores. There was of course Japanese writing all over the place, but we didn't know what it meant. The Japanese all had long swords and "*uri saram*" (our people) would have to walk behind them. Even in the schools there were only Japanese children. At that time we didn't have the resources to send children to school, because the Japanese built them all.

I lived in Chinju until I married on December 17. It was one month before I turned eighteen. I went to my husband's village, a bit away from my hometown. A while later he went to Japan to find a job. I joined my husband in Japan a year later.

My birthday is July 15. . . . I'm not sure exactly what year I was born in the Western calendar, but I am eighty-three years old. I was born in the fifth year of Taishō (1916). When I had my first daughter, I was nineteen years old. Then I had seven more children. I have three boys and five girls.

My name is Kōda Sumi. My husband chose this name. He said that it would be better if I were to call myself "Sumi"—a Japanese name—because we live in Japan. Sumi is written in *katakana* (a Japanese syllabary).[1] The name "Kōda" is from the Korean name "Hong." I am not a Hong, but my husband is a Hong. So that name was read in the Japanese pronunciation as "*kō*," and the Japanese sound "*da*" was attached to make it sound like a Japanese name. When the children were born, my husband gave all of them Japanese names. We didn't give them any Korean names, because they aren't useful. Also, it seems that was what the children wanted. Sometimes there would be a letter from the *Mindan* office with our Korean name on it. It seems that the mailman went next door and asked if there were any Koreans living around this neighborhood. So I told the people in the *Mindan* office that if they were going to send us a letter or a notice, I would prefer that they write our Japanese name. Those people, who know that we are Koreans, know, but I suppose most think that we are Japanese.

As for my children, none of them understands Korean. They only speak Japanese. Their citizenship is still Korean,[2] but I don't know how long that will be. In the old days, when my eldest daughter was going to school, a Japanese child bullied her, saying, "*Hey, you are a Chōsen-jin, right?*" But my daughter was tough. . . . *Ha, ha.* She would never lose. She would get into a fight even with a boy, and they would throw punches at each other, but still she would never lose. If she came back home crying after she lost a fight, her father got very angry with her. So she stood her ground and fought and made sure that she won. We never really told them that they should feel proud of being a Korean, but whenever they were bullied and came home crying, my husband would get very angry. I remember my husband used to tell them that if they got into a fight because they were called names such as *Chōsen-jin*, and if they were to lose, then they shouldn't come back home.

Childhood

When I was little and living in Korea, I really liked playing with the other children in the neighborhood. We were a small family. There were only five of us. My parents, my oldest sister, older brother, and I. I was the youngest. My parents sent all of us to school. But I came home crying all the time, because I wanted to see my mother. When I first started going to school, I couldn't stand it for more than a week. I always came home crying, because I hated to study. Even now I hate having to write. My father would get so upset with me. When all the students arrived at my house to study with my father in his *sŏtang*, I would run away and hide before my father called me to join them.

My father taught Chinese classics and writing in his *sŏtang*. People came to study every day. My father used to say that if I didn't learn as a child, then when I grew up I would have a hard life. If I had at least studied with my father, then now I would probably be able to read. My brother and sister both attended school. They both also learned how to write Chinese characters. The only one who didn't study was me. I thought, why should I study? What am I going to do with it? I think that I caused my own ignorance. Many people couldn't attend school even if they wanted to, because they didn't have the resources. But I think how ridiculous it was that when my parents wanted to send me to school, I refused to go. I think that I put a knife into my own heart. Probably at that time, I didn't imagine that times would change like this. *Ha, ha, ha.* . . . You know, probably this is also a part of my *p'alcha* (fate/destiny). . . . I managed to somehow memorize the *han'gŭl* by myself, but after that there was no occasion for me to read and write. After coming to Japan, I slowly began to forget everything. So now my head has become empty and dumb. . . . *Ha, ha, ha.* . . . Not only that—now I'm old, so I've even started to forget the things that I knew before. Just looking at the complicated letters makes my head hurt. This is also my destiny. . . . It's hopeless. *Ha, ha, ha* . . . (she laughs quietly).

Marriage

My husband was three years older than me. I was seventeen and he was twenty. We didn't see each other's faces until the day of the wedding. The matchmaker was my husband's great-aunt, who also happened to be my mother's friend. Well, she asked my mother to allow me and her grandnephew to marry. Until the day of the wedding I didn't know what he looked like. Back then, many people were married this way—meeting each other for the first time on the day of the wedding ceremony. In the old days in Korea, parents decided everything. The children weren't supposed to ask any questions. You just did as your parents told you to do. For the wedding, all the people from the neighborhood gathered and the wedding ceremony was held in my house.

When I went to my husband's house, my mother-in-law had already died. So I didn't have to take care of a mother-in-law. They said she caught a very bad flu that developed into pneumonia, and that is how she died. She was only twenty-seven years old, and she left two sons. My father-in-law left at that time for Japan.[3] My grandfather-in-law had already passed away, so in the house there were only me, my grandmother-in-law, my husband, and my brother-in-law. My grandmother-in-law was very strict. She was quite old. She was seventy-one years old when I went to my husband's house. I remember when she coughed; she spit out her thick, yellow phlegm in a bowl. She couldn't go to the bathroom by herself, so I had to carry her on my back. Although I took care of her like that, she was still very strict with me.

At mealtimes, she would sit in a room with a small window that connected to the kitchen. She would open the window and ask if the rice was done, and when I told her it was, she would order me to scoop it and then slam the window shut. Sometimes, she would leave the window open and watch how I worked in the kitchen. She would tell me to scoop all the rice for the elder of the house and the men, and that if there was not enough rice for me to eat, I should scrape around the pot for each flake and then eat it, and that would be enough. I wondered why she was so strict. . . . I thought how was I supposed to survive on so little food. . . . *Ha, ha, ha.* . . .

Sometimes when we had a guest and I cooked rice, my grandmother-in-law would come into the kitchen and ask for the leftovers. She would take the bowl and put it on top of a shelf right outside her room where she could keep an eye on it to make sure that I didn't eat it. *Ha, ha, ha.* . . . Sometimes I wondered whether there was another household like ours. I heard that my mother-in-law was rarely allowed to eat to her fill, either. Well, even if I was a bit hungry, I couldn't say such things out loud. It seems that my mother-in-law suffered a lot too. That is what the neighbors told me. My grandmother-in-law passed away when she was about seventy-three years old. After she died, I was able to come to Japan.

From the start, my husband and I didn't have a good relationship. If we were people of these times, we would have separated for sure. We just didn't like each other. You know in Korea, we often go to a fortune-teller. . . . Well, the fortune-teller said that we had such a bad relationship because my husband's uncle's jealous spirit stood between us. This uncle, who was twenty-four and single, passed away without having the chance to get married. My mother was quite worried about us and so she went to a fortune-teller and that is what she was told. Several other fortune-tellers, believe it or not, all said the same thing. My mother was from a rural part of Korea. So whenever there was something, for instance, a sickness or something like that, we would call in a *mudang* (shaman) right away, and she would go around the house banging on drums and rubbing her hands together[4] in front of the gods. In order to cleanse our relationship and appease my husband's uncle's spirit, she hired several of them, and they did all sorts of ceremonies. But regardless of all of that, we had to separate. My husband came to Japan alone a year after we married to look for work.

Coming to Japan

After my grandmother-in-law passed away, my brother took care of all of the paperwork for me to come to Japan. I came by myself to join my husband in Ōgaki City in Gifu. My husband was living there doing manual labor. Well, from Chinju I went to Pusan, and then I took the boat. I arrived at Shimonoseki and then I took the train to Gifu-prefecture. I showed my husband's address to this person and that person and that is how I finally arrived. Even when I had to change trains, I would just show the address and people would tell me to either wait here or go there. Well, riding that boat didn't take so long, but riding the train to Gifu took quite a while. I remember it was raining that day and I had to get off at one of the rural stations. There wasn't even a rickshaw passing by so I stood there not knowing what to do. When I looked to my side, there was a small building, which turned out to be a police box. I showed the policeman the address and I spoke in Korean. Also I used my hands and so did he. I couldn't speak Japanese, but I guess he was able to understand my sign language. . . . *Ha, ha, ha.* . . . The elderly policeman told the younger one to take me to the address that I had in my hand. He was really kind. The younger police officer rode a bicycle and I put my luggage on it and hurried along behind. We went for just a short while and we came to a house. A person from my *kohyang* and his wife and two kids were living there with my husband. My husband was just about to leave for Ōsaka. He told me to stay with those people until he came back. They were living in a small farmhouse rented from a local farmer. I stayed for about a week, and then we rented another small room closer to the city.

In Gifu there were many Japanese manual laborers working in the country-side, building roads and such. When I walked outside, these people would yell out things to me and to other Koreans, especially to the elderly, who only wore *hanbok*. At that time, you didn't buy clothes, you bought fabric to make clothes. Older Koreans I guess felt more comfortable in their traditional wear. So those workers used to see the elderly and the women with their dresses and say things. I also wore Korean dresses back then. In the countryside there weren't many Koreans, but in Gifu city as well as Nagoya, there were many.[5] So those laborers would yell out, "*Chōsen-jin, Chōsen-jin.*" Other people like the farmers or neighbors never said anything. Maybe they said things behind our backs, but they never said anything directly to us. When I first came to Japan, we all were made fools of by the *oenom-tŭl.* . . . You know, we Koreans have really come a long way.

Work

Well . . . when I first came to Japan . . . I didn't know a word of Japanese, and until we were able to get settled it was quite hard, because there was not so much work. And the thing about my husband was that he hated to work under other people. He always had to be the boss. So that's why we moved here and there, following different types of jobs and businesses.

From Gifu, we went to Aizu in Nagoya. We went there for work, but it wasn't so good. After that we moved to Nagano . . . it was just in time for the heavy snowfalls. In the beginning my husband used to go to different companies and buy cotton undershirts and then sell them to different shops wholesale. He didn't want to do manual labor any more. In Nagano my husband knew of a person who was involved in building a big factory. He was Japanese, and through this person, my husband was able to make further connections. He would find out what the factories were making, and then he would buy some of the merchandise and resell it to shops and stores. But we didn't stay in Nagano very long either.

The following October, we moved to Gunma. I had my first daughter in Kiryū City, Gunma. After that we came to Mitsuke City near Nagaoka in Niigata. At that time my husband was strictly in the wholesale business and so most of the work he did was on his own and we didn't need workers. After we came to Mituske, we opened up a bigger business, and also one in Nagaoka City. While we were in Mituske, we heard that by starting a legitimate business my husband could avoid the *chōyō* (conscription)[6]. So we started a business loading and transporting goods and materials. We had a couple of oxen and we would load up goods and merchandise for people and haul them to the countryside. At the same time, my husband was also involved in wholesaling kimono materials. This city is famous for weaving fabrics for kimonos. Sometimes he bartered with farmers, and came back with white rice and food. Even during wartime we didn't go hungry, and we even had enough to help those around us. And because we were selling fabrics and materials, we always had enough clothing. In those days people suffered so much because of lack of food, and had to wait for the state handouts of potato and radish. But when we received these rations, we gave them away. We never had to depend on state handouts.

After the war we came to Nagaoka. We settled in Kanda-machi of Nagaoka and ended up staying there for over twenty years. At this time, all the Koreans were trying to get out of Japan. We heard rumors that the Japanese were going to kill all the Koreans. I myself never experienced such bad things, I only heard about such incidents. Everyone was planning to go back to Korea and many did go back, but we decided to stay in Japan. We heard rumors of people having to return to Japan illegally because they couldn't get food. Besides, there was nothing waiting for us in Korea. My brother had died quite young when he was in his thirties, right after sending me off to Japan. My sister had married and so she had no rights to any of the property, so after my parents had passed away, all our land and everything had been divided up by relatives and neighbors. So this is how we decided to stay in Japan.

In Nagaoka we ran *pachinko* parlors and also did other businesses. We also had businesses in Sanjo and Kashiwazaki City in Niigata. At that time there weren't many Koreans doing *pachinko*, because you need a lot of cash to start up the business. But we managed somehow. We ran *pachinko*s and also cafeterias and during the summer we made and sold ice cream. We tried all sorts of things. We did all types of businesses, and then after that we came permanently to Niigata City. We lived here the longest—thirty years.

After coming to Japan, I suffered quite a bit. We did have food and clothing, but I had to work so hard in order to survive. I had to work in all of our stores and factories, and especially I had to work hard to take care of all of our workers. We had to be able to read and write and take care of all the paperwork for our businesses, but I couldn't do that. I always had to ask others about everything, and that was one of the hardest things.

When I was young in Japan, I was so busy trying to make a living that I had no time to study Japanese. In the morning I had to get up at about four, and I couldn't sleep until about midnight, because I had to help take care of the *pachinko* parlor or the cafeterias. In those days, workers used to live in dormitories provided by the workplace, called *sumi-komi*. All of our workers stayed on average seven to eight years. We had to feed them, and I had to clean up after them. Of course I did have helpers, but we didn't hire them around the clock, and there was always something to be done. At that time there was no running water in places such as Mitsuke or Nagaoka. So every morning I carried big buckets and fetched water from the nearby river. I took the men's clothes down to the river, washed the whole load, and then dragged it back and hung it up to dry. After that I cooked rice, and the men wouldn't be able to eat all together, so I prepared the table several times until all of them were fed. I didn't even have time to step out of the house in order to learn to ride the bicycle. Can you believe it? At this age, I still don't know how to ride a bicycle. *Ha, ha, ha. . . .*

When I think about it now, I wonder how I was able to survive . . . I wonder how I managed. Now when I watch TV, I think that people really lead an easy life these days. Young women now can't live in the times that I did—there is no way they can do that kind of work. There were so many things to do that even if I fell ill, there was absolutely no way I could lie down. Times have really changed.

Husband's Death

Even after I came to Japan, my husband and I had such a bad relationship that it was hard to bear. We never sat together face to face even to eat our meals. We never talked to each other. I would just cook and then whenever he thought the meal was ready, he would sit at the table. Whenever I brought out the bed sheets, if the blanket was too thin for him, he would just go and get another blanket. We said hardly a word to each other. *Ha, ha . . .* (she laughs quietly). But yeah, you're right, we still had eight children. You know, it's not only couples with a good relationship that can have children. You have children because it's something that can't be helped—the *Samshin halmŏni*[7] makes the children for you.

In the beginning, no matter who you are, you go through hard times, coming all the way here to another country, because you don't know the language, and work is hard to find. So, I guess you can say that we had a hard time. But luckily we didn't have to worry about not having enough clothes to warm us or enough food to eat. My husband was really a kind person. If he saw someone who needed something, he would give the clothes off his back. Even now during the New Year, from places like Nagaoka where he had a lot of friends and acquaintances, all sorts of gifts are sent to our home, like coffee, delicacies, and spices.

My husband died sixteen years ago when he was sixty-nine years old. He was in a car accident and he didn't live too long after that. If it weren't for the accident, he might still be alive right now. We were living in Nagaoka and we also started a business in Koide, so he was driving from one place to the other. In Koide, he stopped his car and was waiting for the light to turn, when a truck crashed into him from behind. He was rushed to the hospital. The telephone call came at night from the doctor. The doctor said that my husband was in critical condition and whether he lived or died depended on his condition that night. I received such a shock that I fainted and then I too had to go into the hospital. My husband managed to recover and leave the hospital, but he was not a man to keep still. As soon as he started to feel a bit better he started to move around. He pushed himself too hard and his health began to fail. He went in and out of the hospital. After the accident, he couldn't move his body very well. But still he pushed himself and got worse and worse. I think he really suffered a lot . . . a lot.

Children

Whenever I had children, I had them by myself. My children were all breeched, and so when the babies were about to come, I couldn't stand the pain. I had my first baby in the middle of the night all alone. In the old days there were no doctors. There were midwives, but it was late at night and there was no one to call the midwife for me. My husband was not at home. Even if he had been, he wouldn't have been able to help. He was never around for any of the children's births. If all of my children were living, I would have a total of twelve. But now I only have eight. From the top, there are three daughters, and then after that there are three sons, and then after that two daughters. I lost four children—one son lived for one week and died, then afterward, I had a child that I miscarried, and then my second daughter was born upside down, and another daughter was born upside down and died. So I guess there were four of them that I lost. *Ahhh* . . . (she sighs) this really is talk of the old days.

Well, I guess I thought I was going to die myself so I couldn't feel so much sadness for the babies. My neighbors said that it was a good thing that I, the mother, didn't die, and I was lucky. I always gave birth during the night. That was unlucky. The babies were all quite big, and because they were breeched, there was nothing that could have been done. If I had given birth to them during the afternoon, then maybe I could have called for help. I can't think how many times I almost died giving birth. Whenever my mother asked the fortune-tellers, they always warned me to be careful when I gave birth, because I might die doing so.

When I was giving birth to my children, I pushed them out, and often I forced them out. When the babies were about to come, it would hurt so bad that I would literally roll around on the floor. When you are pushing out the baby, you need to hold on to something in order to brace yourself. So I held on to the dresser and pushed. When I had enough strength to look down, I saw the baby's feet, and then when I pushed with all my might, I saw the baby's face—blue with the umbilical cord wrapped around it. So I guess that's how the babies died even before coming all the way out. . . . *Ahh* . . . (she sighs heavily). I just lay there with half of the baby sticking out of my body, and I was afraid that I might die just like that. So I held onto that dresser as hard as I could and I pushed the baby out. That's when I saw the baby's blue face. I saw death in the eyes several times. There was also one child that I lost when I was five months pregnant. I was carrying something really heavy and that night my stomach started to hurt so bad I thought I was going to die. When I went to the bathroom, it was just blood, and then a big lump covered in blood just dropped out. It was five months old. I just pushed with all my strength and that's when the clump of my five-

month-old baby came out. . . . For me, in my life I have overcome so many en-
counters with death. I would just do the only thing that I could, and that was to
gaman, gaman (endure). . . . A lifelong suffering. . . . *Ha, ha, ha* . . . (she laughs
quietly). Now I can utter these words, but when I was faced with these things, I
couldn't say anything. It was the same as being dead. I guess it was just the
times, and there was nothing that could be done about it. Well, it's all about the
past and the kind of life that I have led. But now, my life is almost over. The
time is coming soon. I think it's coming quite soon. You know, it's amazing that
I have come to live so long.

Reflection

I think the only reason that I was able to survive is that I am a person of those
times, and I had to keep with the traditions and customs of that time. No matter
how good or bad, you just couldn't speak out, you can't argue. That was just the
way it was. You don't think of things as good or bad. You didn't consider back
then whether you had a good or bad relationship—if you were married you just
had to accept it and live on. Regardless of whether a couple had a good relationship, they never showed it in front of others; and if it was bad, they never uttered
a word. Even after a couple had children, they could never hug their babies or
talk sweet to them in front of the elders. It was quite strict in the old days in Korea. That is how I have come to live up to now.

When I say *kosaeng*, it was mostly mentally and emotionally that I have
suffered. I never had to worry about things like food, clothes, money, and
whether we had to borrow money that we couldn't pay back and things like that.
The fact that my husband and I never shared any affection or love for each other,
that was one *kosaeng*—the fact that I had to give birth to my children alone and
had to lose so many of them was another *kosaeng*. Also, during the times when
we were expanding our business and I had to take care of all the workers and
cook and clean for all of them plus our own family—that was another *kosaeng*. I
guess the hardest things for me was taking care of my children and working so
hard. There were too many people to take care of. But since I am a person from
the old days, I just had to endure, "*Gaman, gaman*." Enduring, that's my only
strength. How do you say *gaman* in Korean? *Ch'ama*? Whatever happens, you
just have to *ch'ama*. You know, of course there were times when I wanted to say
all that was on my mind, but there wasn't a time when I told my husband how I
felt, no matter what. . . . *Ha, ha, ha* . . . (she laughs quietly). Anyway, he is not
the type of person who would listen and try to change his ways for me. . . . *Ha,
ha, ha* . . . (she laughs quietly).

After coming to Japan in order to make a living, my husband went here and
there and worked to his bones. If he was the type to go to work for someone, and
simply receive his pay—this much for that many hours of work—then I think
that he wouldn't have had to work so hard. But when you have your own business, there are so many things that need to be done, taken care of, and worried

about. And just when I thought that things were settling down and that he would have an easier life, then the car accident happened. . . . I just felt very sorry for him. . . .

Whenever I think about the past and all the hard times, the tears just come. Before there were always people around or my children, so sometimes I would just cry alone quietly at night. I would just sigh and the sobbing would follow. I would cry quietly by myself for a while and then stop, swallow hard and go to sleep. You know in my life, everything was about *gaman*. *Gaman, gaman*, that was all that I could do—that was all that I knew how to do.

You know, there is an old saying that people with money suffer, because they work hard to acquire and maintain their wealth, but people who don't have much suffer, because they don't have enough. So I guess while human beings are alive, they constantly face *kurō* (suffering). . . . Whoever they are. When I think about it now if you don't suffer at least a little bit, it's no good. I guess that is why I have lived so long. I guess this is part of life. When I think about the fact that I have spent my life in this way, going through such hard times—more than regret I think to myself, "*yoku yatte kita—I have done my best. . . .*"

Notes

1. During Sumi's time, many women's names were written in *katakana* rather than Chinese characters.

2. On April 28, 1952, when the San Francisco Peace Treaty formally ended the U.S. occupation of Japan, Koreans were officially stripped of their Japanese nationality. Since Japanese citizenship is granted through bloodline rather than through place of birth, Koreans born in Japan only inherit their parents' citizenship. However, the number of Koreans in Japan who are willing to naturalize as Japanese citizens has been increasing. In 1997 alone, more than nine thousand were naturalized. See Ryang (2000a: 6-7).

3. Sumi's father-in-law went to Japan in search of work when a boom in Japan's industrial economy during World War I resulted in a labor shortage that was filled in part by cheap labor from Korea in industries such as coal mining, construction work, and textiles. See Weiner (1994: 113).

4. "Banging the drums and rubbing their hands together" refers to the rituals that the shaman conducted. "Rubbing one's hands together" means to pray.

5. Large Korean populations formed ghettos in the outlying areas of the industrial urban centers of Tōkyō, Kyōto, Nagoya, Kōbe, Yokohama, and Fukuoka. The heaviest concentration then and since was in Ōsaka, Japan's industrial center, where Koreans made up almost 10 percent of the population. See Lee and DeVos (1981a: 44).

6. By 1944, all males aged between twelve and fifty-nine and unmarried females aged between twelve and thirty-nine were required to register in order for the government to monitor labor mobility. See Weiner (1994: 190-191).

7. The domestic deity *Samshin halmŏni* (old lady Samshin) is the protecting spirit of children. According to Cha, Chung, and Lee (1977: 115), Samshin embodies the spirits of fertility. See also Kendall (1985, 1988).

Chapter 3

Through His Grace

Pak Sam-Yang

Pak Sam-Yang lives alone on the second floor of a two-story apartment complex in Ikuno Ward, Ōsaka.[1] She is a small, plump woman whose skin color, unlike that of most women her age, is a rich brown. She has a high-pitched voice that breaks into little giggles and alert eyes that show a trace of mischief.

When I mentioned what I had heard about the diving skills of Chejudo women, her face broke into a wide grin. Even when I was quite young, I traveled to many different places to dive. I wasn't afraid to go deep. Ahhh. . . . But that was long ago. . . . There are so many things. *She touched the side of her face with her rough hand.* In my younger days, I never even had to put on any makeup; people always thought that I had makeup on. But you know there are so many reasons why my face looks like this now, that's for sure.

I reassured her that I could still see why she received many compliments in her youth. She let out one of her giggles, paused for a minute and asked, "Hey, do you attend church?" I nodded and told her that my family attends church. Sam-Yang nodded her head approvingly. Now, eat some of this. You must be hungry. Studying and going all over the place, you must not be eating too well. Your mother must be worried. Here, eat some of these oranges. *In exchange I placed a small plate of cake in front of her.* Well, before we eat, let's not forget to pray. Let us pray. . . .

We both closed our eyes and put our hands together before us on top of the table. Sam-Yang sighed heavily and after a few seconds began to pray. Our Father and our Protector, thank you very much. Today, we have once again by-

31

passed our hardships and we are blessed by your love and presence. Tonight, a beloved daughter has come to talk to an old lady like me. We are sharing a wonderful conversation, sharing our company and our love for You. . . . We have come far from our *kohyang* and we have left everything that we know of but allow us to always to know that our true *kohyang* is up in heaven with You. . . .

My name is Pak Sam-Yang. I am eighty years old. I was born in Taishō 6 (1917), July 7, in Chejudo, Hallim-myŏn, Wŏllyŏng—I don't know what you call it now, but in the old days it was called that.

My parents, well mostly my mother, worked on the farm doing manual labor. She also used to dive. I also did *muljil* (diving) from when I was little. I was the youngest child. My mother thought that she was finished with being able to have children and it seems that I happened unexpectedly. I had two older brothers, then the rest were girls and including me there were five of us. There was a big age difference between me and my brother and sisters. As far as I can remember they were all married and living with their own families. My eldest brother moved to Kyoto when he was very young. He worked as an apprentice for making kimono, and after that he owned his own business. My father thought that sons should be well educated, and he didn't want them to do anything but study. After they finished their studies in Japan, I heard that they decided to stay there.

Family

My mother was really a good person. She had to do such hard manual labor on the farm, and she also did *muljil*. She really tried to do her best in everything, no matter what she did. My mother passed away when she was quite young. She passed away when she was sixty-five years old after she fell ill. She was really a good mother to me. My father was quite strict. He was really a frightening father. He didn't allow me to do anything. He didn't want me to learn my letters. He didn't want me to go to school and didn't even let me attend night classes so that I could at least learn how to read. He always said that a girl has to be raised in a very strict manner or she will be ruined. Even going to the water for *muljil*—he said that kind of work was for the ignorant peasants. He said that in a *yangban*'s home such work isn't permissible. I used to think even as a child that *yangban* or not, my mother worked like a dog—slaving over the farmland, and also going to *muljil* in order to make a living for us.

It seems that my father's family in the old days, from the time of my grandfather, had a lot of property. My grandparents died when my father was very young. A while after my mother and father married, and when my eldest brother had just been born, it seems that during one night of gambling, my father lost everything by pressing the *tojang* (seal)—all the house, farmland, and land that my grandfather had left him. . . . He lost it all. My mother wondered how she was going to live her life with a man like my father who gambled away all of his property. But every time he lost what little they had, my father promised her that he would never gamble again. He would beg her not to leave. . . . He even went as far as cutting his finger to write a letter of promise in blood to my mother, saying that he would never gamble again. So my mother would think that this time for sure he would give it up. But within a week or two, once his friends came around and called his name, without saying anything to her, he rushed out. . . .

My eldest brother was just born then and was still suckling at her breast, but she decided that there was nothing else to do but to go back to her *ch'inchŏng.* When my father found out that my mother was planning to leave, he took the baby away from her. My mother thought that there was no other way but to leave. . . . All of their property was gone and no matter what she did, he couldn't stop his gambling habit. She decided that she was going to go back to her *ch'inchŏng* with or without the baby. In one week, her breasts were so swollen, and all she could think about was how thirsty and hungry her baby must be. She decided to go back and somehow try to get the baby away from my father. When she went back, my father refused to let her go back. So she ended up staying and working so hard all her life—farming and *muljil, muljil* and farming. Through her money management and hard work, she built several houses and bought a lot of land all on her own.

My father was especially strict with me. He absolutely refused to allow me to go to *muljil. Ha, ha. . . .* My father was so pleased with me when I helped around the house and on the farm, feeding the cows and the horses and such. He would tell me to do those kinds of things, but all of my friends were at the sea playing in the water and making a little money for themselves. I couldn't even go out of the house. I was so frustrated and I disliked my father very much. I thought that if I couldn't go to school during the day, then at least I wanted to go to night school to study, but he wouldn't even allow me to do that. He used to say that a girl should not go outside at night. Still, even though he was strict about such things, I was really spoiled when I was little.

In the old days, I had a lot of hair, and back then, especially during the hot summer, there used to be lice. I remember my father would take me aside and put oil on my hair, and then take a very thin comb and brush strand by strand to make the lice fall off. Then, afterward, he would brush my hair neatly and then braid it.[2] In things like that he was very kind and gentle to me. But the fact that he did not allow me to do the things that I wanted to do—for instance, study or go out to swim freely—made me dislike him so much. *Ha, ha, ha . . .* (she laughs quietly).

My father used to travel a lot and go to all sorts of places like Taegu, and even to China. . . . My father had three other siblings and there were four of them in all. His siblings all went abroad. One even went as far as America. My father, too, went abroad quite a bit. My mother used to say that just when she would give birth to one child and then a while had passed when she could lie down comfortably again, my father would return in time for another baby to be conceived. Sometimes, he would be gone as long as three years. As soon as he returned, my mother said, it was time for another child to be born. So my mother had in all eight children.

My mother took care of the babies all by herself. My father had no relatives to help her with the children or the work. My mother did farm work, *muljil,* everything. When the seaweed harvest was good, then she would take all of those many strands of seaweed and hang them one by one and dry them in order to sell them. Those who had relatives living with them had some help, and the elderly might look after the children. Most of the women would either work in the field or go out to do *muljil,* and when they came back with the catch, then the rest of the relatives would help clean and sort the seaweed. But my mother had to do everything by herself. She would work all day in the fields, harvesting, taking care of the livestock. Then when the women went out early in the morning—she would never be late, but always be on time or earlier. She worked like that all her life without any help and that was how she increased our properties. My mother really endured a lot of *kosaeng.* Thanks to my mother, I never had to suffer for lack of food to eat or clothes to wear. My mother provided for us quite well.

I heard that my father went all over the world to buy things in different countries and then traveled to many places to sell them. . . . I guess for him, traveling to many different places to try to sell things was hard as well. In the old days, there were many people who came to Chejudo as traveling merchants. Many outsiders came to Chejudo believing that life was convenient and that people were really kind. Eventually, the outsiders started getting rich off of us building houses that were several stories high. But many of us locals became almost like beggars. Well, anyway many people came to Chejudo hoping to get rich. But as soon as they arrived some of the unlucky ones realized that things weren't as easy as they heard. They wandered around from place to place with nothing to eat. Sometimes, when beggars would stop at our house, or whenever my mother would see people from the outside who looked like they were having a hard time without a place to stay—whoever it was, she would take them in. She never refused a person in need. She fed them, and she lodged them. My father, too, whenever he came back home, also told us that we should take in people who were in need. I guess himself as a traveler understood their hardships. My father was also quite kind in this way, but he was so strict with me. . . . *Ha, ha, ha* . . . (she laughs quietly).

Muljil: Diving

We lived near the water and all the girls, even the first-graders in elementary school, used to go into the water to swim. I myself learned it naturally. . . . When we were little, we played near the shallow areas, and learned how to hold our breath and swim strongly. I would go into the water with friends and we would teach ourselves how to float and swim and hold our breath for a long time. That was how I learned. Slowly I began to get used to holding my breath, seeing underwater, and swimming. Then, step-by-step, I would go deeper and deeper. You don't go deep right away. My mother was really an excellent diver. Although my mother was so successful due to her diving talents, my father tried to make sure that I did not dive. He was really against it. But I wanted to go to the water so much. All of my friends started diving. Whenever my father was away—of course, the first thing I did was run to the water. Through those opportunities, when he was not around, I learned how to dive. I guess my mother's blood was running thick in me because from the time I was just ten years old I was able to go to very deep areas where only adults could go.

I used to go way under, wearing only goggles. You stay underwater looking for things until you feel as if you can't breathe anymore. In those days we didn't have equipment like the oxygen masks that people use now. In the old days you wore a simple suit and goggles and stayed under as long as you could hold your breath. During February and March there was a lot of seaweed to pull out and then after that when the water got warmer there were all kinds of things. The big catches were *sazae* (turban shells) and *awabi* (abalone). For things like seaweed you would dip your head and see where to go. When you get to the bottom, you just head in the direction that you saw the seaweed, get your knife and grab a whole bunch and cut it and bring it up. But things like *sazae* and *awabi*, you can't spot from above. You have to go all the way down and look underneath rocks and behind corals because usually that's where they stick themselves. You have to swim all around to look for it with a little *pich'ang* (jackknife) that you scrape and dig with. Things like *sazae*, you can find underneath rocks and such, but *awabi* you have to dig and scrape off, because it sticks underneath the rocks and corals. Sometimes, without enough strength it's really hard to get it off. When you spot the shells you scrape them off, and then you come back up for air and empty your net. Then, you take another deep breath and go under again.

When you go with the adults and go where it is quite deep then you can have a chance at a big catch like a huge *awabi*, not a small one, but a *k'ŭn-nom* (huge sucker) *hee, hee* . . . (she giggles). And even for *sazae*, there are big shells as well. When you stay in the shallow areas, the shells are quite small, but I looked forward to the big catch, so I went where the adults went. They used to scold me terribly, saying that a child should not go somewhere so deep, because it was too dangerous. But still I went with them.

One of my relatives actually died while doing *muljil*. . . . She was running out of breath but didn't want to abandon the catch, and so by the time she scraped it off, it was too late. She couldn't swim up fast enough. You know when you are trying to scrape off the *awabi* and if you feel that you are running out of breath, you just have to abandon the catch and come up no matter how close it is. But the thing is once you come back up and you go back down again, then the tides change and you can't find the same spot—so your catch is gone. I guess sometimes it's tempting to see the abalone as money, and you don't want to lose the catch. Even when your breath is about to be cut off, you continue to try to scrape it off. . . .

Sometimes it's too late, just like what happened to one of my relatives. There have been many cases like that. That was the reason why the adults try to make sure that children don't go with them to such deep places. They either chase you off or get really angry. But still no matter what they did, I followed from behind because I loved to catch the big suckers. *Ha, ha, ha* . . . (she roars with laughter). Even if I could only catch one, I wanted to get a big one. . . . It wasn't exactly that I was greedy—I just thought if I was going to catch anything, I wanted to catch a big one. *Ha, ha, hee* . . . (she laughs out loud). So in order for me to do *muljil,* I went here and there and traveled a bit from the time when I was quite young. From the time I was sixteen years old, I went to places like Bukhoedong, Hwanghae-do, Sŏbong, Wŏnsan, and Kyŏngsang-do, and I even went to the northern coast of Japan. When I was seventeen years old I went to dive there. When I was twenty-one, I went to Kyŏngsang-do and I lived there for one year.

I would go and swim, and when I got a catch, there were wholesalers to whom I could sell it. Even in my *kohyang,* when I caught expensive things like abalone, I was able to sell it to wholesalers for pretty good money. The wholesalers then sold it to big factories for canning. The seaweed brought in good money, too. The seaweed from Chejudo has been exported all over the world. Most of the seaweed that is cut and dried in Chejudo is consumed by outside people.

Marriage

While you are doing *muljil,* if you think for one minute that what you are doing is dangerous, then you wouldn't be able to do that kind of work but . . . (she lets out a deep sigh). But . . . I got a disease from the sea. Getting the illness from the sea, I came to believe in Jesus Christ. . . . *Ahh.* . . (she sighs again). When I was nineteen years old, I got married. But even after we were married, my husband was living in Japan, and I was still living in my *kohyang,* going here and there with many job offers. My husband's mother had passed away when he was five years old, and he had a stepmother. My husband, although he was a son, was not sent to school and actually his father was against the idea of him learning his letters. His father told him that all he had to do was work. He was also from Chejudo, from the next town. My husband said that he wanted to study so much that sometimes he would secretly go to a school just to see what it looked like inside. So when he was twelve or thirteen years old, he came over to Japan all alone, so that he could work and also go to school. Luckily, he was taken in as an apprentice by a Japanese person. He worked during the day and studied at night school.

So it was in my *kohyang* that, through a person we knew, my parents and his parents arranged for us to marry. About two years after the arrangements were made, we were supposed to marry. About three days before our wedding, he returned from Japan for the ceremony. After the ceremony, my husband went right back to Japan. But I stayed back in my hometown for four years . . . *hew* . . . (she sighs).

I was the youngest in my family so maybe I was spoiled, but living together with a man—I didn't want to do that. My way of thinking was still very immature, and perhaps that was why I just couldn't imagine myself being someone's wife. Although I was really past the marrying age, my mind was like a little girl. I couldn't understand the custom of a man and woman living together. So I used to always say that I was going to live with my mother. Although I had married, because of my insisting that I didn't want to go right away to my husband's home, my parents told his parents that I would go to Japan a little while later when I had fully matured. My husband went back to Japan in January and I stayed at home. In February, I went to *muljil* and this was when I got the illness from the sea. After trying anything and everything to cure myself, I finally started believing in Jesus. That is how I have come to live this long. . . . *Ah* . . . (she sighs).

There are so many things . . . but in order for me to describe everything . . . there is no end. . . .

Religion

For one year in the midst of my illness, my parents tried everything—calling a *mudang*, doing a *kŭs* (exorcism ritual), everything that they could think of. . . . But I didn't get any better. . . .

In the beginning when I had that illness. . . . It was an illness that can't really be explained. . . . Shall I say it could be an illness that came with shock or trauma? One day I went out to *muljil*, and I went out pretty far as usual where all the adults were swimming. I was following behind and in the middle from afar, I saw something that looked like a high mountain moving toward me. . . . Then, in a second, before I could even think . . . the mountain fell on me and covered me. . . . It must have been even higher than a mountain because I couldn't see the sky. . . .

During that time I don't know what happened . . . maybe it was God allowing me to live . . . all I could feel myself do was spin and turn as if I was in the middle of a tornado. . . . I couldn't go down and I couldn't go up, all I could do was spin in the middle. . . . There was an older woman who was swimming nearby, and I guess when she looked over she saw that someone was spinning. Finally, while I was being spun, my body was pushed up to the surface, and then I went down again. On top of the spin there was just a gurgle of bubbles. Then as the bubbles started to subside, the water turned a thick white color. And as it turned this color I guess you could glimpse a person spinning in the water. So that woman who was nearby and saw the sea turn white swam over to me, grabbed me out, and dragged me to shore. She was hitting me and trying to get me back to consciousness. I didn't know or feel anything for a while, and then I suddenly awoke.

I suppose if I were to have gone really far out and this kind of thing had happened, I probably would have died there and never come back. But on that day, I was halfway between the shore and the place where everyone had swam ahead to. That's where it happened. The person who had dragged me out, luckily, was an older woman who could no longer go too far out and was staying close to mid-distance when she saw me spinning round and round. So I was with her for a little while until I came to consciousness, and then I was able to go back home. I don't know how I managed to walk back home that day.

When I got home, I locked myself in my room. Soon after that I couldn't stand to look at any person's face. . . . I hated the sound of talking. . . . My head was pounding so much. . . . *Ai-hyoo*. . . . *Ha* . . . (she sighs). I couldn't stand to listen to my parents. . . . Even when it was midsummer, I closed all the doors and windows and locked myself in. . . . I stayed under a heavy blanket and just lay in the darkness. I couldn't move. . . . I lay there and stared at the ceiling with my mouth open, and sometimes I could see a fly buzzing over my mouth and then it would disappear for a moment and fly out. It was as if I was paralyzed, and I couldn't move a limb. The fly would lay its waste on my tongue, and I could taste the bitterness as it slid down the back of my throat. . . . *Aigu . . . aigu* . . . (she shut her eyes tightly and shook her head side to side).

My parents—after trying everything they could think of, thought that there was no hope and that it was only a matter of time before I would die. They asked if I would like to eat this or that and whatever I wanted they said they would give me. But just listening to their voices made me feel so much hate. For a while, my parents brought things for me to eat and tried to feed me, but I just got frantic and crazy. They would bring something to me and beg me to open the door, but after a while, they stopped doing that as well. I guess they just gave up and thought that there was nothing else for me to do except to die. . . .

One day, it was in the middle of September, and it was the busiest time for them because of the upcoming harvest. I was in my room as usual with the door locked, staring into space. It was about three o'clock in the afternoon. In the old days, in the country there wasn't such a thing as a clock. I must have for some reason looked out the window, because I remember the day was getting a darker color of red, and it looked like it was heading into the late afternoon. I got up and went to the window and opened it up and looked outside for the first time since my illness. The sky was getting really bright red, which was a sign that the sun was about to set. Then suddenly I heard myself think. I remember this day so clearly because it was the first time in a long time that I heard myself think. What I thought of at that moment, as I looked up at the clouds, was that if I continue like this I will certainly die.

Out of the blue, for some reason, I thought about these two old women peddlers I met in my childhood who were selling thread and cloth out of sacks. They were carrying *pottaegi* (sacks) on their heads. We were, as I said, living quite well and there were always plenty of things to eat. One day there were these two old women whom my father had brought home to feed. My mother set the table for them with all the rice scooped high that we had prepared for the next morning. I remember that before they ate, the two women put their hands together in front of them, closed their eyes, and then were saying something. At that time I was so little—barely ten years old. But I still remember thinking how funny the two women looked. I wondered why it was that they sat in front of the table and instead of eating right away, just sat there with their eyes closed. I really thought that it was strange but funny. I thought maybe they were sleeping. . . . *Ha, ha, ha* . . . (she laughs quietly). After they finished, what I know now to be prayer, I asked them, *"Grandma, what are you doing closing your eyes before you eat?"* One of the ladies said to me, *"Oh,* agaya *(child), we are believers in* Hanŭnim *(God)."* I asked, *"Hah . . .? Where is* Hanŭnim?*"* The lady smiled and said, *"*Hanŭnim *is always with you no matter where you are.* Hanŭnim *is everywhere."* I thought about what she said for a while. *"What happens, if I become like you and believe in* Hanŭnim?*"* The lady said, *"If you believe in God, then you will become a really good person with a good heart. If you believe in God, when you die, then you will go to a wonderful place called Heaven."* I said, *"When you believe in God, you become a good person, and when you die you go to a wonderful place?"* She nodded her head and smiled at me. *"That's right."*

Since that time, of course, I had forgotten all about this meeting with these two old ladies. But on that day when I looked up in the sky and was watching the clouds, for some reason I thought of that time during my childhood. . . . I remembered it as if it were yesterday. Then, I thought out of nowhere that maybe I should go to a church. That day I slowly crawled to the door and unlocked it. I was so weak because for several months I had barely eaten. I was half human, half corpse. . . . I just sat there and I was waiting for my parents to come back home from the fields. For months, I had hated the looks on their faces, I had hated to hear their voices. I had been cursing them, yelling at them like a crazed animal, but on this day as I sat there—I could hardly wait until they came back.

Finally my parents came back home from the fields. I tried to open the door, but I didn't have enough strength. I called out to my mother and I whispered, *"Ŏmŏni . . . ŏmŏni. . . ."* My mother was very shocked, and she flung open the door. She had this fearful look on her face. She thought that finally it was my time to die and that was why I was calling out to her so gently. They say that when people are about to die, their behavior changes drastically. Even though I had been yelling and cursing at them, now that death was near I became the way I had been before my sickness. She rushed inside and dropped to my side. I told her that if I were to die I would surely fall into hell, and even if I were to live I would have such evil thoughts, hating my parents, cursing them, and hating everyone in sight. I told her that maybe if I went to church I would feel better.

My mother, I guess, felt so happy she was willing to try anything. My father, too, said that once I felt strong enough, I should try attending church right away. They told me later that when they were working in the fields they discussed church several times as the last resort after trying everything and failing. So, when they heard me say the same thing, they were both very happy and in full agreement. The only problem was the fact that I was married. This illness occurred soon after I got married, and so we wondered what my husband's household would think about the fact that I wanted to attend church. But my father—a father who was so strict that he never allowed me to do anything—said it didn't matter what my husband's family said, and that he would give me permission to attend church. He said that if they didn't like it, they could simply cancel the marriage and get a new bride. All he cared about was that I became healthy and normal. He told me not to worry about anything and do what made me happy.

In our neighborhood, most people went out to their fields every day, naturally including Sundays. But there were two or three people among us who did attend church, and on Sundays, these churchgoers would dress up very nicely and stroll to church, even when it was in midsummer and everyone was busy getting ready for the harvest. Back then, I heard that these people were attending a place called *kyohoe* (church), but I had no idea what it meant. I, myself, had never seen a church. Then, one day my parents went to those people and asked them if it was possible for them to take me with them. So that was how I went for the first time when I was twenty years old. Those neighbors gave me a small red hymnbook and they told me to bring it with me the next day, which was a Sunday. Back then there was no electricity of course, and we used a tiny oil lamp that barely lit up the room. I opened the hymnbook and I looked into it, but I couldn't read and didn't know what it was for.

I hadn't realized how far the church was. We were living in Wŏllyŏng, and in order to get to the church we had to walk past two other villages, Kŭmnyŭng and Hyŏkchae. The church was at the third village. The night before I had thought that to have enough strength for the walk I had to eat something, and so for the first time I asked my mother to make me some gruel. For some reason, I felt really good, and I felt stronger than ever before. The next day when the family came to call for me, and the man was going to put me on his back, I said that I wanted to try to walk there by myself. Until then, for months I had lain flat on my back, unable to move. But for some reason that day I felt very strong and energetic. Although we had to go a long way to church, I made it all the way there on my own two feet without the man having to carry me on his back. In the old days, in the country, there was no such a thing as a bus. You had to walk everywhere. On the way to church, the family would suggest stopping to rest, but I wasn't feeling tired at all that morning. Finally, we made it to the church. It was a regular-looking house with several rooms. It was a small congregation of only a few people. In fact there was no minister, nor an elder, and the sermon was given by the person who held the position of *chipsa* (deacon).

Well, I went inside the church, but I don't know what was wrong with me. . . . It sounds crazy, but when I went inside and saw the others in the church . . . they didn't look human at all, but looked like some kind of animal. When they spoke to me, their language didn't sound like human language, but the weird sound of animals. . . . The people who I went with motioned for me to sit down, and one of them pulled me down. When I sat down . . . I couldn't stand the pain. My body felt as if it were being stabbed by a thousand needles from head to toe, and all I could hear was a voice telling me to get out. My body started to twitch with pain. . . . It felt like I was losing control of my body and mind, and I could barely handle myself. So I just told the person who had brought me that I was feeling so bad that I couldn't stay any longer. I just stood up somehow, and rushed out. . . . When I was walking back home, I felt I was going crazy. I would walk for a while, and then I would trip for no reason, and just lie there. I got up again and staggered a little farther and then the same thing would happen. In the end I don't know how I got home. . . . I must have crawled. . . . But you know the amazing thing was, as the days passed, I would actually feel hungry, and feel calmer in my mind. Believe it or not, the following Sunday I decided to give it another try, and I began to feel better. In time I felt normal again.

My father-in-law, hearing all sorts of stories and rumors around the village, came to my house and brought with him a shaman. . . . After the ritual where this *mudang* danced and carried on, my father-in-law said he wanted to sit down and talk with me. He said he was afraid that I might have a disease that could be infectious, and that I would bring the disease into his home and make the other children and even his own wife ill. Then, he said that until I cured myself of the disease, I should not set foot in his house. As a matter of fact, he said that he was going to contact his son and have him marry someone else. I guess he was trying to say that he wanted to cancel my marriage to my husband. He said that his family and household had been for generations devout Buddhists, and not one of them ever had the disease of believing in Jesus. In the village they were from, in Kŭmnyŭng, the Yangs were quite prominent in the village. So what he was saying was that there was no need for a person like me, who was starting to attend church and believe in Jesus.

Although I hadn't yet lived with my husband and his family, still to hear my father-in-law say those things certainly didn't make me happy. I thought to myself, why did I have to get sick and then have to hear this kind of thing from these people. I felt so frustrated with myself—I just wanted to die. . . . I got married to this man whom I have never lived with—whose family I have only seen once or twice, and then a month later I became ill. I thought what was the use of living. . . . I felt very depressed for a while. But I continued to attend church every Sunday without fail. Perhaps because of the peace that I found through faith, my body got stronger and stronger. I was able to move, the heaviness in my head was slowly disappearing, and my hair started to grow back. . . . By the following New Year, I was fully recuperated. When spring came, several of my friends started going to the waterside to do some *muljil*, and I went with them to swim a little bit and then once again got used to the water. My parents encouraged me to go and my father ordered all kinds of Chinese herbal medicine from Seoul. Soon I was back at work and had gone to Kyŏngsang-do for *muljil* with my cousin. There I met some of the people in that village who were attending a church up in the mountains. During the week, they worked very hard, but on Sundays they dropped everything in order to attend church. On regular days when the weather was good I went out to dive, but on windy days I went to church instead. On the days I went out into the water, thanks to God, the weather always held up.

For Cheju people, it was the tradition to go back home during the winter months, no matter where you work during the diving season. So all of the divers would take a rest for about three months. I decided to go see my parents. I took a few things that I needed and went back home. A diver from my hometown who was passing through said that in Chejudo on that year there was heavy rainfall. Due to the rain many divers lost their lives. The mountains were crumbling and the ocean was overflowing. So I went back home, and I stayed there with my parents. But I stayed far away from my in-laws' home. Then, while I was out walking, I met my father-in-law on the road. He used to always look at me with such a terrible expression, but this time when he saw me so healthy and strong, he greeted me first and asked how I was feeling. I guess after seeing me so healthy he had a change of heart. He asked me when I had come back. I had been back home for five days, but to my father-in-law I lied and said I had just gotten back home the night before. He told me to come to his house for dinner, because he had something very important to say to me. I went back home and I told my father that what had happened. My father got upset. *"What is he saying? When you were sick, he said all those terrible things. He said he didn't want you to come near his family, and now that he sees how healthy you are, he is greedy for a hardworking daughter-in-law and now is changing his tune! Don't go there! Now that you are healthy, you don't have to settle for that kind of a family. You can live a better life without them!"* My father got very angry, but I went for the visit around five in the evening.

When I walked in to their house, I found that my father-in-law had bought a heap of expensive herbal medicine, and they were cooking meat, which was quite a delicacy. My father-in-law was sitting in front of the dinner table with a knife in hand waiting for me. When I walked into the room, he had me sit down and he cut the meat into small pieces and put it on my rice bowl. He then started apologizing. He said in his Yang family no one has ever bowed his head in apology to anyone. But to me, he said, he felt he had to apologize. He said he had believed in temples, *mudangs*, and praying to spirits, but after seeing that I was able to recover by believing in God, he realized that there is indeed God. Then he told me to go to Japan and join my husband there. I told him that I was very sorry, but I couldn't go to Japan because I still had everything back in Kyŏng-sang-do, and I was planning to go back. I said I wouldn't be ready to go to Japan for another year. He quickly waved away my explanation. *"Never mind about all those things. I want you to go to Japan and join your husband right away!"*

Coming to Japan

When I came to Japan the hardship that I had experienced in my hometown was nothing compared to what was waiting for me. My husband was living with his brother and his family. From the first day I lived there I was the target of such harassment by my *tongsŏ* (sister-in-law), my husband's brother's wife. My *tongsŏ* was so wicked. I came not having a clue what was waiting for me there. What did I know? I didn't know how to speak Japanese or how to behave in this new land. I didn't know the roads or how to get anywhere by myself. . . . If only I were to have known the roads and how to get away, I wouldn't be here in Japan right now. No matter how strong your faith is, even if you are an angel from heaven, there is no way to withstand that kind of abuse. No matter how much faith you have, still you are human.

When I arrived at my husband's home, no one said anything. I didn't even know which was the man that I was married to. It seems that after my husband heard that I got sick and didn't know exactly when I was supposed to come, he came to his brother's place in Nishinari (Ōsaka) and started working in his shoe factory. The first day, my husband and I said nothing to each other. No one said anything. I couldn't even look up at my husband's face. Everyone else was walking around doing their own work, but nobody said anything.

So it seems that my husband was sharing a room with his younger sister. My brother-in-law and his wife were living upstairs. I had just arrived and was sitting in the far corner, my husband sat in the middle, and his younger sister was at my side. Then all of a sudden from the stairs my sister-in-law was shouting at my younger sister-in-law to come upstairs that instant. She was shouting at the top of her lungs. I couldn't say a word. I was feeling so scared and embarrassed about staying in my husband's room that in panic I grabbed my younger sister-in-law's dress. I felt very frightened at having to sit face to face with my husband. I grabbed her dress as hard as I could, hoping that we all could sleep together, instead of just my husband and I. *Ha, ha.* . . . My *tongsŏ* was going crazy yelling and shouting that my sister-in-law come upstairs that instant. So I just let go of her dress and she went upstairs. I just sat there with my head down. I didn't lie down all night. I just sat there in the same position until the next morning.

I couldn't stand it. I got sick again. I couldn't eat, and with every little sound my heart would start to jump through my chest. There was no one I could talk to. I didn't know how to speak the language, and I didn't know anyone. I didn't know the roads or how to get around, and what was worse, I could never leave the house. It was like a prison, a real prison. She would call me all sorts of horrible names, and if it were now, maybe I could talk back to her. But back then, I was such a dummy. I couldn't even open my mouth to answer back.

There was nowhere that I could go to be alone except the outhouse. I would go in there and cry until I thought I had better get out before she started looking for me again. When I think of those times, all I can remember is how many tears must have dropped from these eyes. I would call out to God. *Oh,* Hanŭnim, *set me free from this hell. What sin have I committed that you have put me on this foreign land. Ha, ha.* (She laughs sadly.) I was so stupid to have brought all of my books and my Bible. If I were to have even opened my Bible, terror would have fallen on the house that day. In our little community, several houses had to draw water from the same pump. Whenever I drew water, there would be some other Koreans from Chinju and elsewhere. Each time I drew water, I talked to them about God. Then, I learned that these people talked to my *tongsŏ* about the things I told them. One day she came home and started yelling and shouting to her husband, my husband, and also their younger sister. She was carrying on and saying that when their father dies there will be no need for me, because I was a "Jesus lover" and I wouldn't pay respects to our ancestors by participating in the *chesa* (ancestor worship) ceremony. So for the first time I got up my nerve. *Even people who believe in the church conduct funerals. We pay respects by having a nice funeral and memorial service.* Then, she got even more hysterical.

One day I caught my husband in a place where I was able to talk to him without anyone listening. I begged him to take me to my brother's house in Chiku-shi (Ōsaka). He didn't say anything. The next day, I felt tired and hopeless, and I just sat down near the water pump where I had gone to fetch water. I heard somebody coming and when I looked up it was my husband. He wasn't so good in speaking Korean because he had come to Japan when he was quite young. But with a mixture of Korean and Japanese he managed to say, "*If you plan to live with me, then you have to quit going to church. If you do not want to quit attending church, then you should go back to your hometown.*" He told me to choose one and to give him an answer. I was so happy I didn't know what to do with myself. *Yes, of course, I can't quit church, so I should go back to my hometown. Ha, ha. . . . Please, take me to Chiku-shi. If you just take me there, then I won't ask anything else from you.* My brother was living there and also my second sister. Once there, I would have no difficulty getting back home, and that was my ticket to freedom. After we had that talk, I thought it would be only a matter of a day or two until my husband took me. I would think that maybe today is the day, but the day would pass. Then I thought for sure he was going to take me and more days passed, one after another but nothing happened. I had already packed all of my books and clothes and was ready to go. But it didn't seem like my husband was planning to take me any time soon. I thought I was going to explode.

Then about a week and a half later, one afternoon, a little pedicab pulled up in front of our house. My husband came in and told me to get in. I got into the taxi, and I couldn't hide how happy I was feeling. I thought to myself that now I was set free. You can't imagine how happy I was at that moment. Then, the cab didn't go too far before it pulled up at a house. I thought, "*Wait a minute, this isn't Chiku-shi! Where am I? I've never been here before.*" I began to panic. I was wondering what was going on, and I got out of the cab. I walked up to the small house. I looked around the back, and I couldn't believe what I saw—there was a small, tiny cross. It was a church. I was so happy.

It was a Japanese church. But can you believe it never opened its door, day or night. It was closed all the time. I thought to myself, "*What kind of church is this?*" The back lawn where there was the cross was filled with bright yellow *na-no-hana* flowers. Well, I got tired of waiting for the church door to open, and it didn't seem that it was going to be any time soon. So in hopeless desperation, I got on my hands and knees and put my head on the ground and prayed. There wasn't a church I could go to. I was really like a mute dummy. I thought, "*What am I to do? Where am I to go?*" I came back home riding the same taxi, and I went back into that hellhole. I couldn't look at anyone, I couldn't talk to anyone, I just lived everyday like that. I had come to my husband's house in April, and I didn't allow him to even lay his hands on me. Well, we would sleep in one room, my husband and I, side by side, and below our feet was his sister.

One day my *tongsŏ* and her husband got into a big fight. My *tongsŏ* turned to me and told me it was because I came into their household that there was so much discomfort and disturbance. She said it was my presence that had caused the Yang household to turn upside down. . . . *Hyaaa* . . . (she sighs). What could I say to that? Well, on another day, it was a holiday and my husband had gone out of the house. I was alone upstairs. All of a sudden from downstairs there were shouts. It sounded as if someone were getting murdered. The woman's voice was crying out, "*You wench! You are killing me and eating me up alive!*" I guess *tongsŏ* was yelling it out at me. It got really quiet for a minute. Then, suddenly I could hear the sound of a hand against flesh, and then a sound of a body being thrown and the impact was like thunder. It got harder and louder and more frequent. She was yelling and yelping, then it became soft moans. It was my brother-in-law losing his temper, and I guess for men their last resort is the fist.

I rushed downstairs and I guess he had just punched her in the face because her nose exploded with blood spurting all over. I was shocked. I ran into the kitchen, grabbed a towel, and rushed over to *tongsŏ*. I tried to put the towel over the nose to stop the bleeding. Then, she shoved me hard across the room and looked at me with a deadly look. "*It is because of you that these kinds of terrible things are happening. Does eating my flesh taste good right now?*" I was so shocked at her cruelty and venom that I just dropped the towel and ran upstairs. Just then my husband came home. She started yelling and crying to him and shrieked, "*Now that there is someone who is able to give you and your family a child, you put her high up like she's some kind of a princess. And just because I can't have children, you all treat me like a dog!*" I sat in the corner and shoved my head between my shaking knees to drown out the sound of my pounding heartbeat. . . . That is how I lived. . . .

One day soon after that day, my husband told me to go. He said he would take me to my brother's and from there I should go back to my *kohyang*. But he said that in exchange he wanted me to wait for him for three years. He said by then he would have enough money to leave his brother's house. He said he would work and find a house where the two of us could live. Well, I told him not to make that kind of a request. I said once I go, I will not come back. I pleaded with him. *Please, you don't need me. Let me go and please find a good person who will make you and your family happy. You don't need me.* I begged him. But he told me that after getting married, he too had to wait and live alone until I came to join him. He said that he didn't plan on living with his brother and his wife, but that was how it worked out. . . .

So on the day I was to leave, I just sat on the stairway thinking whether I should at least say goodbye before I left or if I should just not say a word and quietly sneak out. There was one of the elder workers who was my *tongsŏ*'s cousin's husband and that *ossan* (older man) lived with us. So, of course, he knew everything that had happened. When I was sitting on the stairs thinking about the best way to leave he told me to come down stairs. "*You are planning to leave today?*" I nodded my head. He said he didn't blame me for wanting to go back. Then he called my *tongsŏ*—her name was Chong Yong-Meng. He said, "*Yong-Meng, she is going to be leaving today and never come back here again. So, if she is leaving why don't you leave, too, because you have no right to live here either.*" Then, once again she started to get hysterical saying that if I was intending to leave, I should do so quietly without turning her household upside down again. She was making so much noise that her husband came into the room and started yelling at her. "*It is because of you, you wench, that my household and our name are going to collapse! You can't even give me any children, so why are you staying in my house. You can't even give me one child. When there is someone who can continue our line by being able to have children, you just have to chase her out. You are set to make this house collapse!*" She got even more hysterical and started throwing her body at her husband, asking him to kill her.

Ahhh . . . (she sighs). I have never seen anything like it. The *ossan* was quiet and he took me aside and told me to just wait a few more weeks until things calmed down, and I could leave quietly. He said if I were to leave now, he doesn't know what would happen to *tongsŏ* and my brother-in-law. . . . I couldn't believe my ears. I was all packed and ready to go! How could I wait any more than this! He said, "*If you leave today, you will have freedom and you will have your life back but for your brother-in-law and his wife, your departure will be the end of them.*" So if I stay then they will be together, but if I leave they will separate. . . . He said it was up to me. . . . If I am a bit more patient and continue living there with them for a bit longer, then he said they would think of me as someone who saved their marriage and their lives. . . . *Ha, ha . . .* (she laughs quietly).

I was trapped even deeper. . . . I already had one foot out the door, an inch away from independence. . . . But I was told if I were to endure a little bit more *kosaeng*, the household would not be divided. . . . I had no choice but to stay. But a few days later without them knowing, I slipped out with my brother's address in hand. I didn't care if I couldn't speak the language or how afraid I felt. I was desperate, and I was going to somehow meet my brother. Believe it or not— I finally made it to his house. I told my brother nothing else except that I needed his help to get back to our *kohyang*. My brother said he didn't know what had happened between my husband and me, but unless my husband brings me to him personally, he couldn't do as he liked even though I was his sister. "*Once you are married, the person who has authority over you is your husband and without your husband here I can't do anything. . . .*" There was nowhere to turn.

Until then I had never uttered a word to anyone about what was going on in my husband's home. But finally, I told my brother everything. I told him that I couldn't take it any more. My brother was very upset. He sat for a while and then told me to follow him. I just followed him with my head down. To my surprise, he bought me a new *yukata* (summer kimono) to wear and also new *geta* for my feet. Then, he took me to the photo shop. I got my picture taken for the permit to get on a boat. With the photo in hand, we went to the police station. My brother was quite respected by the police, and it seemed they were on really good terms. When we walked into the small police box, the policemen greeted him. My brother's name in Japanese was "Arai." He told them he needed a permit for me to go back home. The policeman said, "*I'll make the permit, but when she comes back to Japan, please, let me marry her.*" Ha, ha. . . . Then, in a few minutes they were finished. It was as simple as that. . . .

Going Home

At this time I was only about twenty-three years old and the war hadn't started yet. . . . My brother gave me the permit and told me to go to my husband and his brother and tell everyone that I had a permit, and I was able to leave at anytime. When I went back that night, I showed them the permit and said bravely that I have taken all that I could, and I was leaving the very next day. But can you believe . . . ha, ha . . . (she giggles) from that night, my *tongsŏ* changed her tune right away. It was like day and night. I guess she did some thinking and realized that if I were to leave and go back to my hometown, my father-in-law would find out everything that had happened. Once that were to happen, because she couldn't have any children anyway, and had caused the one chance for their family to have legitimate children to come back home in tears—she knew that she would be kicked out of the house not only by her husband, but also by his family. She would have nowhere to go. But now there was no turning back. I had the permit, and so I went home.

But life is funny. . . . After staying there for about three months, I decided the best thing for everyone was that I come back to Japan. Well, I have been here ever since. When I think about it now—because of me—my *tongsŏ* got a lot of beatings from her husband. I often thought that if only I had not gone into that house then everything would have been fine. The couple got along really well, although she couldn't have any children. *Tongsŏ* was two years older than my brother-in-law. They really seemed to love each other very much. But for some reason, they couldn't have any children. Maybe that's why my brother-in-law had numerous affairs. But the strange thing was when the other women got pregnant, they would lose the baby midterm, or the baby would die as soon as it was born. My brother-in-law also kept a *ch'ŏp* (mistress) who gave birth to six children—all girls and one boy. Also, there were several other women. So after counting all the children he had with various women—there were altogether thirteen children. My *tongsŏ* brought in a boy and a girl from one of her husband's women who died. Although the children were not her own, she raised them with as much love as if they were her own. She bullied and harassed me, but she raised those children really well. One of them grew up to be a really fa-

mous doctor in the city. She gave money to all of the other children as well. She
made sure that they were fed and sent to school. Of course, it was money earned
by her husband, but still she supported all of them. They were also all registered
under her name in the family registry. Although she was very cruel to me, once I
was out of her house I really started to feel sorry for her. *Ah* . . . (she sighs). Just
because she couldn't have children. . . . My *tongsŏ*, she really endured a lot of
kosaeng, too. When she wanted to eat something, she would sacrifice and not eat
it, so she could save a little more money for her husband's children. She didn't
buy any new clothes for herself and would almost look like a beggar in order to
save enough money to support all the children equally. People like her are
rare. . . .

Wartime

Then the war began. . . . In those days there was no work—especially for
women. We were too busy going here and there as we were told in order to
avoid getting hit by the bombs. During those times, there was no work, no
church. . . . We had to escape and ended up in Chiba prefecture near Tōkyō. We
all went—all of our family along with my brother-in-law's women. . . . That was
just when all the bombing was going on. So we left everything, taking just what
we could carry. We stayed in Chiba until after the war. One of the women who
had come with us was pregnant with my brother-in-law's child. She stayed in
the same house with us. My *tongsŏ* really hated her, and all the bullying and har-
assing went to her. So while my *tongsŏ* was out of the house, the woman and I
started talking and we became very close. She told me about her childhood and
all the *kosaeng* she had to endure. It seems that she didn't have anyone to talk to
except me and I felt the same about her. Soon she gave birth. Afterward she
would constantly say that her stomach hurt. A short while later she fell ill and
died. Then, the baby caught the same kind of stomach problem and was near
death. The baby finally died. Then, I too had a baby—my third child, a daughter.
Back then, living was not living at all. At any time a bomb could drop, and you
didn't know whether you were going to live or die the next minute. I felt it was
only a matter of time. Then, after the war, we somehow came back to Ōsaka.
The many dead all over the place. . . . I can't even talk about it. . . . We just
entered any house that was standing and started living there.

Reflection

I have two sons and a daughter. My husband passed away about forty years ago.
My youngest son was in the second grade of elementary school then, and my
daughter was in the first grade. My eldest was in the first year of high school. I
had four children but the youngest one died when he was very little. I raised

them all by myself. They were really good kids. . . . I did all sorts of things. I sold things on the black market, worked at home sewing for factories, and made children's shoes. Through the grace of God, I was able to raise the kids all by myself. I could never have done it alone. . . . The only thing that weighs heavy on my mind is my eldest son. While he was going to school, he was very active in church. He had quite a strong faith, and he even went as far as attending theology school to become a minister. But all of a sudden one day, he quit. Then afterward, he stopped attending church entirely. I pleaded with him to talk with me. But I don't know what's going on with him. . . . I haven't spoken to him in a long time. His wife is from Korea, and although we are from the same country, the ones who have come recently are different. And I guess my son needs to keep his wife happy in order for them to have peace in their home. Anyway, it seems that they feel more comfortable not keeping in contact. But no matter what, whether or not I am able to see my son, in my heart I pray for him. This is the most important thing in my prayers, that one day he will once again find God in his life. I pray that he will find his way back. . . .

I have never had the feeling that I should work hard in order to live well or be rich. I never felt envious of people who had plenty. I guess you can say that I am lazy. I always felt that if I had enough to eat and did not cause trouble to anyone, then I was satisfied. You live with what you are given. . . . Even if you have a lot, when it's time to go you have to leave everything behind. When my father was ill, after the war, I rode the *yami-bune* (illegal boat) so that I could see him once more before he died.

Soon after my father passed away, my mother also fell ill. She was such a devout believer. . . . A woman of true faith. . . . When my mother passed away, I didn't get to see her for the last time. But my relatives said she passed away so beautifully. On that day, she said she needed to lie down for just a little while and closed her eyes. They said she looked like she was sleeping very peacefully. One of my relatives went to wake her and saw that she was gone. They said that when she was lying there, her face shone brightly like an angel's. . . . *Ahh* . . . (she sighs). I have run into death several times. But through the Will of God, I have come to live until this age. But when it is my time to go to my true *koh-yang* . . . I want to go the way my mother did. . . . I think that will be when I am the happiest. . . .

Notes

1. The highest concentration of Koreans presently lives in Ōsaka, numbering over 180,000. There are approximately 36,000-38,000 Koreans in the Ikuno District alone. Approximately 3,600 are older than sixty-five. See Shōya and Nakayama (1997: 28) and Ōsaka-shi gaikoku-jin kyōiku kenkyū kyōkai (1992: 41). Ikuno Ward also has a large population of Koreans from Cheju Island. With chronic unemployment on the island, a large number of Cheju natives rode such ferries as the "*Kimigayo-maru*" to Ōsaka in search of jobs as well as to join family members.

2. Within the island culture, fathers frequently looked after the children, as the mothers worked in the fields or went out to the sea for diving. Such care described by Sam-Yang where a father would brush his child's hair would be extremely rare, or even nonexistent within the mainland culture.

Part II

Journey of a New Bride

Chapter 4

No More Tears

Tanaka Kimiko

You know, all my life, I worked and worked, and that's all I know. Sitting still and not doing anything like a *kongju* (a princess) sure is hard work! Ha, ha. . . . *She laughed as she began to talk about the bicycle accident that she had had the previous year while she was going to work at the* yakiniku *restaurant in Niigata city. Afterward her daughters insisted that she quit working and for once in her life take a rest. I told her that she should now sit back and collect an allowance from her children.* Huh! What allowance! It's the other way around! I always have to help out here and there. If I didn't have my own money, do you think they'd let me live here? They won't look after me once I get much older and dirty my pants, not unless I have money! My daughter says, "*Kāchan* (mom), if you get too old and hard to handle, I'm going to send you off to older sister's place." . . . Ha, ha. . . . She always teases me like that. But they are all good kids. My girls all know what I've gone through. As you get older, you need money, and you know, people like me, we don't receive the national pension. My husband never received a pension either, because he didn't work for a legitimate company.[1]

After eating the lunch she had prepared, we settled back in comfort at the kotatsu. *Kimiko let out a deep sigh.* You are a young lady, and you have so many chances to study, and do all the things you want to do. People in my day, we never learned our letters. Even at my age, I have to carry around my name and address written down on a piece of paper like a child. *She brought out the neatly folded paper from the side pocket of her wallet to show me. I was watch-*

ing TV the other day and there was a story about this Japanese *halmashi* (grand-mother), and the kind of hard life that she led during the war. She had written her diary every day, and they made it into a book. I was watching that sad story and I said to myself, "Aigu, at least you knew your letters and were able to write down everything in a diary." Ahhh. . . . *She sighed as she picked up some of the orange skin's white flakes with her forefinger, dabbing them onto the edge of the ashtray. When I told her that I would write down her life in a book, she roared with laughter.* Sō kai? (Really?) *When I turned on the tape recorder, Kimiko giggled and put her hand over her mouth. I feel so nervous like a dummy. She began by reciting her name.*

Ima de mo irŭm to mo'tss-ŭnda, aigu ch'am![2] Even now I don't know how to write my own name! My children told me to practice writing it, but there was never any need. When I had my own business, I used the *hanko* (signature seal). When merchants asked me to write my name, I just pressed the seal. So now I can't even write my name.

My Korean name is Chung Ki-Sun. I am seventy-six years old. In Korea, there is a place called Namji. I was born there. From Masan, you have to go a bit farther, past the *ch'ŏltto-tari* (railroad bridge). I was about nine years old when this *ch'ŏltto-tari* was built. We had to cross this bridge to come to Japan.

When I came to Japan, I thought my husband was ten years older than me. But later I found out that he was more than twenty years older. Back then my cousin worked for the city. He was kind of like a city mayor. He knew some people who lived in Japan and through their introduction I came to meet my hus-band. My mother-in-law came to Korea from Japan with my husband-to-be and we were married. He was from Yŏngsan, Porum.[3] The day after the wedding, we came to Japan. It was March 1939, and I was seventeen years old.

At that time there were many rumors about how you could earn big money if you went to Japan. . . . In the old days, people said that Japan was a good place. Of course, even now they say so. Back then, Korea was a very poor coun-try. People said that if you came to Japan you could almost pick up money on the streets. Before I came, I heard that rooms were spacious and there were even indoor toilets and electricity, and I thought how great it would be. But you know these days when Korean women come to Japan after they marry Japanese men, they say *"Hey what is this? This place isn't any better."* Well, it was the same for me. After I came I thought, *"Hey, this is not what I heard about Japan."* I always thought it was strange that we lived in one tiny room and that the toilet was an outhouse far from the house. When I came, yeah, there was electricity, and of course the toilet—a hole in the ground where you scoop out the business. When you go deep into the countryside, there are no toilets in the house, only an outhouse far from the house itself. At that time Koreans believed that in Japan everything was advanced and good.

Coming to Japan

Well, when we got on the boat, *Aigu*. . . . It took at least five days to get to Shimonoseki, on a steamboat that gave off such black smoke. All of our clothes became literally black. *Aigu*. . . . We couldn't take a bath or wash ourselves for days. Anyway, in Korea we didn't take a bath very often. In Japan we went to the bath on occasion, but my mother-in-law used to say that we shouldn't go so often, because we were washing away precious body oils. . . . *Ha, ha*. . . . The three of us, my husband, my mother-in-law, and I got off the train in Nagoya, and can you believe it—we ran out of money for the connecting train. By chance we met a Korean neighbor at the station—we were so lucky, those people lent us the money for the train to Nagano. . . . My husband's sister who was living in Korea gave us forty or fifty won for the trip. It must have been one or two yen back then. My husband and I didn't have a single yen. And when we got to Japan, there was so much debt to be repaid.

I was told that Japan was such a great place and so I came and then, *ai*. . . . Trying to tell you all that has happened leaves me breathless. . . . When we reached Pusan to take the boat to Japan, there were peddlers pulling our arms for us to stay at their inn. It was getting quite late, so we followed one of them and stayed overnight until the next day. I was carrying our sack on top of my head. . . . I just followed. . . . They said in Japan I could wear kimono, so I didn't even bring any clothes. My mother-in-law and my husband said I would be wearing Japanese clothes, so there was no reason to bring Korean clothes. *Ha, ha*. . . . I bought one traditional Korean dress to wear on the journey, and I packed one other dress. Well, I ended up wearing only these two dresses for about three years. . . . After coming to Japan, I tried to make *hanbok* by myself, but I didn't know how, and anyway we didn't have the material. . . . *Aigu*. . . . My mother-in-law turned sixty and, although I was a young girl, I still knew the Korean tradition. So I gave her a proper sixtieth birthday celebration.[4] There was a war going on, but somehow I got my hands on a whole chicken and some other dishes, and I made sure to give her a decent party. I had two daughters— my eldest daughter was born in the mountains in Nagano and then I had a son. My mother-in-law was quite pleased that I had a son. She passed away soon afterward and until then she lived with us.

I spent my life paying off my husband's debts, and that started from the first day of our marriage. When we married, he took out a loan to make a decent suit for himself—the one he was wearing for the picture. That was the start, I guess. . . . He kept on getting loan after loan, spending here and there. He took out a loan for his suit, his shoes, his watch. . . . So when we got to Japan, it was the same as if he were nude, because if we couldn't pay off the loan, we would have to pay it back with whatever he was wearing.

When I came to Japan at seventeen, I was *panjil panjil*—shiny and young. . . . All the neighbors used to say that there was no way I would be able to live with my husband. At that time I didn't know what they meant. *Aigu*. . . . When we got to Nagano, where my husband and his younger brother and wife were living, there was just a six-mat room and a three-mat room—for all of us. When we first got home, my husband looked in all the cupboards and yelled that there wasn't anything to eat. My sister-in-law was shaking. . . . There was nothing to eat, she said, because her husband was gambling and lost everything. . . . Down to their very last blanket. . . . Back then they would even take your last blanket if you lost in gambling. The men would pawn the clothes off their backs. *Ha, Ha, ha* . . . (she roars in laughter). If they could pay back the money, they got their clothes back, but if not, oh well. . . . There had been two blankets to cover the floor and two additional blankets to cover ourselves, but my brother-in-law lost all of them. It seems that he had lost to one of us—a Korean. My mother-in-law, my husband, and I had just arrived, and there was my sister-in-law and their two small kids. Well, she was happy to see us, but there wasn't even rice to make dinner. . . .

In order to pay off the debts, we went all the way to Gunma where they were cutting down forests in order to pave roads. And to put some food on the table, my husband borrowed more money, and as collateral, he gave the clothes that he brought from Korea, and also the first thing I bought in Japan—my red *geta* (wooden slippers) with these little flowers in the front. Every time I see red *geta* I still remember that time. . . . So then, we had some rice and miso (bean paste). My sister-in-law and I made some kimchi from the green vegetables. Luckily for us we didn't ever have to starve. I still remember that little black rice pot. . . .

Wartime

We came to Japan right before the war. Soon, we heard that bombs were landing in Ōsaka, Nagoya, and other places, and there was commotion everywhere. I heard that Koreans were brought to Japan as workers to dig tunnels, dig out trees, and do such manual labor. A lot of our people were crushed while digging these tunnels. Many Koreans were brought from Ōsaka to work in the countryside. I knew of Koreans who dug tunnels and uprooted trees. The Japanese lumber companies had the workers dig tunnels and put the trees inside to be used later. I heard that sometimes the workers, when they were off, would sneak inside the tunnels and take some of the really good trees and sell them. Even after the war, there were people who used to take the trees out and sell them for money or to trade.

There were about fifty people who were doing this kind of work near my town. When my husband and I started running a boardinghouse for these workers, I heard such stories. The workers said that there were several other boardinghouses, but mine was the cleanest. I did their washing and ironed their clothes with one of those big irons that you heat up on top of charcoal. There were several workers in one room, and there was also an old lady who stayed for a while. She used to smoke this long pipe and always teased me by saying, "*Hey this place uses the same barley and beans with their rice—not anything special.*

So I don't know why all the workers say this house is the best." Ha, ha. . . . I used to go way into the countryside and buy vegetables and make different dishes for them. They all said that my cooking was good. When Japanese people try to do such work, they can't even last two days. I had small children, but still I did such work.

The workers were really homesick because they didn't know the language. Most of the workers I served were brought to Japan by the government.[5] After the war, people who had enough money to pay for their transportation to the ports all left to go back to their *kohyang*. The people who were left were the ones who couldn't afford the trip. Those people who still had their own house and their fields in Korea took some money back home with them, but the Japanese money was worthless. I heard that they endured tremendous *kosaeng,* and I know some people who later came back to Japan. At that time my mother-in-law was still alive, and she kept saying that we should go back. But I told her, *"We don't even have enough money to pay for the train ride, so how do you think we are going to get there?"*[6] Anyway, we had nothing in Korea.

Luckily we never really went hungry, even during the war. I used to sell alcohol that I made illegally at home. I went into the countryside, and farmers gave me all sorts of vegetables and rice in exchange for the homemade brew. I would bring the food home and feed my children. I heard of people whose children went hungry, but ours didn't. At that time we were allotted *paegŭp* (rations) for food such as sugar and miso, and a certain amount of rice per household. Even after our boarders left, we still received their share. When we needed other things, we went deep into the countryside and bartered what we had for what we needed. *Butsu butsu kōkan*—barter trade. Many people almost starved, but we didn't experience that.

Learning Japanese

In the countryside in Nagano, the Japanese never gave us a hard time. Actually they were quite nice, and they tried to help my family and me by giving us rice and vegetables and such. So I've never experienced prejudice. Our Japanese neighbors helped enroll my five children in school and they did all the paperwork for the city. I guess that is why I remained such a dummy, because I had everything done for me. . . . *Ha, ha. . . .*

Before I came to Japan, I worked for a little while for a small Japanese soybean factory. Because of that I knew the words *konnichi wa* ("Good afternoon") and *konban wa* ("Good evening"). But that was all that I knew. After coming to Japan, I didn't study anything, I only learned how to speak. In my time, there was hardly anyone who studied and could write their names. When I came to Japan, I didn't know how to say anything. But you know, you listen to this and that, and after a while you can figure out the meaning—for this occasion you say this and for that situation you say that.

When I was living in Nagano, there was a Japanese woman from Toyama who was my neighbor, and her husband was a Korean. That woman used to always say "*O-tsukare! O-tsukare!* (You've worked hard!)" And she would say it morning and night. Usually, Japanese people would say "*good morning*" in the morning and "*good evening*" at night but this woman from Toyama would always say "*o-tsukare*" for everything. At night she would say "*o-tsukare,*" and in the morning she would say "*o-tsukare.*" The public bathroom was at that time quite far. You had to pass several houses, and each time I passed her house she would say "*o-tsukare!*" I thought, "*What does* 'o-tsukare' *mean?*" I thought that it was so strange that she said this each time I saw her. In Japan I was always with Koreans, so there wasn't much chance to speak Japanese. My husband couldn't speak Japanese very well either, so he couldn't explain what these words meant. . . . *Ha, ha, ha* (she roars). *Ai. . . kurō shita wa yo*—those were some hard times. . . .

Work

You know, it was a hard life, but at the time I lived it without thinking that it was hard. Still, when I look back now I think that it was a hard life. . . . After the war we went around the neighborhood picking up everything—glass, shoes, anything that was lying around. There were many people who did that. We sold whatever we picked up—whatever that was in the trash, anything. . . . There was also a time when I worked in a factory that cut blocks of wood into small pieces. I received thirty yen a month. When I think back now, I really wonder how I lived on that thirty yen. . . . I would lay my eldest daughter in a small box near where I worked. The other workers said that it wasn't fair that I, looking after a child at work, got paid the same amount as them. Then the supervisor told them, "*Hey, this person does twice the work that you do. When you go up once to get the block of wood, this person goes up twice. It's not that we are paying her too much, we are paying you all too much.*" Ha, ha. . . .

I did all sorts of work, I did it all. . . . I also did manual labor up in the mountains and my husband used to get so upset, because there were a lot of young men who worked there. He was so jealous. That was harder than the work itself. I also worked at home for my boarders, then I would go work in the factory. That is how I saved enough to pay the loan for a house. I did everything, all kinds of work. . . . I sold rice, too. There is not one of our people who didn't sell rice in the black market in Nagoya, Ōsaka, and those cities. We carried it on the train and if the train was stopped by the police we would throw the rice out of the window. Even on the trains we traded the rice for other things. The buyer would take the rice to places like Ōsaka and then sell it for a bigger profit. Yeah, there were such things. . . . Black market, I sold a lot of things in the black market.

When I used to stand in line to be chosen for work, some of the bosses would say I was too small and not pick me for jobs. But when I did get picked, they always said that I was a good worker. I worked at the city hall paving roads, pouring cement and things like that. I also collected rocks by the load. I got assigned a particular amount, and I rushed to get my share done. Then I would come home to do other work and just go back to collect the money afterward. The city paid me about two hundred yen per day for that job. You know it was only two hundred yen, but I was happy that I could get that money every day. I used to make pig's feet to sell as well. . . . Eventually I paid back all of our debts. Afterward, I was even able to buy a small house. And then, we kind of settled down and raised pigs to sell. We tried everything. . . . We tried to sell hard sugar candy, alcohol . . . there is nothing that we haven't tried.

My husband was sixty-one years old when he passed away, and I was forty-one years old. He drank too much. I built a house after he passed away . . . 700,000 yen back then was quite a lot of money. I paid it all back by raising pigs. I bred them and slept with them . . . oh, yes, I had to lie right next to those piglets. . . . *Aigu.* . . . You know the pigs were quite big and their babies were so tiny. So while sleeping, the mothers would crush the babies. I used to go around and sell the pigs, and also do manual labor, paving roads and digging ditches. The Japanese people used to say that when a job takes five hours, *Chōsen-jin* do it all in one hour. I did exactly what they told me to do and concentrated on getting the job done. I used to hurry and do all the things that I needed to finish by lunchtime. After that I rushed back home and did other work. That's how I was able to raise pigs. . . . That was really hard work. . . . In order to get food for the pigs . . . I used to have to go around to butcher shops to pick up all the fat and bones. I boiled and mixed it with tofu (bean curd) extracts to give to the pigs. I raised about fifty pigs. Then they had babies. You have to make all sorts of attempts to keep piglets alive. You have to cage them all in and then clean up after their mess all the time. . . . *Aigu.* . . . In order to tell you everything, several months wouldn't be enough. To live like that. . . . It was frightening. . . .While raising those pigs, I was never able to sleep in my own room. I wasn't even able to sleep next to my own kids. Sometimes when the mother pigs wouldn't breastfeed them, I held the little piglets up to the mother's nipples and let them suckle. If the mother rolled over and I wasn't there watching, they would all be crushed to death. When the piglets didn't survive, it was that much more money that I was losing. We had debts up to the ceiling . . . children to be fed . . . *ah.* . . .

Husband

Sometimes my husband, when we got older, said, "*Let's eat some rice with barley instead of just white rice.*" Then, I would tell him, "*Hey, why did we come to Japan? It's so that we can eat white rice as much as we want!*" There's a saying eat white rice and smoke good cigarettes. . . . *Ha, ha, ha.* . . . When I think back, I don't know how I did it. There is no way that I could do it now. *Aigu.* . . . There were some hard times. . . . The work was very hard, but also at home. . . . I can't even begin to tell you. . . .

My husband. . . . he used to get so jealous. He would drink and then come home and badger me about looking at other men. . . . You know my children saw their father's drunken stupor so often that they said they would never drink alcohol. My husband had a bad temperament. . . . I guess now that you ask, it wasn't a matter of whether I liked him or not when I first saw him. I just thought that if I were to be able to come to Japan, I would be able to make a lot of money. . . . My family also thought so, and they just told me to go with my husband and his mother. When he didn't drink he would work here and there, but then, he gave me such a hard time whenever I went somewhere, accusing me of meeting other men. But I still went out, because when I worked for the city or for the factory, I got paid in cash that I could use for food. If I stayed at home like he told me, then we would have really been in trouble.

I guess people in the old days drank a lot. . . . When my husband didn't drink, he was fine, but once he drank. . . . *Aigu.* He drank and gambled and drank some more. Sometimes, after getting drunk, he came all the way to where I worked. . . . Then a coworker would say, "*Hey, your husband is here, go somewhere to hide, hurry, go and hide.*" At that time, I was working in the fields— you know when it rains, all the rocks tumble down from the mountains, well, I picked up the rocks and cleaned up the area. . . . Well, so my coworkers would lie and tell him that I wasn't assigned to that area. They would do that for me, because they all knew what he was like. Sometimes he did spot me, and that was the end of it. The other workers would try to stop him. But even when they tried, do you think he would listen. . . . *Mushira, mushira* . . . (Its frightening, it's frightening). I can't put it into words. . . . He had a bad drinking habit. I guess, back then, there wasn't much work for men.

After awhile he started having a hard time using one side of his body, his arm and leg. . . . This was when we were in that old house. One night, he came back home after drinking, and started yelling again. So the kids and I hid under the blanket, or wherever we could. Suddenly he fell down and was yelling in pain. I thought, "*Good, maybe that will sober him up.*" I just left him there. After a while he fell asleep, so I dragged him into the room. The next morning, he woke up and said one side of his body felt funny and his lips felt tingly. Then the next day he went to the bathhouse and they didn't want to let him in. At the entrance he took off his slippers, but only on one side. On the other side where his leg felt numb, he left his slipper on because he couldn't feel that it was still there. When he went to see the doctor, he was told to check into the hospital. He lived a little while longer and then passed away after falling down a second time. But I'm glad that before he passed away he was able to see two of our daughters married and also our first grandchild. After he died, I thought I would have some peace, but my sons behaved so badly. . . . Sometimes, I wished that he was around when my sons were giving me such a hard time. I guess children are like their parents. *Kurō shita, ima de mo*—I've really suffered, even now. . . . I don't know where my two sons are right now. . . . Until I close my eyes I don't want to see them. . . .

Children

I have five children. I had three sons and three daughters but my oldest son died of high fever when he was in the sixth grade. My children all went to Japanese school, and they all used their Japanese names. I don't think my children experienced the kind of thing that goes on now, bullying and such. When my first son was still in school, for instance, if there was an event, the teachers used to ask me to wear the *hanbok*. Well, after he died, they held a memorial service for him at school. All the flowers from first to sixth grade. . . . There were buckets—at least a hundred buckets full of flowers. They all said what a good child he was.

I remember, though, in the third grade, there was a Japanese teacher who gave my son a hard time because he was Korean. That son never missed school for one day, even though he got beaten by that teacher quite often for absolutely no reason. He would call my son a *Chōsen-jin* and find some excuse to beat him. But even then my son would go back to school the very next day. Luckily when my son went into the fourth grade, he got a better teacher. My son used to go to this teacher's house all the time. This new teacher had just come back to his hometown, and he was quite lonely. So he would invite his students over to eat, but nobody went except my son. I used to tell him not to bother the teacher. But every time my son went to his teacher's house, he used to tell me all about it after he came back home. . . . *Ah, ah* . . . (she sighs quietly). The good child dies first, I guess. . . .

There was a time when my son was playing with his friends and the front door of his classroom came loose. The new teacher scolded all of them and not just my son in particular. My son said he was really surprised, because if it had been the other teacher—even if he was not at fault—he would be blamed and beaten because he was a "*Chōsen-jin*." But the new teacher scolded all of his friends and defended my son. My son felt quite bad that his friends got scolded more than he, and so he fixed the door himself. The teacher told him what a good boy he was. From that time on, the teacher felt very kindly toward my son. It seems that even now, five or six of my son's old school friends still bring flowers and visit his ashes at the temple. They are really kind.

My son died when he finished elementary school and was just preparing to go to junior high school. He died in August. My husband had a hard time accepting his death. Every time he drank, he went to the doctor's house and yelled, "*It was your fault! Why did you keep saying he's okay, he's okay and not transfer him to a bigger hospital!*" Now sometimes when I think about it, I think it was my fault, too. *Ah* . . . (she sighs). I was so busy taking care of the pigs . . . the child, if I took him to the doctor earlier . . . if I knew how to get around on the bicycle like I do now. . . . At the time I didn't even know how to call for a taxi. . . .

In the old days we didn't have refrigerators. We used to eat some things raw, and so I thought that he got food poisoning. But it turned out that he died of high fever. Back then there were a lot of diseases. In our neighborhood, three or four people died of the same illness as my son—there was one older person and the others were children. My husband used to go to the doctor's house each time he drank and yelled out, *"You idiot, you killed my son!"* These days, there could be various ways to treat it, but back then it couldn't be helped, I guess. . . . *Ah* . . . (she sighs).

You know that Japanese teacher hit my son in front of me like that until his nose bled! But I couldn't do anything or say anything. I just sat there and watched like a dummy. If it was now . . . I'd really like to tell that teacher what I think. . . . You know, when I brought the child home I scolded him too. *Ah*. . . . Japanese children would sometimes get hit, too, but that teacher would hit my son especially. At that time I thought my child must have done something bad. But now I know that it was the teacher who had the problem. So although my son complained about going to school, when I told him to go, he would just nod his head and go. He would finish all of his homework and take it to school, but still his teacher always found something wrong. Now when I think back I really hate that teacher. . . .

Ahhh . . . (she sighs). My other two sons, I don't know where they are. . . . I guess for about fourteen years, I don't know where they are. They must be somewhere near Niigata. But my daughters don't tell me where. And if they come to our house, my daughters tell them not to come. They really put me through so much. I feel so ashamed, *Aigu* . . . (she whispers). You know recently, there was a news story about a parent who beat a child to death. You know when you hit your kids, it is because you feel so frustrated. And can you imagine how frustrated that person was to beat his child to death. You know, I raised them without them having to beg from anyone. I fed them the best that I could, and I put them through school, but . . . (her voice trembles and shakes). You know I went through so much *kosaeng* in order to raise them, but I guess they don't know. They could have gone to high school, but they didn't want to. . . . So they only finished junior high school. *Aigu* . . . my sons, I don't know why they were like that. . . . *"Kosaeng do, kosaeng do, kosaeng do* (so much *kosaeng*)." *Aigu* . . . me . . . an old woman, just so that I could live. . . . My daughters told me to escape, and then finally I did. *"Aigu. . . . Really* . . . (she sighs)." That is how I came to Niigata to live with my daughter and started working for Seoul *yakiniku*-restaurant.

I don't know why it happened that way. My daughters are quite good with their hands and are quite talented and smart, and there is nothing that they can't do. . . . My eldest daughter, she got married, and unfortunately she can't have any children, but still she is living well. The daughter I am living with now, because of her *p'alcha* separated from her first husband and is now living with her second husband. But she seems happy now. But my sons . . . I don't know why they became like this. My sons, I haven't seen them in fourteen years, but I don't feel *sŏpsŏp'he* (sad). Why should I feel sad? Just imagine what I went through . . . (she weeps). A child that hits his parent can't be considered a child. *Haa* . . . (she sighs deeply).

My eldest son is a little over fifty and the younger one, maybe he just made fifty now. You know, I just live day by day. If today is good then it is good, if tomorrow is good then it is good (she weeps quietly). *Aigu.* . . . It's because you ask me, but I can't tell this to anyone because I am so ashamed. . . . People around my neighborhood told me that if I wrote a book about my life, it would surely become a movie. They said, then, I wouldn't have to work so hard anymore and be able to eat while lying down (she cries). My neighbors saw all of my suffering. There wasn't anyone who didn't know. If only I were able to write, I would write it all down. . . .

Kosaeng . . . I didn't want them to go through *kosaeng.* . . . I just wanted them to be happy. . . . But my younger one keeps showing up in my dreams. I don't know why! *Ahh* . . . (she sighs). In my dream there is this tremendous shaking, as if we were in an earthquake. And then I look to my side and he is lying together with a woman, and the whole house is shaking like it is going to collapse. I start yelling, "*It's an earthquake!!!!!*" Then, my son says, "*Mother it's not an earthquake.*" The woman is nude and then she jumps up and hides in a corner. . . . *Aigu,* it was such a disturbing dream. (She whispers.) I wondered for days if he was all right and not into some kind of trouble again. My younger son, he's the one who gave me such a hard time.

He was into drugs . . . *Mayak* (narcotics). *Aigu* . . . (she breathes out). You can find those nasty things in Japan, too. It's all over the place. It makes me shiver. . . . I don't know whether he does it now or not. . . . He even has children of his own . . . but. . . . The younger one, he had a wife and his own children and he was still into those things. . . . His child now is twenty-six or twenty-seven years old. He's even a grandfather, now.

Mmmm . . . (she moans softly). Maybe he couldn't stop using it. . . . He used to see things all the time and feel like there was always someone after him. He used needles. He was doing it in the house, and I caught him several times. I don't know where he bought the stuff. He got caught by the police several times. . . . He used to not be able to sleep, and he kept on saying that there was someone up on the ceiling waiting to capture him and put him away. He became like that because he got into the *kŭn-tŭl* (gangsters) . . . the *yakuza.* . . . *Aigu* . . . it's so frightening. . . . I can't put all of these things into words. . . . When my younger son was still in school, he got involved in gang activities. He followed them around and then he got into it deeper. My older son, he was never able to stay with one job. He just wonders around from place to place. I have no idea where he is either.

Ah . . . (she sighs). I ended up saying it out loud. . . . You know I am always laughing and so people always tell me, "*You look so happy, you must not have any worries.*" No matter where I go, I always laugh, and so I guess I look like somebody who has no worries . . . but because of my two sons, I can't sleep at night. . . . My mind is so heavy. . . . You know, although I see a lot of rich people, I'm not envious of them. . . . What I do envy is the love between husband and wife, between parents and children, and between siblings, that's the only thing, the only thing that I am so envious of . . . parents and children who have love between them. . . .

Now there are no more tears. In the old days, I cried easily, but now I have no tears left. *Ahh.* . . . Really. . . . There were so many things to think about in the past, but now I want to forget everything of the past and think only about the future. . . . If today is good, then it is good, if tomorrow is good, then it is good.

Notes

1. In the postwar period, due to the loss of citizenship, Koreans were denied veteran's pensions, rights of political participation, and social welfare benefits such as national health insurance and social security, as well as broader opportunities in the realms of employment. However, by the mid-1980s, Koreans as well as other resident aliens could access public sector housing and housing loans, child care allowances, the national pension plan, and the national health care plan. See Kashiwazaki (2000: 28).

2. *"Ima de mo"* is Japanese for "even now," *"irŭm do mo'tss-ŭnda"* is Korean for "can't even write my name" and *"aigu cha'm"* is an exclamatory Korean phrase to show exasperation or frustration.

3. This place could not be verified. It is possible that the name changed throughout the years.

4. One's sixtieth birthday is referred to as *"hwangap"* in Korean and is celebrated with a feast prepared by the children to commemorate the elder's longevity. This birthday derives its special importance from the Chinese calendar, where the years are divided into a combination of ten calendar signs and twelve zodiacal "animal" signs. After sixty years a person therefore has lived through every possible combination of this cycle.

5. During the later stages of the war, in 1944-1945 the government resorted to forcible methods known as *kyōsei renkō* (forced migration) or *kyōsei rōdō* (forced labor) to supply workers for industries such as coal and iron mining, construction, factory work, and other manual labor. See Weiner (1994: 193-194).

6. Many Koreans who were far off in the rural areas could not afford to transport themselves and often their extended families to the assigned ports, where they would be repatriated.

Chapter 5

Blessings Came Later in My Life

Kim Ch'ae-Yun

Kim Ch'ae-Yun is a woman of small stature, with a round face that lights up into a quick smile that often turns into a loud roar of laughter. She lived far away in a small town, which she referred to as a village compared to Ōsaka.

At first reluctant to give an interview, she finally agreed. I guess if old people like me don't talk about the past, how else will the young ones know about what we went through. There is no way they could read about things like this in history books.

Ch'ae-Yun whispered that in the rural area where she lives no one knows that she and her family are Korean. She said that for the sake of her children she prefers to let it remain that way and therefore revealed only her Korean name.

My mother died when I was seven years old. My brother was ten, and my youngest brother was two years old. My mother died on February 12 in the *ŭm-ryŏk* calendar. So I guess when you calculate it according to the Western calendar, I was just barely five years old. I don't even remember her face very well. I'm from Kyŏngsangbuk-do, Kim-chŭng district, Ap-po, Sŏng-sang village. I was born on October 13, Taishō 13 (1924). Now I'm seventy-four years old.

In the old days, we *Sŏng-sang Kim-ga* (the Kim lineage of Sŏng-sang village)[1] held a really high position. My grandfather held an important and high post, and there was no one who did not know him.

My father was eleven years old when he married my mother who was five years older than him. My brother was born when my father was fifteen. I was born when he was eighteen. When my father was about twenty-three years old, my mother passed away. So my father had to remarry in order to get all of us raised and have someone to take care of the household. My *kŭn-abŏji* (oldest paternal uncle) got married when he was nine years old. Back then in Korea, boys would marry very early and continue with their studies, and many women were betrothed to marry younger men. That was the way things were, I don't know, maybe it was because they needed the women to come into the household to work.

I still remember my father going to school and studying when I was little. My father finished all of his studies in Korea and then he was sent to Japan to study. But my mother stayed behind. When he came back, he brought home some Japanese cloth made from *asa* (linen), and there were *pin-dae* eggs in the box. *Pin-dae* is a bedbug. We didn't know that and in the night the bugs started to hatch. Well, you don't know how it feels to be bitten by one of those bugs—it is so itchy that you can't sleep for days. I was bitten till I had red welts all over my body, and those things hatched so fast that they were all over our neighborhood. Although I was still very little then, I remember this incident quite well. A short while after he came back to Korea, my mother died.

She was lying down with a towel wrapped around her head because she was very ill. She said that her head hurt. I guess I was too young to know anything. I remember her lying there and calling my brother to constantly tell him to go to school, and she would repeat herself several times. She said when she died she would become a bird and then sit on the branch of the big tree in front of our house and watch him. I wonder how old I was then. . . .

It was February when she finally died. For the *chesa* (mourning ritual) there was a big rice cake, and being so little then, I didn't know what was going on. I loved rice cakes and so I went to my grandmother and asked her if I could have some. My grandmother said softly, "Aigu, *this rice cake was made because your mother just died. Do you want to eat this rice cake that much?*" All of a sudden, my throat became very tight and tears just started to flow, and from that time I have never put rice cake in my mouth again.

Stepmother and Family

After my mother passed away, my new mother came into our household. She was from the *Wijŏng* Pek family (the Peks from Wijŏng). My stepmother was sixteen years old when she married my father. She was from a very poor family. I heard that they had lived very well before, but her father went to China to study and he got addicted to *a-p'yŏn* (opium) and sold all of their land and everything they had to feed his habit. They were left with nothing, and he didn't even have enough money to get his daughter married in a decent way. That was the reason why she had to come to our household where there were already three of us when she was only sixteen. She was quite young so she didn't even know how to make rice. My grandmother taught her how to do everything.

In the old days we had to make our own thread and weave our own clothes. My stepmother didn't want me to attend school so that I could help her with all the housework. Besides that, I practically raised all of my younger siblings before I got married. Since I was the only daughter of the house, she and I were always together. My stepmother and I had to work in order to clothe everyone. Day and night it was weaving, weaving, weaving. Now these days you don't know all the work that it takes to make clothes. . . . Back then—you had to peel the cotton and then pound it, boil it, weave it. It wasn't like now where you can simply buy materials in the stores. You had to go and get the cotton from the fields and then weave it, and that is how you made clothes.

Well, I heard that when someone from my stepmother's family went to ask a fortune-teller about her future, they were told that since she was a "tiger" who was born at night,[2] if she were to marry someone who had not married before, the marriage would not work. I heard that a tiger born at nighttime has to endure a lot of *kosaeng*. And it was true, she did have to endure so much hardship—I know it, I saw it with my own eyes. We had a lot of land that needed to be farmed and tended to. My father studied a lot and was very learned but he didn't know anything about work.

You know, my grandmother's sixtieth birthday was such a grand event. My father was very talented and he loved to play. He beat the drum so well, and could he sing. . . . I don't know why I didn't inherit his voice or his love of playing. Although we had fifteen *kisaeng*, the guests didn't want to hear them. They wanted to hear my father beat the drum and sing. He really had a beautiful, rich voice. His voice was so smooth that people said it could melt the autumn rain.

My stepmother, after coming to our house for the first time, had to pay respects by setting up the ceremonial table and serving up the rice and soup to my dead mother's memorial altar. I still remember her shaking because she was so scared. . . . When she was supposed to serve the soup, she came running back to the kitchen saying that she couldn't stand being alone in the room. She was still quite young and maybe it was her first time having to do such a ritual. What's more, my stepmother was afraid of my father. She was terrified of him. She said that even in death she didn't want to sit face to face with my father. So my father beat her and told her to leave the house, and it was quite noisy for a while. That really put a lot of strain on their relationship and the family. The funny thing was after their arguments, my stepmother used to beat me furiously. Neither my father nor my real mother ever laid a hand on me, but my stepmother—I don't know what it was, but she took everything out on me, I guess because I was the eldest girl.

Then after my stepmother's first year in our household, the one year *chesa* ritual was held for my mother. All of a sudden my stepmother said that she wanted to sit and pray to my dead mother's spirit. She just fell before the altar and with her head touching the ground she started praying. Then, right afterward, my stepmother said that my mother's spirit turned her fearful heart around so that she would be able to feel love for my father. It seems that my mother's spirit allowed my stepmother's feelings toward my father to change just like day and night. She didn't feel afraid of my father any more. She said she no longer felt afraid even when she had to sit in front of the altar all night. That was really a funny thing. My stepmother was very young, not even ten years older than me. At night when she had to go to the bathroom, she would wake me up and have me walk with her to the outhouse. But right after the *chesa* ceremony, she lost all of her fears.

You know, when my real mother married my father and came to his household, she brought a lot of new clothes. But she didn't get a chance to wear any of them before she died. So they were still in her closet-chest. I think that maybe she put them away so nicely as if she was keeping them for someone else to wear, because she somehow knew that she was going to die early. My stepmother wore all of them after she got over her fear.

Childhood

So from the time I was seven years old, I had to cook and do a lot of the housework. As soon as I woke in the morning I worked and that is all that I did. Look at these hands. . . . That's the reason why my hands look like this. I had to do the laundry and also iron the clothes. I would have to beat the clothes with a stick that was heated up in a pot full of charcoal in order for the clothes to straighten with no wrinkles. I really suffered a lot. From the time I was seven to seventy all I did was work.

There was never a time when I grew my hair as long as you have your hair. When I was thirteen years old, I had my head shaved. My hair was quite curly, and you know in the old days there was no such thing as a bath. You don't know how it was in those days. People now can't even imagine it. About once a year we were allowed to go near a stream and wash ourselves. Once a month, we would draw water from the well and wash our hair. Very often my stepmother hit my head so hard that the blood caked on my scalp. Then the sores would get infected and the pus would be all over my scalp. After that, lice would feast on the wounds. My grandmother came to comb out my hair with one of those very thin-toothed combs and the lice fell out of my hair like black snowflakes and covered the old paper. The remaining ones in my hair started moving around like crazy, and it was so itchy that I couldn't stand it. Finally, my grandmother grabbed the big scissors and started cutting off my hair. She was cutting so close to the scalp, irritating the wounds that it started bleeding, along with the flow of the pus from the sores. Then my grandmother took some oil and started rubbing it on my bald head. I guess that was supposed to be the medicine against lice. After that, I never had to shave off my hair again. But still I never had my hair as long as you. I remember that time so clearly. I didn't want to shave my hair and I yelled and cried. My grandmother told me that if I didn't shave my head, then my hair would fall out and never grow back again. Even now, I can still see myself when I was thirteen years old, crying as if I was going to be killed at any minute. *Ha, ha. . . .*

In the old days, even though we were better off than others, how much we had to eat depended on the harvest. If there was no rain that year we were in trouble. I remember one time when I was little, there was a major drought and for almost five years there was hardly any rain. People were starving. Nowadays, even if there is not too much rain, still there could be a harvest, but back then there was nothing that could be done. When there was no rain we made *muk* (jelly-like bean curd), and we would just eat that. Even if we could harvest a little bit of rice, still we couldn't eat it because we had to sell it in order to send the kids to school and have some money to pay for things. During those times we made noodles out of flour. I was so used to making noodles from when I was little that even now I can make the best handmade noodles. We didn't have white flour like now. I would pound beans and make noodles out of the powder. There were many mouths to feed and I had to roll out a lot of dough. When we ran out of the little bit of white rice, we only ate barley. So after feeding everyone else, I would save just a little bit for myself and put it away. Later, when I was alone, I would shove a fast spoonful in my mouth. Sometimes, during the warmer seasons there were huge flies flying out of the bowl leaving a few black spots. When I think about it now . . . I just can't believe that there were those kinds of times. *Ha, ha, ha. . . .* I just shoved it in my mouth and swallowed without barely even chewing. . . . Back then I didn't know about such things as bacteria. . . . All I knew was that I was hungry. So believe it or not the reason why I was happy about getting married to someone in Japan was because I heard that in Japan everyone was able to eat pure white rice.

Marriage

One day my grandfather told my father that he was going to send me off to Japan to get married. I heard my father say, "*Who are we going to marry her off to with her runny nose, she is still too young.*" I still remember hearing my father say that to my grandfather while I was ironing in the other room. . . .

My husband's relative was living in my village. One of my friends in the neighborhood was fifteen and was at a perfect age to get married. But for some reason, they wanted to have me come into their household as the daughter-in-law rather than my friend. This is also one's *p'alcha. P'alcha. . . .* So that is how my grandfather decided that I would get married and move to Japan. My mother-in-law came to see me and my family. After her visit, my parents and my husband's parents decided on their own. That is a *p'alcha.* After about one year, my husband-to-be and his mother and father came out to Korea from Japan when I was sixteen years old. I stayed in my parents' home after the wedding for about half a month. I came to Japan in January with my new husband and mother-in-law. I was not able to go back to Korea for over twenty years. Right after I came to Japan the war broke out.

My husband was four years older than me. During the wedding, I didn't get to see what he looked like. Even during the ceremony you were not allowed to look at the other person's face. After you spend the first night with him, then you kind of have an idea of what he looks like. The first night after the wedding ceremony my relatives and neighbors shoved me into the room. I remember crying so much because I was very scared. My relatives scolded me very harshly saying that I was going to ruin our household if I kept crying and refused to go inside the room. They said that if I didn't go inside and be with my husband, then terrible things were going to happen to my family and our household. . . . I was told once I marry, for three years I am to be blind, for another three years I am to be deaf, and for three more years I am to be dumb.[3] . . . And after enduring it all for ten years, I would be able to live through anything. . . . No matter what kind of hard times, I would be able to survive through it for the rest of my life. . . . That's how my parents sent me off to Japan.

Coming to Japan

We got on a boat and then got off at Shimonoseki. We rode a train to Kōbe. My husband was from Kōbe. My mother-in-law and my husband and I rode the boat late in the evening. It was very dark and I couldn't make out anything. The night wind blew strong which made the water very rough. It was the first time I ever saw a boat, let alone boarded one. I peeked over and it made my eyes open wide. We were surrounded by water and it was the first time I ever saw the ocean. I was so shocked and frightened that I opened my mouth to say something and nothing came out. All my life growing up in the mountains, I had never seen such endless water. After a short while, the boat was rocking back and forth so much that I threw up everything I ate and drank. I was so sick. I couldn't eat anything for the day and a half when we were on that boat. I remember I was given a small mandarin orange, but I threw that up as well. I couldn't keep anything down. The cold night wind was rocking the boat so much. The wind was blowing very hard because at that time it was still quite cold.

My husband and I, we didn't say one word to each other. He never said anything. Anyway, he didn't speak Korean so we couldn't really communicate. He only spoke Japanese and at that time I didn't know how to speak Japanese. *Ha, ha.* . . . You know even if I want to tell you everything there is not enough time. . . .

My husband was very scary. When we had to spend the night together, it was frightening. It was the same as dying. I didn't want to do the things he told me to do. Even if I were to die, I didn't want to do the things he wanted me to. . . . So he went and got another woman. He hardly ever came home. Well, for the children. . . . The one child we had during one of the struggles was my first daughter who is now fifty-seven years old. I had my first child when I was eighteen years old. I had my menses after I came to my husband's household. Three months after that I became pregnant. I wasn't really scared when I first got my menses. I had heard about it from my friends. Well, I was skinny like a stick, so I guess mine came quite late. Anyway, my first child was a daughter. I didn't even know to be happy to have a child. I didn't know anything. My mother-in-law raised the child and I would just work. My husband was coming back and forth between me and the other woman and we eventually began living separately. Then, a couple of years later, he came during the night and he laid his hands on me again. That was how I had my second daughter.

Before coming to Japan, my stepmother told me that once I am in my husband's household, no matter what, I was to live there. I was told that if they told me to die then I should die, if they told me to live, then live, but no matter what, never talk back. . . . That was the reason why I didn't say a word. I just thought that was what being married was all about—you work and you are given food to eat. . . . *Ha, ha.* . . .

Well, my husband died after we had two daughters. One day he was found beaten to death. At that time, he was living with the other woman and I was living with my two daughters and my mother-in-law. The woman that he was living with was Japanese. One day I heard the news that he died, and my mother-in-law and I went to identify his body. He was lying in a box. . . . The woman said he was beaten to death by several Japanese men who accused him of stealing.

I was twenty-two years old. My mother-in-law told me to go into the countryside with her. I didn't know anything, and so I was just going to go with her when a trusted friend held me back. I didn't have any money, where was I to go? Then, can you believe that friend gave me three thousand yen? Back then, that was a lot of money. In the old days even when one's husband died a woman had to live with his family. But that friend was telling me that things were different now and that I should forget about going back to the countryside with my mother-in-law. What was even worse was that the house that she wanted to move into in the countryside was where my husband and the Japanese woman had been living together. She had gone back to her hometown after he died.

I decided that I would try to live on my own. This friend showed me how to make money. I bought shoes at wholesale and sold them in the countryside. So that was how I saved up a little bit of money. After one year, I returned the three thousand yen to my friend. Then one day, an older man came to my house and said that if I came to live with him, I would be taken care of for the rest of my life. All of my friends told me that I should take the offer. I told them that if they said that again, I never wanted them in my house. At that time, just thinking about going through another marriage like the previous one made me turn away from all the money in the world. I thought I could earn money on my own and support myself, so why should I depend on someone. Even going into debt, I really hated to borrow money from anyone.

When I was younger, you know I had a different face than this. . . . *Ha, ha.* . . . Until I was in my thirties, I never put on any cream or makeup on my face. But still people used to say that I looked like I was wearing makeup. Now my face is all scrunched up but back then when I was twenty-two years old . . .

ha, ha. There were several such offers. . . .

But soon I began to realize that although I felt like I could survive on my own, I couldn't continue to live alone forever. I guess it is because I am a woman, and people think that I am weak and powerless. If I do a good business and save up some money then someone suddenly appears and cons me and ends up taking everything that I have. This happened to me several times.

Remarriage

One day a letter came from my father and in it he said, "*It is no longer days of old when a widow has to live alone. In today's world, a woman cannot live alone.*" That was what my father wrote when he found out about my husband's death. At the time I married, if a woman became a widow, she had to live by herself for the rest of her life. Even though my father wrote this kind of letter, I wasn't particularly thinking about remarriage. So for several years, I tried to live on my own and support myself. Then I met my present husband. He was very smart. Back in those days to have a college education was a big deal. He graduated from college and he worked as a kind of an accountant for a very wealthy man from Hiroyama in Kōbe.

A friend of mine introduced him to me saying that he was very honest and kind. I was in my twenties. At that time I couldn't imagine marrying again. So actually I refused the offer of marriage for the second time. Then one night in my dream the dead man, my first husband, appeared. He appeared to me so clearly. He said that no matter what happened, I should not miss this chance of marrying this man. The dead man said that he had sent this man to me and yelled, "*Don't lose this chance!*" Right then I woke up. I thought what a strange dream it was. I was so disturbed by this dream that I told my friend about it. My friend suggested that I consult a *shinpang* (shaman). Well, as soon as I walked in the old woman looked in her book and said, "*You saw your dead husband in a dream.*" I was so shocked. Can you believe it? She told me exactly what the dead man said. I was so shocked. I didn't say anything to her, but she knew everything. . . . She told me everything that the dead man said in my dream and the fact that this new marriage offer had come in. . . . It was really amazing. Even to this day I think even going to that shaman was also the doing of the dead man. And just at that time I was conned in business a second time and again I had lost all the savings that I had. So that was how it happened. . . .

My second husband was so kind to me. No matter what I wanted to do, he would allow me to do everything. He was one year older than me. He was really kind. Of course, he was Korean, but he was so smart. . . . He graduated from college. His parents were also living in Japan, but during the war they all moved back to Korea. But he stayed back in Japan by himself. He worked for people's businesses doing accounting and taking care of their paperwork because he was so well learned. We were together for over thirty years until he died. From him I have five children. I had several sons and I have daughters as well, and my daughters are so good to me.

Children

All of my husband's family and their burial grounds are in Pusan. His family's burial grounds weren't very good, but I took care of that. I went to visit my father-in-law's burial site and it seems that when there was rain, the site would get completely flooded. Perhaps that was the reason why I lost two children by drowning. My husband and I . . . we lost two of our children by drowning . . . (she whispers). We had a restaurant and in front of it was a stream. They both drowned there. I ran a *yakiniku* restaurant for over twenty years. We were living in Okayama, and there is a large stream that leads into a lake. In one year several people drowned in that water, and especially during the war, so many people lost their lives there. So after I lost both of my children, I put a small *hotoke-sama* (Buddha, or spirit of a deceased person) in front of the lake and after that there was no more drowning. Even though now I live here in Hiragata, it seems that many people in the neighborhood still put flowers in front of the statue.

We went to Okayama for *sokai* (evacuation) during the war when all the bombs were being dropped. I earned some money there, and that was how we came back to Kōbe again. I lost both of my children when they were three years old. Can you believe it happened at the same age for both of them? After one died, then within ten years the other died.

When I visited my father-in-law's grave in Pusan, I thought that maybe I lost two of my children because my father-in-law was made to lie in that bed of water. So I decided that before anything else bad happened I should fix his burial site. But one of my husband's sisters refused to allow me to touch it. I couldn't convince her and so finally not being able to do anything, I came back to Japan. Then, my sister-in-law lost her husband and also her child. After that she contacted me and asked me to go on with the repairing of the site. I went back to Korea and had it fixed. Afterward, water was able to irrigate much better, and it didn't flood any more.

Altogether I gave birth to seven children including the two I lost. My husband was a really good person because he didn't mind that I had two children from the previous marriage. My eldest daughter, she lives very well and owns a very big business. When my daughter was in the third grade, I took her with me to visit my ex-mother-in-law. She asked me to leave my daughter with her for the summer vacation. My mother-in-law also lived in Okayama at that time. Everyone who was living in Kōbe and near my neighborhood all had to escape to Okayama during the war. My daughter was just a child, but she was really good at taking care of the customers and helping in the restaurant. At that time my mother-in-law also did a *yakiniku* business. The child was helping her and also was doing such a good business that my mother-in-law asked me to leave her there. She said that since she was getting too old to do the business alone, she wouldn't be able to continue to support herself. I left my daughter with my mother-in-law and kept my second daughter. My eldest daughter went back and forth between my house and her grandmother's. My mother-in-law died in Okayama.

Work

In Okayama, although I did well in business, I lost two children. So I didn't want to stay there because of the terrible memory of it. I think that daughter, if she were living now, would be in her mid-fifties. The boy that died, too, if he were alive he would be about fifty. So I came back to Kōbe. My husband wanted to try a *pachinko* (pinball) business, but it went down. We didn't have much money, so I took what we had and started a pig farm in Hiragata, way in the countryside. I did the pig farm business for over twenty years. We earned some money from that and a while later my husband passed away. Then, I paid off all of our debts with our savings. What was left over is what I am now living on. The children are all taken care of. The two daughters from my first marriage are living very well. I had my last child quite late when I didn't want another child, but then it turned out to be a son. He is now thirty-eight years old. So that is the story of my *kosaeng*.

Reflection

When my husband passed away, I was fifty-three years old. He passed away quite early. It seems that short life runs in his family. His father passed away when he was forty-nine and also his younger brother passed away when he was in his forties. When he died, we were in so much debt trying this business and that. I had to support not only my family here in Japan, but also I had to send money to my family in Korea as well as my husband's family in Pusan that was having such a hard time financially. In order to help them pay off all of their debts, we started getting in more debt. So when my husband passed away, with debts up to my head and with all the children to support, I couldn't even drop a tear thinking what I had to do in order to survive. But you know the amazing thing was right after my husband passed away—I guess he was watching over me and helping me—I was somehow able to repay all of our debts. Every yen.

Now, whenever I see someone suffering, I just feel so sorry. I guess I endured so much *kosaeng*. . . . I just want to live right. I don't want to cause distress to anyone. Whenever I have some money I want to share it. No matter what my own situation is, when I see people who are hungry, I want to share with them whatever I have. Maybe this is the reason why I have been blessed with the fortune of always having something to eat, although these blessings came later in my life. That is how I have come to continue to live until now.

Notes

1. Korean family names are identified by the lineage as well as district.

2. Girls who are born under the astrological sign of the tiger are said to lead a life of harsh *p'alcha*, which is even more severe for those who are born during the night with this sign.

3. This is a famous Korean proverb meaning a woman must endure.

Chapter 6

Dear General Kim Il-Sung

Kang Yang-Ok

She stands head to head with me, her back slightly bent. She must have been quite tall and slender in her youth. Her hair is gray with occasional black strands, cut in a neat but simple boy's cut and parted to the side. Her eyes behind gold wire-framed glasses are slit low, so that they almost close when she smiles a broad generous smile, which never elevates to a full laugh. It is a smile that disappears fast before it even reaches her eyes.

As she talks she sits with both knees up to her chest, leaning on a sliding door that separates the small kitchen from her dark room, displaying only the dresser, an old telephone covered with a quilt, and a small TV against the wall. There are no pictures hanging, no clothes laid out or casually hung over a chair. It is a very neat and simple room, a room that displays no clutter of a life being lived, suggesting rather one that has been lived—with its reminders perhaps discarded, put away, or stored neatly in a box.

Her voice is soft and shaky and her head hangs low, and you fear to speak too loud lest you blow away so frail a presence. Then she speaks and you have no choice but to listen, not with your ears but with your eyes as she slowly tilts her head to the side and then looks straight into your eyes.

Yang-Ok lives in Ikuno Ward in Ōsaka in a small two-story apartment complex. It houses many elderly Koreans who due to various individual circumstances live on their own in very modest rooms connected to a small kitchen and a community toilet, with bathing done elsewhere in a neighborhood sentō *(bathhouse). When I entered her room, Yang-Ok was in the middle of a solitary game of* hwat'u *(playing cards) with the blare of the TV keeping her company.*

My name? I only use one name and that is the name I was given at birth. *Mmmm*
. . . Kang Yang-Ok. I'm eighty-nine years old. I was born on June 29, 1910, in
Chejudo, Choch'ŏn-myŏn, Shinchŏn.

I have no brother or sister. There is only me. When my mother had me in
her stomach, she and my father separated. Although they parted, she couldn't
erase me. My mother gave birth to me alone. They said my father died when I
was three years old. This is the reason why I don't have any siblings. My mother
never ever talked about my father or what happened between them. *Mmm. . . .*
My mother never talked about that with me. Sometimes, I used to think about
why my parents separated. . . .

My mother married when she was eighteen years old. After she married, for
about two years she went back and forth from my father's house to her
ch'inchŏng. During one of those times she got pregnant with me. Then she
found out my father was living with another woman. I guess that is the reason
why my mother separated from him. So I was raised in the *oeka* (mother's natal
household). That was why I never knew any of my father's relatives and know
nothing about his ancestors. My *oe-halmang* (maternal grandmother) and *oe-
harabang* (maternal grandfather) raised me since I was a baby.

When I was fifteen years old, my mother came to Japan alone. I stayed behind with my grandparents. There were many rumors floating around about how
easy it was to make money in Japan. That's why my mother decided to come to
Japan. At that time you had to have a permit. A parent, a relative, or a spouse in
Japan could send you the entry permit. A very good friend of my mother who
lived here for quite a while sent her the permit. My mother worked on a farm in
the countryside somewhere near Hirano in Ōsaka.

Family

My *oe-halmang* and *oe-harabang* were farmers. In Chejudo, there were farming
villages, and villages where the people went out to sea to dive for seaweed, abalone, and shells. In the village where I grew up, farming was the main source of
survival. We harvested wheat and barley, and ploughed the fields. After my
grandparents passed away we didn't farm anymore. There was no one to do it. In
Chejudo there were two very important things for farming—your own bull and
your man to turn the dirt in the fields and plow it. My mother didn't have any
siblings, just like me. My mother was alone, and I was alone. . . . When my *oe-
halmang* and *oe-harabang* passed away, my mother and I only had each other.
Even if you tried to hire someone to work the land for you, it wouldn't work. So
those families that did not have enough hands to work the land couldn't farm,
and had to find other ways to feed themselves. I remember when I was fifteen
years old, during that year, we didn't have much success in farming. That year it

wasn't just us. Basically all over Chejudo farming was quite unsuccessful. So all the people, unless they were extremely rich, went hungry. Nothing would grow that year. We used to pull *ssuk* (sagebrush) and then boil it to eat. We mixed it up with other edible grasses and ate it. There were times like that. . . .

After my mother passed away when she was seventy years old, a relative from my mother's *shika* came to see me from Seoul and wanted the rights to hold the *chesa* ceremony for her. So her *chesa* ceremony was held by one of my father's relatives.[1] Although my mother separated from my father, she never re-married. She lived with me until she died, depending on me, her only child. Be-lieving only in me. . . .

My *harabang* passed away when he was sixty-four years old. My *halmang* passed away when she was eighty-eight. I was thirteen years old when my *hara-bang* passed away, and I was in my thirties when my *halmang* passed away. Our relatives took care of their funerals and *chesa*. But these days, I don't think that they do any of their *chesa* ceremonies. If they were still holding the *chesa*, they would at least write to me once a year, but there have been no letters for a long, long time. So I guess the *chesa* for my grandparents has long been forgotten. . . .

My grandparents were really good people. They didn't have much, though . . . not many children, nor much money, or many relatives. But they tried to lead good, honest, hardworking lives. I was very close to them. My favorite per-son in the world was my *halmang*. I used to sleep in the same room with her. Sometimes during winter, when I used to lie next to her and my feet felt really cold, my *halmang* would take off her vest and wrap it around my feet very tightly and then massage my feet and say softly, "*pal shiri chi . . . (your feet must be cold)*." I grew up in my *halmang*'s hands. That is why even now at this age when I close my eyes, I can still see my *halmang*. We didn't have much, but she raised me with so much love. When I think about my past and the people of my past, the first person who comes to my mind is my *halmang*. Then, I think about my mother. She and I, we survived through her sheer strength. . . . So I guess until I die, and I have breathed my final breath. . . . When my lifeline is cut and I can no longer breathe. . . . Until then, the only thoughts that come to my mind are of my *halmang* and my mother . . . the only people who really loved me.

Marriage and Giving Birth

As a child, I never knew what studying and school meant. . . . Maybe that was the reason why I do not know the ways of the world. In my world there were only my grandmother and my mother. After my grandmother passed away, it was just me and my mother. I lived for my mother and my mother lived for me. So that was how we came to live all of our lives together . . . always. Even when I was married and I had a husband, it was just the same as if I didn't have one. He was a gambler and could never find a job. . . . *Aigu* . . . (she sighs). I married when I was fifteen. One of my neighbors brought me and my husband together.

My husband-to-be was living in Japan. My neighbor said that he was from a really good family and was a very good man. She said if I were to agree to the marriage, it would definitely be to my advantage. My grandparents gave permission for me to marry. I didn't know what he looked like or what kind of person he was—whether he was good-looking or bad-looking. I didn't know anything about him, but I had to marry him. We were four years apart in age. He was also from Chejudo, and his *kohyang* was a faraway village. He was living in Japan, and so it meant that I would have to leave my *halmang* in Chejudo.[2] The neighbor who introduced me to my husband said what a wonderful man he was and what a good family he was from. So I guess although my grandmother didn't want me to move all the way to Japan, all she had in her mind was that I, her only grandchild, would be able to marry well.

I came to Japan when I was sixteen years old. My husband returned to Japan a month after we got married in Chejudo. I stayed behind for a year. I came to Japan alone on a boat to Ōsaka from Chejudo. I left my *halmang* behind. From the first day of our married life in Japan, I lived with a husband who gambled for a living and did nothing else. A big-time gambler! I heard he started gambling when he was quite young. You know in Japan, then and now, there is no way to live in this country without your own money. But all he did was gamble. He never worked. Gambling was his job. We had to pay the rent, two yen and fifty sen, but no matter how cheap the rent was, we couldn't pay it. We had to live somehow . . . but how? I couldn't take it any more. I went back to my *kohyang*. My mother continued to live in Japan.

I went back to Chejudo when I was seventeen years old. But as months passed, my stomach got bigger and bigger. I had absolutely no idea that I was pregnant. Although I soon turned eighteen, I had no idea of these things. One day one of my friends said, "*You could be pregnant.*" I didn't know anything. . . . All I knew was that my stomach was getting bigger and bigger. . . . *Ahh.* . . . Then, I had a baby. *Ha, ha* . . . (she laughs quietly).

I had the bright red thing coming out for the first time when I was fourteen years old. It really shocked me terribly. I thought, maybe I had a disease, because I was bleeding so much. Nothing hurt, but I continued to bleed. You know, back then you wore thin underpants under your skirt, and one day it had blood on it. Finally, I went to my mother and I told her that nothing hurt but I was continuing to bleed. My mother said my body was coming of age. She brought out a piece of cloth and showed me how to make it into something that looked like a diaper.

Well, so I had my first child in my *ch'inchŏng*. My mother stayed in Japan. My *halmang* was with me when I was having the child. She had seven children of her own, but they all died except for my mother. She was the only one who survived. My *halmang* was so happy. "*Aigu . . . aigu. . . . I'm so happy, I'm so happy.*" *Ai* . . . (she sighs). In Chejudo the women work, and we work hard until it gets quite dark. That night when I was to give birth, I worked until about midnight, weaving these things we call *yangt'ae*. I decided to go to sleep and got under my blanket. Suddenly, I felt like I wanted to go to the bathroom to urinate.

Then when I squatted to urinate, my stomach started hurting all of a sudden. When I went back into the room, my stomach hurt more and more. "*Halmang, halmang, my stomach is sore . . . halmang.*" I called out to my grandmother who was sleeping next to me. She woke up with a start, and then told me to lie down. She started rubbing my stomach. "*Aigu, your body is splitting,*" my *halmang* whispered quietly to herself. I thought, "*My body is splitting? What is that supposed to mean?*" I was feeling very afraid, but still I remember wondering how my body could split. I know now that she was saying that the baby was going to come out. I didn't have such a hard time having the baby. I just put a little pressure down there and then when I pushed down on my stomach, the baby soon came out. "*Aigu, it's a boy, it's a boy,*" my grandmother said happily. "*It's a boy. . . .*" (She whispers.)

I had the baby when I was eighteen years old, but it was like a baby having a baby. I was eighteen but I didn't know anything. . . . I didn't know how to mother a child. I still felt like a child myself. A woman has a baby, and she has to take care of it, but I didn't know any of that. My stomach hurt, and then the baby came out, and when the baby came out my stomach didn't hurt anymore. . . . That was all that I could think of. . . . There was no feeling like it was my baby and that I was the mother of this child. . . . None of that. My grandmother brought out the blanket and told me to lie down, and I did as she told me. I just lay there and watched my grandmother give the baby a bath and wash him. When I looked at the baby, it was so tiny, but *aigu*, the baby looked so ugly. I didn't want to even look at it. I don't know why, but every time I looked at the baby, I would think, how did this thing come out of me. . . .

My grandmother would bring the baby for me to breast-feed it. She would bring it up to my breasts. My breasts were swollen out to here, leaking milk, but I didn't want the baby to come near me or suckle on my breasts. To me it looked so ugly. . . . I didn't want to even look at it. About two months later, the baby fell ill. It cried all day and started having clear bubble-like diarrhea. That put my grandmother into a panic, "*This is terrible, this is terrible. Maybe the baby has a cold. Put the baby up to your breast and see if it will suckle,*" she said. So right away, I brought the baby up to me, but this time the baby refused to suck on my breast. The baby continued to cry and we had no idea what was wrong with him. Finally, my grandmother went to call an old lady[3] in the neighborhood who sat by the baby and said prayer-chants. And believe it or not, the baby got better soon after that. We didn't have any medicine to feed him, and there weren't any doctors, but after the old woman sat and recited her chants in front of the baby, the baby recovered. The baby began to suckle on my breasts and became quite strong after that, and you know, that child up to now has never gotten sick after that one time. I don't know what the old lady prayed or chanted. She was very, very old, and she walked half bent. She sat down and said something like "*moshin, moshin, moshin. . . .*" I don't know what she said, but since that one time when we thought he was going to die for sure, he has been the healthiest.

After I gave birth to my first child, my mother called me back to Japan. I told her that I didn't want to go. But she said that my husband had changed and he was working. . . . She said it would be better for me to live in Japan. So, finally, unable to go against my mother's wishes, I came back to Japan. For a few months I thought maybe he had changed. But soon he quit his job and was gambling full time again. . . . Even now when I see a person who gambles, *ch'ika ttŏlryŏ*—it makes me shake with disgust. But I must say that although he was obsessed with gambling, he wasn't a bad man. He had a good heart. The only problem was that he didn't want to work, and all he could see before his eyes was gambling. But no matter how much I complained about his gambling, he never laid a hand on me. He was a quiet and gentle person, but gambling was his disease. He lost everything . . . so much money . . . money that we didn't have. . . . But we didn't live with each other for very long. He died when he was thirty years old. His parents were living in his *kohyang* and he had a few siblings, but they all died quite early. My husband was a lover of gambling and hater of work, and I guess his life span went as fast as the lifestyle he led.

When you marry for the first time and things don't work out, then you should just learn to live alone. If you think that by marrying once again you will somehow be happy, it doesn't work like that. I remarried when I was I think twenty-eight or twenty-nine. With my first husband I had two children, and with my second husband I didn't have any.[4] We lived together for a while, and then one day he just picked up and left. Soon my thirties passed and then my forties . . . *saaaaa* . . . (she lets out a deep sigh).

Chongryun

I had to feed my kids and send them to school, *jyaaa* . . . (she sighs) . . . all I could think about was how I was going to survive. The only kind of work that I could do was sewing and tailoring. Since coming to Japan, I have never worked outside of the home in factories and such. I would receive the work from the factories and do *naishoku* (work at home). People told me about jobs here and there in factories, but what kind of work could I do? . . . I didn't know how to speak, and I had no other skills. The only thing I knew how to do was sew. Then a couple of my friends told me that I should try to work for "our people" instead of being stuck in the house. I didn't know how to speak very well, and I was not educated. I thought what could a person like me do to help our people have a better living environment and society. But believe it or not, I have come to work for our *Chongryun* for about forty years now.

Right now it is called *Chongryun* but back then, right after the war it was called *Ryŏngmeng*. The first *chojik* (organization) for the *Chosŏn* people was called *Ryŏngmeng*. Then the Japanese government dissolved *Ryŏngmeng* and didn't allow us to continue working in our organization. I think it was 1953 that *Chongryun* was again established as our *chojik*.[5] So that was how I started working for the *Jo-Chongryun* (women's group) going from one neighborhood to another telling this person and that person, anyone who would listen, about the new *Chongryun* organization. It was part of my daily activity and I didn't see it as work. So I guess that is the reason why there was never a limit, or a feeling that I should just do this much or that much for the day. There was no limit to how many more people I could tell about the *Chongryun* organization. *Aigu . . .* (she sighs).

Whenever the organization was building schools or doing something to benefit our people living in Japan, I tried my best to help. I could not contribute much money, so I gave all I had of my body, my strength, my ability to work and move about. For example, to build schools for the children—you know for the second generation, it was the first time that we were able to educate them in our own schools. We couldn't continue to borrow people's houses to educate the children. In order to plan for a school, we needed land, money, donations, contributions, and so many other complicated things. I guess when you start there is nothing too hard to accomplish, but it was a hard road, to build schools, offices. . . . Of course with money we were able to build and get everything going, but what we most needed were people and everyone's strength. There was no way to get these things done with only one or two people.

Our General Kim Il-Sung

In southern *Chosŏn*, every several years they changed leaders and each time the country went through a lot of changes. But our Kim Il-Sung *Changgun-nim* (General) is always the same. Whether we Koreans are in Japan, or America, or India or wherever . . . his guidance and leadership is always the same and never changes. We *Chosŏn saram* (Koreans) live in Japan, but if it wasn't for our *Changgun-nim* we wouldn't be able to live here so comfortably. The Japanese have taken us *Chosŏn saram* from our countries and brought us to Japan by force, making us work, and even killing us.

We endured so much *kosaeng* being pushed around here and there, and basically they have taken our country away from us . . . the Japanese. But after independence from Japan, we reclaimed our country, and our *Changgun-nim* made sure that we *Chosŏn saram* who were living in Japan were protected and allowed to live comfortably. So that's why our *Chongryun* was organized and our leader in the central office is able to provide good guidance and leadership. That is why we can live so freely here in Japan, and this is all due to our Kim Il-Sung *Changgun-nim*. There isn't one bad thing that he has allowed to happen to us . . . not one bad thing. . . . He has always protected our livelihood here in Japan, and he has never turned us away. Our *Changgun-nim* has accepted all of us no matter who we are, and he has done everything that he could possibly do to establish our organization here in Japan. So that's why not even the Japanese government can touch our *Chongryun* organization.

In the beginning there was *Ryŏngmeng,* which the Japanese government dissolved, to make sure that we couldn't build our own schools and such, and in the midst of all of that confusion, *Mindan* came about. The *Mindan* organization became a separate organization, but I have continued to be on the *Chongryun* side.

I have never walked another path. All of my children attended *Chongryun* schools throughout. They didn't go all the way up to the Chosŏn University, but they all attended *Chongryun* schools. Our children were born and raised in Japan, but because of our schools and our education, no matter where they go they can express themselves perfectly in their own *Chosŏn* language.

For me, living alone with my children—I received a lot of help from *Chongryun*. If I didn't know of *Chongryun* and had to do everything by myself, I am sure that I would have had to endure more *kosaeng* than I have had—I would have suffered a lot more for sure. . . . You know, I do not know how to read or write, and I certainly can't speak very well, but I do have ears and so I was able to at least listen, and out of a hundred things, I was able to pick out at least one of his words and then get it into my head. And no matter what kind of a time I was facing, I was able to think about his words. This is what I think is faith. Through this belief you are able to lead your life the best way, and make up for the things that you don't have. My belief in Kim Il-Sung *Changgun-nim* has given me more strength than a husband, my parents, or anything else. . . . If I walk this path then it is the right path, and it is the most comfortable, safe, and only path to follow until the end. Now I am too old and I can't move around so much, so I stay in my room most of the time. But whenever I sit, I always think, *"Aigu, our Changgun-nim has left us and the world. . . . If he were to be living now everything would still be good. . . . He has finally left this world. . . ."* All the other things . . . even my own children . . . never mind all of that . . . when *Changgun-nim* was living I believed that I could live in peace for the rest of my life. That was the only way I could think and that was all that I knew. . . .

I have tried many things, but there has never been anything that worked. I guess the fact that I am able to feel like this for Kim Il-Sung *Changgun-nim* has been a part of my fate . . . my destiny. When our Kim Il-Sung *Changgun-nim* passed away and I heard the news,[6] I received such a shock, and that is the reason why my health became this weak. In the morning I got up and then I received a phone call, and on the other line, before I could say hello, was a woman's voice wailing saying, *"Our Kim Il-Sung Changgun-nim has passed away, turn on the TV!"* So without saying anything, I hung up the phone, rushed to the TV, and I turned it on. There it was . . . the news of his death. I stood there in my nightgown and I didn't know what to do. I tried to change into regular clothes, but I couldn't control the trembling of my whole body. . . . I can't put it into words. . . . *Aigu*. . . . My body was shaking and fluttering all on its own. I thought, *"Aigu . . . did somebody kill him? We didn't hear anything about him falling ill or anything that was wrong with his health. . . . How did he end up dying and leaving us like this?"* I ran as fast as I could to the *Chongryun* office, and as soon as I walked in, all I could hear was the *"Wong, wong . . ."* (crying) of so many people's voices. For me when our *Changgun-nim* passed away, it hurt me more than when my own mother passed away. After she passed away, I thought to myself that my mother has finally left this world. . . . But when the *Changgun-nim* passed away, from the very first news that I heard of it on the telephone, I felt completely hopeless. . . . I felt lost. . . . You could very well say that I became crazy trying to work out what this was all about. Why did it happen?

Twice I saw the *Changgun-nim* in a dream. In one of the dreams I saw the rising sun. Just when I looked toward it, I saw our *Changgun-nim*'s face, and it was so very bright and clear. This kind of thing, I have never uttered to another soul, until now . . . I dreamt of him like this the year before last year. I saw him twice in my dreams. The second time the *Changgun-nim* was standing in the middle of a farm giving a speech and guiding the people. He was telling the farmers to plant this and that. I could never forget these dreams. . . . *Aigu* . . . (she sighs).

If he was alive, then perhaps the talks with South *Chosŏn* would have been successful, and maybe there would have been a chance at reunification, but. . . . It was less than a month before he was to attend talks with South *Chosŏn*.[7] I think that if he had lived four or five years longer, then things would have been better. It seems that they are having such a hard time now. Our North side is not like the South. In the South you dig the land anywhere and plant something, and it will start to grow, but in the North it is not like that. The land and the soil are not so strong. I have been to the North a few times, but the farming is not so good. Things such as potatoes grow very well, but other things don't grow very well at all. When *Chosŏn* became independent from Japan, many people were going back to their homeland, but I had no friends or family in the North, and that is the reason why I didn't go. But at that time, in the North as well as the South, farming was at its all-time low.

Now, all I wish is for people to be able to go back and forth between the North and the South and be able to talk freely with each other. You know there are people who are separated from their parents and their children and their relatives. It is of secondary importance whether there will be reunification, or that the country become one, but simply that people would be able to meet and talk. That is all that I wish for now. Sometimes I think how my life would have turned out if I had gone to the North during the time when many people were going.[8] But I suppose this is also a part of my destiny, because back then I had absolutely no desire to go to the North. For me when I thought of *kohyang*, all that came to my mind was Chejudo. No matter how many years I have been in Japan, the Chejudo *sat'uli* (dialect) I haven't forgotten.

Chejudo is really a beautiful place. Mt. Halla[9] was my favorite place from the time when I was a child. There is a saying that great people are born on Mt. Halla, having great skills and talents. There is a story that said that because great people were born on the mountain, *yukchi* (mainland) people came to Chejudo and went into the mountain to kill the power of the soil and land. I hear that the hole called "*ko-ryang-pŭ*"[10] is still there in the mountains. It is said that from this hole there came the three original last names—*Ko, Ryang,* and *Pŭ*. People who have these names were thought to be of pure breed from the famous Mt. Halla. This is the story I heard when I was a child.

Japanese Occupation

Near my village there was a big drinking bar. When the *paeknyŏn tŭl* came to our Chejudo, these Japanese soldiers would go up to a bar on a hill with their high boots to the knees, carrying guns, and wearing these funny-looking caps. They would all rush into the bar. It was quite shocking to see them at first. At that time I didn't even know that our country was being taken away from us. I was too little to know all that was happening. But when I saw them near a field that first time, I thought they were quite scary looking. All the other grown-ups would suddenly stop working in the fields and stand by the road with their heads down. No one would look up. I went to one of my neighbors and said, "*Look, the scary-looking people are coming.*" The woman didn't answer and she kept her head down and didn't dare look up. I was too little to know that these people had eaten up our country. . . . The adults knew what was going on, but all they could do was stand there with their heads hung low.

In order to get to my house from this big field, I had to go up the hill along a curved road. The road was surrounded by large plots of fields and right in the center I remember that a pole was built and several other poles went up soon after. I didn't know at the time what it was, but it turned out that the soldiers were putting up telephone poles. I don't remember so much about the Japanese in Chejudo, but that sight I have never forgotten. Then, I guess about a year later, I remember that the Japanese soldiers came and told everyone that we must stick a piece of paper written in Chinese characters in front of our houses. Of course, most of us didn't know how to read so we put it up without knowing what it meant. I guess it was something that showed that we were a part of Japan. Then, they came around and told us to put a small flag in front of our house and it was the Japanese flag. They said that from then on this was the flag of our country.

In my neighborhood, there was an old *harabang* who could speak Japanese. After gathering all the people from our village together, the Japanese put this *harabang* in front of them and said things, and then this *harabang* explained to us what they said. He said that we were no longer an independent *Chosŏn*. We were now part of Japan. From this time on, we should listen carefully and obey what the Japanese soldiers told us to do. If we didn't, they were going to either kill us all or take us to a faraway place. That was when I was quite small, I think about five years old. But I still remember it. Even now I can see it so clearly. I remember standing there thinking, "*I wonder where these people are from. They are really scary. We have to listen to what they say otherwise we will get into trouble. . . .*" Then, a while later, the soldiers said that because we were no longer *Chosŏn*, but a part of Japan, if we have pictures of the *Chosŏn* King[11] on our walls, we must remove them immediately. My *harabang* and *halmang* left it on the wall. My neighbor was shocked and told us that if we did not remove the picture we would all be killed. I remember wondering why we would be killed if we didn't take the picture down. My grandmother said, "*Aigu, let's take it down. . . .*" I thought, "*We have to take the picture of the King down, and we have to listen to what these people tell us to do. . . . What does all of this mean?*' Now when I think about it, I am able to connect that time with the facts. . . . This was the time when the Japanese were swallowing up our country.

Maybe, if I had been a little smarter, I could have thought enough to keep that flag, but now all I have is what I saw and remember. Maybe, I could have listened carefully to what they said or had the grown-ups explain what was going on, but I just remember all the *halmang* and *harabang*, standing quietly with their heads down. Maybe they were bowing their heads helplessly knowing that they were losing their country. . . .

Walking through Hiroshima

When I was thirty-five years old, I packed up everything I had in order to go back to my *kohyang*. Japan was still at war. There were bombings and explosions and people were taking cover and moving away to escape the bombing. In areas such as Namba or Nishi-nari (districts in Ōsaka) there were many explosions. So many people lost their homes, and the livestock were all lying dead. There were dead cows lying on the road, and people were dead here and there after getting hit by the bombs if they weren't fast enough to make it to the dugout. They turned black, burned to death. During the war, this kind of thing becomes normal, and you no longer think that this is anything frightening. You get used to it. . . . At that time, some of my neighbors, who were also people from my *kohyang*, were all busy packing their bags and saying that they were going home. I packed up everything that I had, too, when Hiroshima got hit by the bomb.[12] People were lying here and there dying or already dead. . . . I saw it all. . . .

In order to return to my *kohyang*, I was going to take the ship from Shimonoseki. There were no ships leaving from Ōsaka. So from Shimonoseki, the ship would go to Pusan and from Pusan it would go to Chejudo. Before the trip my mother and I went to Shimonoseki with our luggage and asked when the ship was going to leave. We were told that the ship was going to leave a few days later, and so I came back to Ōsaka alone to take care of the rest of our things. My mother stayed in Shimonoseki and waited for me. In Ōsaka I had to see if there was someone to whom we could rent the house or who could buy the house from us even if it was almost a giveaway. My next-door neighbor said that if no one bought the house, she would look after it for me until we were able to find a buyer. I thought that after I took care of everything, I would be able to leave on the fourth or fifth. So on the fourth, I tried to buy a ticket from Ōsaka, but I couldn't get one. At that time in order to buy a ticket you had to get a permit saying where you were going and why you were going there. That was the only way you were allowed to buy a ticket. So, that put me back a day later until I was able to get the permit saying that I was going to Shimonoseki in order to go back to my *kohyang*. At the latest I thought I could catch the train on the fifth or sixth and after that I wasn't sure if the trains would be running.

From Ōsaka to Shimonoseki, it took twelve hours by train. Finally, I was able to get on the train on the fifth. But inside the train there was an announcement saying that people going to Shimonoseki had to get off. The train came to a sudden stop a few stations before Hiroshima. I thought to myself that this was strange because the train was supposed to go directly to Shimonoseki. Then there was an announcement saying that we had to get off the train because the bombings were getting heavier and heavier. We were told that those of us who were going on from there to Shimonoseki had to either sleep one night in the train station or walk. I thought, *aigu*, how can we sleep one night here in the station when we needed to get to Shimonoseki on time to get on the ship. But we stayed there in the train station. There were rumors that no trains would be running. They said there was a big truck to take us, but nobody knew exactly what time the truck was going to show up. That day, the truck didn't show up at all. People started walking and so did I. This was on the seventh, the day after the bombing in Hiroshima. On the seventh we walked. On the eighth we walked. We were so hungry . . . if only we could wash our feet, if only we could have some water to drink. . . . *Aigu, ijae pae ttŏnan ti*—the ship must have left without us, the ship must have left. . . .

Even though it was the day after the bombing, there were still people lying on the road who had not yet died. I remember so clearly the words "*Mizu kure, mizu kure . . . (Give me water, give me water . . .)*" of a man who reached out to me. His body was already dead, just his breathing was left. "*Mizu kure, mizu kure . . .*," he begged. But we were told not to give them water, because as soon as they are given water, they die on the spot. *Aigu . . . aigu . . .* (she sighs, shaking). Even now when I think about that time in Hiroshima when I saw all those people dead and half-alive . . . I just can't get it out of my mind. . . .

Back then, I was wearing *wara-zōri* (straw sandals). By the time I got to Shimonoseki, my last pair of *zōri* no longer had a bottom left. Although it was a day after the bomb had been dropped, metal poles were still burning red. To describe the dead people covering the roads. . . . *Ai*. . . . I can't put it into words. . . . *Ai*. . . . I just walked right over their bodies. . . . The dead people. . . . I walked right over their bodies. . . . *Aigu*. . . . I still have that dead baby in my mind. . . . I looked up at the train cable, and there it was hanging . . . frozen. . . . On the road another child with the skin blown off her knee. . . . My own children were with me. . . . *Aigu*. . . . I can't think of that time. . . . I just can't think of that time. . . . (She shuts her eyes tightly and shakes her head.)

These days sometimes on TV they have shows about wars here and there, but all of that is nothing compared to that time. I was so hungry. In the midst of all of that . . . I was hungry. I still walked on . . . but when I couldn't walk anymore, I would sit and take a rest, and right next to me would be several bodies. That became normal. *Hooo . . .* (she lets out a deep breath). To be hungry was also becoming a part of me . . . like breathing. There was no one to give us food. Whatever little rice ball I brought, I would walk and then stop and eat, and feed my children, and then again, until there was nothing left. *Pae kop'a* (I was so hungry). You know . . . when children are hungry . . . they don't breathe very loud. . . . It's as if they are dead. . . . My children were so hungry that they had hardly any strength. At night there was no time to rest. There were my two children and two other women from my *kohyang*. After a while the *zōri* strap would break and then we would have to walk for a little while barefoot so that we could save our *zōri*. When I felt the dirt between my toes and on the bottom of my feet, it was still warm. I guess it was left over from the bombing. When I think about that time, I think maybe this year I will be able to forget . . . but at night when I lie in the dark and close my eyes, those sights circle, going round and round in front of my eyes. *Aigu*. . . . *Sensō, sensō* . . . (War, war . . .). These days, young people don't have any idea what *sensō* (war) is about, what *chŏnjaeng* (war) is about. . . .

Sometimes when I think of all the people the Japanese and the Americans killed . . . it really is scary . . . very scary. . . . Right after the bombing in Hiroshima, there were many fires here and there and even steel poles were bright red from the fires. There were bodies that were black, and all you could see were the whites of their eyeballs. There were people whose bodies were mangled but they were still breathing . . . those with arms cut off and legs cut off. . . . *Aigu*. . . . After the bombing when the bodies were being cleared, people who couldn't move and were barely alive were all lifted and laid together with all the dead bodies. *Aigu*. . . . Those with their legs cut off and their arms cut off, and were still holding on to their lives, they were laid together quietly with the dead. "*Aigu . . . genshi bakudan . . . genshi bakudan—atomic bomb . . . atomic bomb . . .*" (she closes her eyes and shakes her head).

In the middle of all of that . . . can you believe it . . . there was a woman who gave birth to a child. . . . This woman pushed out the baby and then afterward, she rolled over. . . . I guess she died. . . . I don't know. But some of the people around her were looking for things to at least cover the baby. You know in August it's really hot. . . . The people were covering the baby with some grassy weed. . . . *Aigu* . . . "*chŏnjaeng, chŏnjaeng . . . (war, war . . .).*" I wondered if this was what war was supposed to mean. I saw the woman lying next to the baby. And you know at that time, I wasn't in the frame of mind to go to her and ask if she needed any help, or if she was okay. I don't know if she was dead or alive, and the baby was squirming . . . squirming. . . . We were sitting there resting and saw all of this . . . *hooo* . . . (she breaths out). I thought I would be able to forget what I saw in a few days, and I tried to reassure myself, but for months, whenever I would close my eyes, these sights would haunt me and . . . that voice asking for water. . . . *Aigu* . . . all those dead bodies all stiff and hard . . . people lying face down . . . babies hanging on the cable lines. . . . *Aigu* . . . *hooo* . . . (she breathes out). But at that time I didn't think of it as scary. . . . I just walked over the bodies. . . . When I felt tired we would sit to take a rest, right next to the bodies. That became nothing unusual.

We'd been walking for three days. We didn't make it in time for the ship . . . we lived . . . but all we had left was our bodies. On the eighth the ship took off and then sank after an explosion. Everyone aboard died . . . all ninety-some people. The ship that I was supposed to be on. . . . My mother loaded our luggage on to the ship and waited for me and the children. Luckily she didn't get on. We were supposed to be on that ship and if we did make it we would have died along with the rest. It seems that some of my cousin's friends were on the ship. When I heard that all those many people had died, and here I was alive. . . . Well, I was physically alive, but it was as if I were dead. . . . I didn't have anything to eat, I didn't have anything to wear, I didn't have anything . . . nothing . . . except my body and the clothes on my back. I thought back then that although I wasn't living like a human being, because somehow I had survived I had to live. I didn't have anything, but just when I needed something to cover myself, someone came to me with a blanket. When I needed a bowl to eat with, someone brought me a spare bowl and that is how I have come to live and survive up to now.

A few months later, we came back to Ōsaka. My next-door neighbor, who said she would look after the house for me, took it upon herself to sell my house to someone else. When we went back, someone else was living in our house. *Ha, ha.* . . . I received a hundred yen for the house. *Ha, ha* . . . (she laughs quietly).

Meeting American Soldiers

While in *Shimonoseki*, I saw Americans for the first time. The *mikuk-nom tŭl* (derogatory word for Americans), when I saw them for the first time, they were all so big, just like their ships. When they marched up like that you could see the frightening glare in their eyes. . . . *Aigu* . . . (she whispers and shakes her head). The Hiroshima atomic bomb was dropped on August 6, and then independence came on August 15. On that day the now late emperor surrendered and I heard the radio broadcast. I remember seeing the *mikuk-nom* coming into Japan and I think this was in October. I'm not sure what day it was but anyway it was in October. I was living with my family in Shimonoseki, where we stayed for a few months after missing the ship. One day I was outside, near the port. All of a sudden some Japanese started pushing everyone who was on the street, telling us to move and make way. Suddenly, I heard "*whajak-chak, whajak-chak, whajak-chak.*" It was the sound of the *mikuk-nom* marching onto Japanese soil, coming in through the Shimonoseki port.

Now these days I wear Western clothing, but back then, I always wore *Chosŏn* clothes. Most of the Koreans back then used to always wear *hanbok*. One day in Nakanoshima Park (in Ōsaka), some friends and I, six or seven of us, decided to get together. We were wearing our *Chosŏn* clothing as usual. On that day, I don't know why, but the *mikuk-nom tŭl* were everywhere. I think maybe they were having some sort of training or gathering there. They were so scary. My friends and I were shaking. We thought that this was going to be the end of us for sure. We were going to be dead at these *mikuk-nom*'s hands. The soldiers started coming toward us and I guess we were a sight looking so shocked and frightened. . . . Several of the soldiers were approaching us saying something, and they were waving their hands in front of them and shaking their heads. Now when I think back, I guess they were saying that there was no need to be frightened. But back then I was so afraid of them. I guess the first time when I saw the American soldiers in Shimonoseki, the unforgettable rage in their eyes up close gave me such a terrible shock. I can never forget the sound of their boots marching up the rocky pavement on that day near the Shimonoseki port. The soldiers kept saying, "*yang . . . yang . . . yang . . . yang . . .*" waving their hands back and forth, and came closer and closer. . . . I thought this was it. Then, one of the soldiers touched my skirt and tugged at it and said something. Now, when I think back, he was saying, "*Korean, Korean. . . .*" Then they waved their hands again, smiled, and started moving away. I guess they were telling us good-bye. We all let out a deep sigh of relief and felt so grateful that our lives were spared.

Reflection

I don't know what you could call it . . . *kosaeng.* . . . I don't know what else you could call it . . . or perhaps, *p'alcha,* your life's destiny. . . . Sometimes when I sit alone and think about the years that have gone by . . . then I really think that everything was according to my own destiny. . . .

You live a lifetime and there are times you live really well and feel happy, and then there are times when you are down on your luck. When you have a balance of these two, then you are able to feel, understand, and explain the ups and downs in your life. But when you live your entire life with only downs then there is nothing more that can be said. *P'yong saeng* . . . (all of my life . . .) all I can remember are difficult times. . . . But I have no regrets. I know of nothing else but the life that I have led up until now. I was born into this life, and my whole life has been about *kosaeng.* So I don't have the ability to think that maybe if I were to have done this, then things would have turned out better. . . . Maybe it is because I am not smart, or I lack the ability to think. I guess I could be too stupid to even be able to regret. I guess when it comes to *kosaeng,* I have endured as much as I could. I think I have tried to live the right way. . . . I can't resent my parents, I can't resent anyone, I can't resent my husbands. . . . When I was created as a human life, I was born into this fate. . . . What was good, what was bad, who was a good person, who a bad person. . . . I don't think like that. . . . Now I can only think that I was born into this life and into this fate. . . .

You know, no matter how much my mother suffered, she never let such words come out of her mouth. She never said anything about her feelings to her friends or even to me, her own child. If she said anything, she would simply say that all of these things that were happening or have happened had already been written in one's book of fate. *T'ako nan p'alcha*—your fate is something that you are born with and keep, from the time of your birth to the end of your life. I was with my mother when she passed away. I was forty-six years old then. She passed away quite early, so I don't know why I'm sticking around like this. It's no good to be living until this age. To live long is not a blessing but rather a burden—it is not a blessing, it is a sin. . . .

My son and I began to live separately from when he was twenty-five years old. One day he didn't come home from his job in the factory. I didn't hear a word from him for a couple of days, and then one day I received a phone call from him. "*Okā-san, sumimasen* (*Mother, I'm sorry*). *I found a job in Tōkyō, and I'll be staying here for a while.*" I was glad to hear his voice and I was happy to hear that he was working. It seems that he borrowed the money from his friend for his train ticket to Tōkyō. Since then we have always lived apart. My son is now in his seventies as well . . . *ha, ha* (she laughs quietly). So we have been apart for a long time. . . . When he was a baby and he would cry and cry, my grandmother would almost beg me to give him some milk. . . . *Mmmm* . . . (she sighs).

My daughter, too—we've lived apart for a long time. After her brother left, she also moved to Tōkyō. I think it has been about thirty years that we have lived so far apart. Before, my children used to tell me to come and join them in Tōkyō. But I have been living here since I came to Japan. I have never moved away from here. This place has become like my *kohyang*. Now they don't bother to ask me any more. I'm lucky if at least I am able to see their faces once a year. . . . I have been living alone up until now. . . . I guess when it is time for me to die, I might as well die alone, too. When you are born, you come into the world alone, and when you leave, you go on your way alone. . . . I think this is the best way. . . .

Epilogue

In the spring of 2002, Yang-Ok collapsed alone in her room. She was found on her kitchen floor by a helper who visited her several times a week. Luckily she had collapsed on the day of one of those visits. She was rushed to a nearby hospital that was built especially for Koreans. It seems that the hospital was constructed about thirty years ago through the funding and donations of Koreans in Japan who wanted to provide medical support for those who did not have national health insurance benefits, as well as enable patients to discuss their ailments in their mother tongue. The majority of the medical staff, doctors, nurses, and administrative personnel, are graduates of the North Korean University, and therefore are fluent in both Korean and Japanese. There are also a few doctors who are Japanese. Currently, the facility is open to both Korean and Japanese patients.

Yang-Ok's condition seemed quite serious. According to her children, she collapsed due to an aneurism of the brain. They were not certain how long she had to live. The dilemma that they now faced was how to take care of her. All of her children lived in Tōkyō, and no one could afford to stay at home to take care of her full-time. Also, the option of a nursing home in Tōkyō was nearly impossible, due to the high costs of private establishments, and the long waiting lists for those facilities funded by the city. Furthermore, Yang-Ok did not wish to move from Ōsaka to Tōkyō.

Yang-Ok lay in bed—her cheeks sunken, her brow stubborn, an oxygen mask covering her small face. A quiet pulse beat rhythmically on the side of her thin neck. I bent close to her, wondering if she would recognize me. At that moment Yang-Ok lifted her heavy lids and peered at me. She let the lids fall and waved her right hand for me to come closer. When I did, she weakly patted the side of my face.

Perhaps her physical endurance is due to the "magical" effects of the acupuncturist whom she met over sixty years ago. The last time I talked with Yang-Ok before her collapse, it was early winter. Surprised at the coldness of my hands, she told me why she thought that she was able to live to such an advanced age. When I was in my late twenties, my hands were just like yours. When people touched my hand they would literally jump back and pull their hand away in shock, because of its coldness. Every month, when the thing would come, I wouldn't be able to move, because of the terrible pain in my stomach and in my back. Then, one day, in my neighborhood, all the old women were talking about the famous acupuncturist who was passing through. I thought I should just give it a try. At that time, I don't know why, but I was quite thin and sickly. When the old gentleman felt my pulse, he said that there was wind within my body. I wasn't sure what that meant. But he treated me a total of three times. Each time he only used about four needles. I remember thinking back then, "What good would these few needles do?" Then, he gave me one month's worth of herbal medicine. He promised that after I drank the medicine faithfully, I would never get sick in my life again. He said that he couldn't guarantee my mental state, but physically, I would be strong until a very old age. Well, so far he has been right. Until now, I have never been ill. Now because of my old age, sometimes, my knees ache a bit, but I have never fallen ill to the point of lying down for even a day. Nowadays you can't find acupuncturists like that. The ones that really know how to heal use only a few needles and a combination of the right herbs. . . .

Yang-Ok recovered physically and now resides in a nursing home for Koreans in Ōsaka. She has been diagnosed with the onset of Alzheimer's.

Notes

1. Izumi (1966: 25-26) discusses a phenomenon of Chejudo, concerning ancestral rituals and burial grounds for women who have married twice or three times. He said that it is most common for a woman's last husband and their children to perform the worshipping service for her. However, there are cases in which the children from her previous marriage pursue the sole rights to hold the ritual. Also, within Chejudo, to be without a mother is looked upon worse than being without a father. Izumi states that this attitude has remained unchanged within the island culture.

2. At this time Yang-Ok's mother was already living in Japan, while she was living in Chejudo and taking care of her grandmother.

3. The old lady she refers to is the neighborhood shaman.

4. Here Yang-Ok said she did not have any children with her second husband. How-

ever, recently when she was in the hospital, I was told by one of her daughters that altogether she had four children.

5. Yang-Ok was close in recalling the date. The actual date was May 25, 1955, one day after the Sixth *Minjŏn* National Conference, when it was decided that *Minjŏn* would cut ties with the Japanese Communist Party (JCP) and align itself directly with North Korea. In order to create a new image, *Minjŏn* was dissolved and *Chaeilbon Chosŏnnin Ch'ongryŏn haphoe* (General Federation of Korean Residents in Japan) or simply *Chongryun* was created, and further endorsed and recognized by the North Korean regime as the sole representative of Koreans in Japan. See Lee (1981b: 90).

6. Kim Il-Sung died on July 8, 1994, but his death was not made public until July 10, 1994.

7. Yang-Ok is referring to the start of the first high-level talks between the United States and North Korea, as well as to Kim's interest in opening up diplomatic talks with Japan and South Korea.

8. The first wave of repatriation of Koreans to North Korea due to their political affiliation with the communist ideology and government began on December 1959 and lasted until 1976, totaling 93,444 people. See Lee (1981a, 1981c).

9. Mt. Halla stands at the center of the island and is looked upon as a sacred place. Izumi (1966: 16) states that in contrast to the iconography of the mainland, where mountains are associated with tigers, the messenger and servant of the mountain god, Halla represents wind and rock, which are extremely significant elements in the minds of the islanders.

10. Within the mountains, there are three sacred holes (*sam sŏng hyŏl*) that are thought to be the places of origin of the divine ancestors of the island, whose names were Ko, Ryang, and Pŭ. See Izumi (1966: 16).

11. It is probable that the picture of the king that she mentions was King Kojong who was forced to abdicate to his son Sunjong in July 1907. Sunjong then was forced to yield up both his throne and the country on August 29, 1910. See Lee (1984: 312-313).

12. The atomic bomb hit Hiroshima on August 6, 1945. According to McCormack and Su (1981), in 1945 there were approximately 53,000 Koreans in Hiroshima, living in slum ghettos and mostly brought forcibly to Japan. It is said that almost thirty thousand died as a result of the bombing.

Part III

Solitary Sojourn

Chapter 7

It's My Destiny

Yasuda Kimiko (Kim Song-Yun)

Yasuda Kimiko's small room is tucked away at the back of an izakaya *(Japanese pub) located among the narrow side streets and alleyways of Sakuramoto marketplace in Kawasaki. The dark hallway between the bar and her room smelt of stale liquor and cigarettes. At the end of the hall was an entrance to a small courtyard. On the left was a beat-up laundry machine and over it hung several undergarments. Kimiko feels that although her living quarters are a bit shabby, she is most comfortable this way, as she does not burden her children. She said the best part of living alone was that her friends could drop in and visit her anytime they wished.*

One day when I visited her, Kimiko greeted me with a worried expression. She said that something terrible had happened. I don't know what I did wrong. I always pay my rent on time, and I don't give that fatso (the manager) any trouble. He did warn me several times that too many of my friends come over, and that we speak too loudly. I told him that's just the way we Koreans speak. But other than that I don't know why he is telling me to move out.

I asked her what she was planning to do. I don't know. It's really convenient here. What's more, it's almost impossible for me to find a new room, because no one wants to rent to an old person. They are afraid that old people will die and then there won't be anyone to take care of it. So I told Fatso, "Hey, you tell me to move out, but where am I supposed to go? You know that landlords don't rent to old people like me."

Kimiko supported herself on a small living allowance from the government.

97

She worried that if she moved in with one of her children, she would forfeit the subsidy by which she retained her independence. She would then have to ask her children for help, something she could not imagine herself doing.

My father passed away when I was eleven years old. When I was separated from my mother I was thirteen or fourteen years old. Now I am *kazoe*[1] eighty years old. I was born on August 14, Taishō 8 (1919) according to the *ŭmryŏk* (lunar calendar). I was born in Kyŏngsangnam-do. I have five siblings. There were five girls and one boy and I was the youngest. My family's last name is "*Kyŏngju Kim.*"[2] My Korean name is Kim Song-Yun. When I was little, I went to *yagakkō* (night school) for just a short while, even though I was a girl. But I really didn't like to study. I would take my little papers and pretend to be going to school, but I always ended up at my friend's house. You know there are people who didn't even get to go to night school, but . . . *ha, ha, ha*. . . . My mother and father got so upset because I didn't go to school, and I always ended up at my friend's house. . . . Whenever I did go, we learned the Korean *han'gŭl*. My family owned farmland. But my father died when I was eleven years old. . . . I don't remember him very much. So my mother did most of the work. All of us had to work and help my mother, because there weren't enough hands.

From the time I was very small, I used to help pull the weeds. There was only one boy in the family, although there were five of us girls. So I was in charge of one whole cow. I pulled weeds and fed it to the cow. My brother didn't work very much. He really didn't like to work at all. My mother, my sister-in-law, and I had to do most of the work in the rice field. . . . When I was little, I don't remember ever feeling hungry, because not only did we farm, but also because I was the youngest so I was quite spoiled. Until I was nine years old, I still suckled on my mother's breast. . . . *Ha, ha, ha* . . . (she roars with laughter).

Coming to Japan

In my hometown, about four blocks away from us, there were several Japanese families. I think I was fourteen years old when I was charmed by stories of Japan told by my next-door neighbor. I don't know why I was so *akogarete ita* (yearning) for Japan. But I was only fourteen, so I guess I didn't know anything. My next-door neighbor's nieces were already working and living in Japan. When they came home for a visit, they told me so many things. They helped me get a travel permit and I just followed them here.[3] My brother, sisters, and mother were dead set against me coming, but I didn't listen to what they said. I really wanted to come, so it didn't matter what anybody said. I was so stupid. . . . Really I was stupid. . . . *Ahh* . . . (she sighs). *Unmei dakara shō ga nai*—it's my destiny, so it can't be helped. . . .

I took the boat to Shimonoseki, and then somehow I got on that noisy train and got off at Nagoya. I lived in Nagoya, Ichinomiya. The person I came with helped me to get a job in a factory. I didn't know any Japanese, I didn't know anything. The Japanese person who worked with me talked with me in gestures. When it was time to eat, she would put one hand up to her mouth to gesture that it was time for lunch. At that time we lived in a factory dormitory. My room-mates were three other Japanese workers. There were about three or four Koreans who didn't live in the dormitory, but who used to work in the factory. So during the afternoons when these people came, I could speak to them in Korean. But after they left, I couldn't say anything or do anything. . . . I cried so much.

In those days you worked all day and night, every day. In the morning we started work at eight a.m., and then, well, I forgot until when, but they really made us work long hours. Well, when I first came, the food was quite different from what I was used to, so I really *kurō shita yo* (suffered). When I came here there were no such things like kimchi, because I was living in the dormitory.

I was scolded quite often by the other Koreans, because I was crying so much, calling out to my mother, "*Ŏmŏni, ŏmŏni.*" Even when I wasn't crying, if I would look like I was about to start, the other ladies would yell at me and say, "*Why are you crying again?*" I was only fourteen years old. . . . I wanted to see my mother so badly . . . so badly. During the afternoon, when I was working, I would hear a voice and then I would turn around . . . I could swear that it was my mother's voice. I could hear it so clearly. When I heard it again, I would look back quickly, but there was no one there. And if I started crying again, the others would get angry, so I would rush to the outhouse and just cry. My mother was forty years old when she gave birth to me. So because my parents had me when they were quite old, they thought that after they died I would be left all alone. I think they felt sorry for me and that was the reason why they spoiled me so much.

My older sister came to Japan a little while after I did. She lived with me and for a while she worked at the same factory. The factory gave me the papers to invite her to come and work in Japan. You know, my older sister was so very strict. . . . Even when I wanted to go out of the house to buy soap, she wouldn't let me walk out of the house by myself without her or someone following me from behind. She was so strict with me. . . . That's why I didn't like my sister at all. So after seeing to it that I got married properly, my sister left Japan to go back to Korea alone.

Marriage

When I got married and came to my husband's house, there were his two younger sisters and also his father living in the house. My husband's mother died early. My father-in-law was really a wonderful person. . . . You know, I'd never had to make rice before. . . . Back then it wasn't like the way it is now—electronic. You had to make the rice in a big pot over the fire. And I don't know what it was, but every time I cooked the rice—in the middle of the pot there would be a big spot where the rice was uncooked and still raw. So my father-in-law showed me how to cook the rice. He showed me how many bowls of rice to put inside the pot, and then how much water to put in. He taught me so patiently, but maybe I couldn't get the degree of the fire right. Always, just right in the middle of the pot it would be raw. I would be so worried after I put the big pot over the fire. And then, my father-in-law, so kind, would tell me, "*It's okay, I'll try to fix it somehow.*" I don't know what happened; maybe it was the amount of water or the fire. But making the rice . . . *ha, ha.* . . . *Kurō shita, nā* . . . (I suffered). My father-in-law passed away when he was eighty-something. If my mother-in-law had been around, I would have had a hard time, because I didn't know how to do anything.

Before my husband and I were married, I hadn't even seen him. . . . My sister heard about him from her husband's brother, and decided to have me marry him. My sister thought since her husband's brother was introducing the two of us, they wouldn't lie and fool us into any bad situation. Little did she know how much he hated to work. . . . My husband didn't have any money, and plus he hated to work, and so there was no woman who was willing to marry him, I guess. *Ha, ha, ha.* . . . There really was no one who could compare to my husband, the way he played around. When I arrived at my husband's home, his sisters were at that time sixteen and eleven. Those two girls went to a glove factory to work, and whenever they got paid, they wouldn't spend a yen. They wouldn't even open their pay envelopes, but bring them home to me unopened each month. I guess they felt that they had to do that, because their brother was so irresponsible. And so I made ends meet and made sure that eventually they were each able to have a small wedding.[4] . . . Not fancy weddings though. . . . We just didn't have that kind of money.

I was nineteen years old when I married. Everybody was actually saying that I married late. We had a small wedding party. I had to wear the bride's ornament on my head and also my husband wore the traditional groom's cap. I had pictures of that, but during the war it all got burnt. It was really a good picture. . . . In Nagoya, because of the *kūshū,* shelling and bombing, it all got burnt. After that I didn't have anything left. If it weren't for the war, maybe I would still have that picture.

During the first night together, people from the wedding shoved me inside the room. I was so scared. I just sat all the way in the corner. All you could hear was the chattering of my teeth, I was so scared. I didn't even see his face. . . . I just huddled in the corner and sat hugging my knees, because my body shook so much and my teeth were just chattering away. . . . *Ha, ha, ha* . . . (she lets out a loud laugh). When I think about it now, I think I must have looked pretty stupid. . . . *Ha, ha, ha.* You know, it was the first time that I entered a room alone with a man. . . . I was so scared, so scared, I was shaking—shaking like a leaf, and then my teeth were chattering so much, "*ta, ta, ta, ta, ta*" so loudly. *Ha, ha, ha.* . . . So until the third night he did not touch me in that way. . . . I think my husband must have thought that there was something wrong with me. For three nights straight, I huddled in the corner and didn't sleep, and at the crack of dawn, I just jumped out of the room. I couldn't lie down even for a minute. I really was scared, that's for sure. . . . So night after night, my husband just fell asleep. He must have thought what a strange creature I was. Actually, when I think about it now, I think it was in a way my sister's fault. I think if she hadn't been so strict with me and allowed me to go out of the house or to meet different people, then maybe I wouldn't have been so scared like that. But really, it was just like living in a box.

In my husband's household, there were two rooms—my sisters-in-law and my father-in-law used one room and the other room was used by me and my husband, whenever he was home. Sometimes he came home at two or three o'clock in the morning, and sometimes not for two or three days. The sister-in-law who is now living in Taegu in Korea was back then eleven years old. She didn't like sharing the room with her father, so when her brother didn't come back home, she was happy, because then she could sleep next to me. . . . *Ha, ha, ha.* . . .

Husband and Children

I think it was about two or three months after we got married. Anyway, although we were married, my husband would never take off his shirt in front of me. One day he drank a lot as usual and then he got into a fight. He rushed home and I saw him hiding in a small corner. He was soaking wet when I saw him and for the first time he took off his shirt in front of me. I glanced in his direction as I quickly handed him a new shirt—both of his shoulder blades and his back were covered with two big blue marks. I was shocked. The next day, I whispered to my father-in-law that my husband must have gotten beat up quite badly because his arms and back were covered with blue marks. When I said this to my father-in-law, he just smiled. . . .

I think he must have wondered if I could really be so stupid. Sometime later, I heard that it was a tattoo. *Ha, ha, ha.* . . . On the right side was a demon's head and on the left side was a cherry blossom—the signs of the *yakuza*—he was an *oyagumi no chinpira,* a lower rank gangster. In the beginning of our marriage, one day, a man who looked like a hoodlum came into our house and said, "*Nē-san, konnichi wa*—older sister, good afternoon." At that time I didn't even know the word, "*onē-san*" (older sister). The guy looking like the hoodlum he was, I thought that he was saying something nasty to me. So then when I asked what that word meant, I was told that because I was the wife of the "older brother"[5] he called me *onē-san,* older sister. I didn't even know the meaning of the whole thing until later. . . . *Ha, ha, ha.* . . . I thought he was saying a bad word to me.

Binbō na seikatsu shita yo—we really lived a poor life. My father-in-law gave me all his earnings for our living expenses. He would give me the money and then tell me to hide it from my husband and use it for foodstuffs and whatever we needed. Then, my husband would come home and ask me if his father gave me any money. I was so stupid, I should have told him that I didn't receive anything, but back then I would just give him the money. Then, my father-in-law would come back home and find out and he would tell me, "*You should have told him that I didn't give you anything.*" He would say, "*I told you not to give him any money and if he asks you, to just flat out deny that you have any money. . . .*" It was all because I was lacking good sense. If I was even a bit smart then I would have had enough sense to run away, but in the beginning I felt sorry for my father-in-law. I felt a certain obligation toward him, because he was so kind. . . . My father-in-law was like a god to me. Then, after that, the children came.

My husband played around like the gangster he was. At that time I didn't even know the feeling of being jealous. I thought that men were supposed to do those kinds of things. My husband used to go to this one bar in the neighborhood. He used to go there all the time. Well, one summer, it seems that the granddaughter of the bar's *mama-san*[6] came for a visit. That's how they met. Her name was Nobuyo. Well, he was going there almost every day, and I guess they started talking and began to like each other. And, of course, she became pregnant. She was quite young, and since my husband was already married with kids, the grandmother of the girl came to talk with me one day. She said her granddaughter had just given birth and asked me to take the child in and raise it as my own. Can you believe that? I told her, "*Jōdan ja nai yo! (You must be joking!)*" I, too, had just given birth to my youngest son, and I was also running a *yakiniku* business. The business wasn't making all that much money, but I was literally running around in the restaurant with a kid on my back, and also taking care of the house as well as my in-laws. All day long I cooked and served in the restaurant, and then when we closed late at night, I had to count the money and prepare it for the bank people to come and pick it up early next morning. This was how I was paying off the bank loan. Then, after that was finished, I had to come to the back of the restaurant where we were living and prepare the next day's breakfast and make the lunch boxes for everyone to take. With all the kids, as well as my in-laws, I had to do the laundry almost every day. Although I was so tired, these were things that needed to be done, no matter what. Then this woman comes and asks me to take another newborn baby in. *Ha, ha. . . .* The grandmother of the woman was begging me for help. She said her granddaughter had promised to marry a man who had gone off to the army and he was due to come back home at any time. Well, I told her the truth. There was no way I could do it. A while later, I heard that the woman went back to the countryside with the child. I don't know if her parents decided to raise it or not. But I never heard from them again. I doubt it if my husband ever kept in touch with her or helped her out with any money. He didn't have a sense of responsibility.

My husband was the only son, and that's why he was so spoiled. There was no other way but to give into him. But if I gave him everything that I had, how was I supposed to feed all of our children. We would all starve. He would tell me, "*Either you give it to me, or you're going to get it.*" So I got beat up instead. Look at this scar. Here just over my eyebrow, it opened up completely, and that's why even though it healed up years ago, sometimes it still aches a bit. It was from a blow with a beer bottle. That idiot got me right here on the forehead with an empty beer bottle. The thick, warm blood gushed out and it blinded my eyes. I just crawled to the other room and I warned the kids to get out. When I went to the doctor I didn't have to say anything, the doctor also knew of my husband. He just said, "*Ano Nonbē-san hidoi koto suru nā—that husband of yours does some cruel things. . . .*" *Ahh . . .* (she sighs). The doctor thought that I might not be able to see through this eye.

As for the children, whenever they heard their father's voice and knew that he was drunk, they hid in the closet, or ran out of the house to hide somewhere outside. During the summer, it wasn't so bad, but during the winter, I felt so sorry for them. He would make the children stand up at attention and have them look straight ahead and then he would grill them, poke at them, and carry on. . . . All throughout the year, the side of my face would be blue, and then when it started to heal, it would get a dull yellow. . . . My husband was known for drinking. In Kawasaki you said the name "*Nonbē*" (heavy drinker) Yasu and everybody would know who you were talking about. His last name was Yasuda, so he was known as Nonbē Yasu. I can't even talk about it. . . . Outside of the home, everybody thought he was such a good man. People who didn't know would say, "*Nonbē Yasu, he's really a good person.*" But once he entered the house, he changed completely.

Oh, I thought about leaving everything and running away often. . . . But if I did that, what would happen to my father-in-law and the children. Of course, I would feel sorry for my kids if I were to leave, but I would feel even sorrier for my old father-in-law. . . . He was such a good person. . . . Because his son was like that, I guess he felt sorry for me and wanted to make up for his son's behavior, and so he was always considerate to me. . . . But I was so stupid, and that's the reason why I endured. Even if I'd had the money, I had no idea where to go.

But we still had five children. I think God must have made them. . . . *Ha, ha, ha.* . . . I had three daughters and then the fourth child was a son. I had two other sons after that. My first child was a daughter, and she lives in Chiba now. My second child was also a daughter, but I lost her before her first year due to measles. I didn't even know that she had measles and that's how I lost her. For measles you have to keep the baby warm, but I didn't even know what she had. . . . I was so stupid, I didn't even know how to take her to the doctor. *Ha, ha, ha.* I guess back then there weren't too many doctors. My father-in-law felt very sad when she died. I had my daughter in September and then I lost her in March. Then, I had another daughter after that and then three sons. When I had my children, we called a *sanba* (midwife). During that time there were no hospitals.

Wartime

During the war we had to escape from Nagoya. Then we came to Kawasaki in Shōwa 20 (1945). We had two cousins who were already living here. So my father-in-law, my husband, my daughter, and I came to Kawasaki. My first daughter was born in Nagoya, and the rest of my children were born in Kawasaki. At that time I was twenty-something. When we were living in Nagoya there were *kūshū* and we had to get into our dugout shelters. When the bombs were dropped you could see them sparkling in the sky as it fell. It really was something else. . . . All of a sudden we would hear, *"Kūshū keihō"* (Air Raid Alarm) over the loudspeaker. They would yell it out, and sometimes they would announce it as it happened. To build the dugouts, you would dig out the dirt from the ground and then pile it all on one side. You take wood and such, and pile it up and get inside. Then you wait until the announcement *"Kūshū keihō kaijo da"* (Air Raid Warning Release) and we would come out of the dugout. . . . *Ha, ha, ha.* . . . We went into that hole quite often. You know words can't describe it. . . . After the warning was called off, we would receive some *onigiri* (rice balls) from the town hall. There was no white rice then. There were only wheat and barley and such things. I still remember my little daughter asking me, *"Okā-san, gohan mō chitto kureru?—Mommy, can I have just a little bit more rice?"* But at that time I was breast-feeding and I, too, was hungry . . . and so I said, *"That's enough for you."* But she said in that little voice, *"Mō chitto chōdai—please, just a little more. . . ."* I still can hear that little voice clearly. . . . It still rings in my ear. . . . *Ha, ha . . . ahh . . .* (her laugh turns into a sigh). Maybe, if I gave her just a little bit more, she would have felt full, but. . . .

Sometimes, I went into the countryside hoping I could buy some rice cheaply, but it was really hard to get the farmers to sell it to me. I would walk around the countryside trying to buy some rice to feed my family. Sometimes I would walk here and there and then I would come upon an elderly farmer who would sell me some rice. Sometimes they would even give me a couple of rice balls. They would slip it in my hands and say to take it with me and eat it on my way back into the city. They would whisper to me, *"When you get on the train, eat it. Don't let my daughter-in-law see it otherwise she'll get angry that I gave you something to eat."* Several times I received these rice balls, and I still remember how good it tasted. It was so delicious. . . .

Work

Well, *ha, ha, ha* . . . I started smoking, I think when I was reaching thirty. Yeah, I wonder how I started smoking as well as drinking. I guess when you are in that business of selling alcohol, you learn the habits as well. I was making *doburoku* (unrefined alcohol). I would have to squeeze the alcohol, and then taste it, and that's how I learned the taste. Now I don't drink. I drink a little bit only on special occasions. When you make alcohol, you take *kōji* (yeast, malt) and *kome* (rice) and you soak it. I had three or four barrelsful, and the customers took it clean. The customers would come to buy it from my place, and they could be jailed if they were caught with the alcohol. So of course they couldn't take the alcohol freely in their hands. You had to hide the bottles well in a cardboard box or wrap it where it can't be seen.

But once one of the customers got caught. He was asked where he bought the alcohol, and he told the police that he bought it at my place. He had bought four bottles. The police came and asked who made it, and there was nothing I could say, because of all the evidence. So they took me into jail, and I ended up staying in Kawasaki police station for two nights. . . . *Ha, ha, ha.* . . . There were mostly Koreans in the jail, who had all been caught making *doburoku*, too. You know at that time Koreans could only do bad things like that. I was barely thirty years old then. I couldn't eat at all for two days, because I was so scared. When mealtime came along, the gruel was barley with just a little bit of white rice. Then, they would take the food right away if they thought that you were not going to eat it. So after not being able to touch it several times, I felt so hungry that I waited until they brought some food again. But for some reason when they brought it, I just couldn't eat again. I couldn't sleep. The children were still very small. And I was still breast-feeding one of them. My breasts were so swollen with milk . . . I really cried. . . . I didn't know what they were going to do with me—whether I was going to live or die in that terrible place.

Actually, with all the evidence and everything, there was no way I could get out of jail after spending only two nights there. . . . But it seems that they shortened my stay. . . . I begged the police officers and I told them that at home I had my children and my old father-in-law to take care of. And what's more, my husband was quite famous at the police station and they all knew about him, in Nagoya as well as Kawasaki. . . . He was really famous. . . . *Ha, ha, ha.* So I was let out after only two nights in jail. But at that time the penalty was sixty thousand yen. I went to the tax office and I told them that I wasn't refusing to pay this penalty, but I needed them to divide it up into several payments. I told them that if I were to pay all of this at once, me, my children and my old father-in-law would die of starvation. So, then they allowed me to make small payments. And I paid it all off. . . . every yen. When I was in jail, I promised myself that even if I were to starve to death I would never ever bootleg again as long as I lived. But then after I came out of jail, a few days later I was making and selling again. . . . If I hadn't, there was absolutely no way we could have continued eating.

Then, somehow I started a *yakiniku* business. Even now when some of my former customers see me, they still say that they think about my cooking to this day. In the restaurant when my children would call me, they would say, "*ŏmma*" (mother). Then the Japanese customers learned the word and they started calling me "*ŏmma*," too. As soon as they entered the restaurant, they would call out "*ŏmma*." *Ha, ha, ha.* . . . I was thirty-something when I started the business. "*Ichiba Yakiniku*" was the name on the signboard—it was famous. I did the business for about thirty years. . . .

The Japanese customers used to eat all the meat and kimchi quite well. But one problem was when Koreans came, they caused so many problems. You can't do business with Korean people. They drink and carry on and then get into fights all the time and break everything. They would tell me that they were customers, too, but I would just tell them I didn't want them to come to my restaurant. Most of my customers were Japanese. If we didn't deal with Japanese customers, then my family couldn't have put food on the table.

I was able to start this business, because in the beginning the meat companies allowed you to use their meat and then pay them back after your sales. Without that you can't start a business. I ran the business right out of my home. For additional things I borrowed money from the bank. In the Japanese banks you needed a Japanese guarantor so I couldn't borrow from them, but I borrowed money from the *Chōsen ginkō*, the North Korean Bank.[7] Before, the Korean bank was small, but now it is quite big. The bank would come to collect money every day, a portion of the sales to pay back the loan. I don't know how I did it, but *yoku yatte kitta*—I really did it. If I got three to four hours of sleep a night, I considered it good.

Chongryun

We were part of *Chongryun*. All of my children went to *Chongryun* schools in Yokohama. So this was why I could borrow money from the North Korean bank. They all went to *uri hakkyo* ("our school").[8] I'm not quite sure why we went to the *Chongryun* side. At that time *Mindan* wasn't around so much, and most people in this area were involved in *Chongryun*. The only one of my children who graduated from high school is my daughter who lives in Nakajima. The others only completed junior high school. We didn't have the money to send them to school longer. And for *Chōsen gakkō* (North Korean ethnic school) you have to have money. If the parents didn't pay the money, the schools wouldn't keep the students. I forgot exactly how much it was but it was quite expensive.[9]

Many people went back to both North and South Korea. I was also thinking about going to the North. My husband's nephews all went back to North Korea. But then my first son and my daughter were so against it and I couldn't go alone and leave my kids behind. Even if I were to die, I couldn't leave my kids behind. My husband didn't want to go back to Korea either. . . . But now in the North, it seems like they are really having a hard time. My eldest daughter always tells me that it was a good thing that we didn't go back then. But it seems that even if we had gone there, as long as we had some relatives here in Japan sending money, it wouldn't have been so hard. But I heard that people who don't have any relatives abroad sending them money are suffering quite a bit.

We have changed from North Korean citizenship to South Korean citizenship. When I went to Korea twice before, I had to apply through *Mindan,* and that's the reason why I changed my citizenship from North to South. My children have not changed to Japanese citizenship.[10] My third son says that he wants to keep his Korean citizenship, because it is his country. My children all attended *uri hakkyo,* so they can speak Korean. They speak pretty well. My third son is quite good. My first daughter and my second daughter also speak Korean fluently.

Reflection

Ahhh . . . (she sighs). I really suffered a lot, but I lived for my children. My girls understand my feelings. . . . My older one, she understands what I went through. She understands from one to ten, all the things that I went through. She lives very well now, and she always tells me to come and live with her, but I tell her no thanks. Where she lives, there are no Koreans in the neighborhood. Also, her husband does a big business there. My eldest daughter really suffered a lot, too. . . . She had to do most of the housework and look after all of the younger ones when I had to work.

I think my children really disliked their father. My first daughter said that when her father died she probably wouldn't drop a tear. But when he actually died, she cried a lot. I think that although he was the way he was, she felt sorry for him. During that time Korean men couldn't find much work. When I think about it myself, it is a wonder how I have come to live my life. . . .

When I was living alone in Ichinomiya (Nagoya), there were many Koreans living near me. At that time I would ask them to write letters for me to send to my mother. I received some letters from her as well. In some of her letters she told me not to get married here and to come back to Korea and then get married. I really wonder why I ended up getting married here—meeting a wonderful man like him. *Ha, ha, ha.* . . . I guess when he was younger, he wasn't so bad looking. *Ha, ha.* . . .

That picture there, when we took that picture, we were married for over thirty years. We had to get our alien registration card[11] renewed and we needed a picture, and so we went together to take the pictures. Then my husband said all of a sudden that since we lived with each other for this long and we didn't have a single picture together, we should take one. And that's how we took it. A week after that he collapsed. . . . He was really a smart person, it's just that he used it for bad things.

I think it has been about fifteen years since my husband passed away. He was bedridden for seven years before he died. Before my husband fell ill, I was quite active, sometimes going to church, and attending classes to learn *hiragana* and *kanji* (Japanese and Chinese characters). But once my husband was bedridden, I had to change his diapers and hand-feed him, because otherwise he couldn't eat anything. I couldn't really leave his side. He couldn't move his body at all. During those times, when he wouldn't do as I told him, I would feel frustrated. Sometimes when I thought about the way he hurt me in the past, I would spank him on the behind or pinch him. . . . *Ha, ha, ha.* But these days, when I turn out the lights and I toss and turn, I really wish that I hadn't done that. I saw him in a dream about three times after he died, and then after that I don't see him anymore. He must have gone to a good place, because he was quite kind to others. People would often say, "*Nonbē-san, he really is such a good person.*"

I really suffered a lot and I'm still suffering. . . . *Ha, ha, ha.* . . . Now, I'm just trying to make ends meet. Right now I'm receiving *minsei* (welfare). The money that I saved up from the *yakiniku* business, working all those years with these little hands, my eldest son and I ended up spending it all. After I gave up my business, I didn't have any other income. Also, my son couldn't work for a while either. So we just lived from the savings.

The owner of this room was an old lady who was a good friend of mine. She was Japanese. When she was alive, she started renting this room to me. But before that when my husband was alive, we lived together with my first son. We have a four-story building, near here. It's the third building right next to the hospital. It's called "*Yasuda Biru.*" But the problem was when my son drank, he went crazy just like his father, and that's why I ended up moving here alone. One day when I talked to the old lady who owns this place about my son and his drunken behavior, she told me that I should just move out and come live here, and that's how I ended up here. If that *obā-chan* (old lady) were still alive, then I wouldn't have this kind of problem with her son telling me to move out. She really was a good person.

It's been only a little while since my first son died. It hasn't been forty-nine days yet. He was born in Shōwa 20 (1945); he was born in the year of the chicken. I remember that when he was born there was nothing to eat. . . . My son has died before me. . . . That's one of the things that *maŭm app 'ŏ* (hurts me). My other sons grew up well, but my first son gave me a lot of heartache. From junior high school he started hanging out with the wrong crowd. *Ahh . . .* (she starts to smoke). That boy in the beginning lived with a Japanese woman, and they had two kids together and now they live somewhere in Tōkyō. And then after that he married a Korean woman. He hardly worked and he drank so much, so the wife's mother took her back home. She was really a good girl. They had four children together. My son had diabetes and even then he was continuing to drink, and that's what did it in the end. He just passed out one day.

My third son lives over there now. He was the one who helped me build the building anyway. He is still paying off the loan. The first floor he lent to a business, and also there are other tenants. The two younger ones are very responsible. My third son is really smart. He tells me to move into his house, because he says he would feel ashamed if his friends knew that he lets his own mother live alone like this. But I like this room, I feel the most comfortable here. If I go into my son's house to live—I can't live over there. I can't breathe easily. . . .

You say I am great, but there's nothing great about living like this. I only have regrets. . . . I don't know. . . . Maybe, when I was young, if I were to have run away. . . . But perhaps it was just good that I stayed, I'm not sure which would have been better. . . . *Ha, ha, ha.* . . . You know, recently, I met a person whom I knew long ago, and then she told me that I look so young still yet. I told her its because I lack something in my head. . . . *Ha, ha.* . . . Because I am stupid, I don't have the ability to think much, and maybe that's the reason why I don't have many wrinkles. . . . *Ha, ha, ha . . .* (she roars with laughter).

Notes

1. This word refers to the traditional manner of reckoning one's age. Throughout their narratives, the women sometimes give an age according to the *kazoe* count, even if this is not explicitly indicated.

2. Kim from the province of Kyŏngju.

3. In order to fill the demand for low-wage labor, recruiters of individual firms and independent labor brokerage agencies, with the help of local assistants, solicited Korean workers. See Lee and DeVos (1981a: 35-36) and Weiner (1989: 54-60). Between 1931 and 1937, as Japan's economy underwent a notable recovery, about 736,000 Koreans, of which approximately 290,000 were women, constituted a substantial portion of the urban population. See Weiner (1994: 113, 148, 187).

4. As the eldest and only daughter-in-law, Kimiko was responsible for taking care of her sisters-in-law's marriage prospects and weddings.

5. Within the organization, the system of hierarchy according to experience, length of affiliation, and age was strictly observed. Older members were addressed as *onī-san* or "older brother".

6. In Japan, the female owner of a bar or drinking establishment is referred to as "mama" or "mama-*san*" by both the workers and the customers.

7. Through this bank, Koreans, especially those affiliated with *Chongryun*, were able to borrow initial capital for businesses. Ryang (1997: 4) writes that Chōsen bank, which divides Japan into 38 blocs with a total of 188 branches, had total savings exceeding two trillion dollars as of 1990.

8. "Our school" refers to North Korean ethnic schools.

9. According to Ryang (1997: 24), students of *Chongryun* primary schools had to pay tuition of about eight thousand yen per month in 1995. At the same time, the parents are requested to give "donations," for which the amount was fixed according to financial situation.

10. For the second as well as third generation Koreans who have attended North Korean schools, the desire to retain Korean citizenship is generally much stronger than for those who are affiliated with the South.

11. Under the Alien Registration Act enacted in May 1947, Koreans were cast as aliens, restricting their legal rights in the areas of public housing, social welfare, taxation, food rationing, and business. Under this law, they were required to renew their residential status every four years and carry an identification card with them at all times or face deportation. See Lee (1981: 138). However, through the mandate of the two International Covenants on Human Rights in 1979 and the UN Refugee Convention in 1981, which required equal treatment of nationals and noncitizens, a number of social rights were extended to resident aliens. In 1991, all permanent residence statuses were unified under the "special permanent residence status," which provided more security and rights. See Kashiwazaki (2000: 28).

Chapter 8
Now I Can Say That I'm Happy

Sŏ Meng-Sun

At church, Meng-Sun keeps to herself. She comes earlier than most and sits at her usual seat near the window. After praying, she waits quietly until the sermon begins. When the service is over, she joins the others for snacks or the monthly meals and then quickly departs. She is not one for small talk. But when she tells the many events of her past, she energetically lifts her hands in the air and dramatically alters her intonation, and sometimes breaks out into little giggles showing her small side teeth.

Meng-Sun believes that living for her children gave meaning to her life, and for the sake of her children, she would do anything. If it meant having to sit and chant the sutra for hours in a language that was foreign, or stand in the cold under freezing water so that her "body felt as if it would break into a thousand pieces," she would do so in order to placate the gods. She defined happiness as being able to raise her children properly and keeping her family together.

Meng-Sun believes in always taking care of others instead of being cared for, giving back after receiving, never being in debt or owing anything, never causing trouble to anyone, and most importantly, taking care of herself and maintaining a sense of pride.

Before I was born, all three of my brothers died, and so my parents were worried that if they had another boy he was also going to die. When I was born as a girl they were quite relieved. Actually they gave me a boy's name, so instead of being called Meng-Sun, when I was a little girl, I was called "Meng-Su." When I was little, my friends used to tease me all the time because I had a boy's name. But after I got married, my name was written as Meng-Sun. My mother said it was because they were afraid that I was going to die, so when I was born, they tried to trick the bad spirit by giving me a boy's name even though I was a girl.

My name is Sŏ Meng-Sun. I will turn eighty-one years old on May 22. I was born on May 18, but during the war all the dates and everything were mixed up so it was recorded as May 22 . . . Taishō 7 (1918). I was born in Kyŏngsang-do. It's close to Pusan. There were seven of us and I was the middle child. I had two older sisters who married when I was very small, and an older brother. I also had one younger brother and two younger sisters. I lived with my parents until I was fourteen years old. In the old days in Korea, every year your mother would go to have your fortune read from a book.[1] It is one of those fortune books that tell about your *p'alcha*. Well, the book said that I was going to die that year, but if I went to another country, my life might be saved. So I came by boat to Shimonoseki. I didn't know a word of Japanese. I traveled with about nineteen others who were also going to work for the same factory. A distant cousin of mine was then living and studying in Tōkyō's Ōimachi. One day he came back to Korea to recruit some workers for a relative of his who had opened a factory in Japan. So I guess the timing was just right. I worked and lived in the factory for about three years. Then my brother settled in Nagoya and asked that I live with him. He worked in a factory.

Coming to Japan

To come to Japan, I needed to get a travel permit from police headquarters.[2] Luckily, my father was quite close to some of the police, and he got the permit for me. My father was well-known in town for being learned. He was well versed in the Chinese classics, which he studied under my grandfather, who built a *sŏtang* in our house. My grandmother passed away when my father was five years old. My father began his studies in the Chinese classics from the time he was *kazoe* five years old. Back then one who mastered Chinese classical learning was considered to have a deeper understanding of things than even a Buddhist monk. In fact, my father had an ability to look at a person's face and know things—for example, he would say this person would be happy or that person will face difficulties in life. My father also could predict if there would be a lot of rain, or sometimes if there would be earthquakes. . . . He knew what the weather would be like for the day, by saying things like "*Today it will rain*," or "*Tomorrow it will snow*." He knew of such things. He would say, "*Today it is going to be rainy, so hurry and clear things away*," and after we did, rain always fell, just as he said. When he saw a pregnant woman, he could tell by the way she walked whether she would have a boy or girl. People now would say that only monks would know such things, but back then, elders who were educated in the Chinese classics knew and understood many things. Men who had finished such high education of Chinese learning would say that *han'gŭl* was only for women who learned it in the toilet.

In those days they didn't allow girls to study. Although there were reading classes and night classes as well, girls weren't allowed to go, because they said when girls went to school, all they did was lift up their legs and start dancing. I wanted to go to school so badly, I would take a little piece of thick paper and pretend to write on it. But no matter how much I begged, my parents wouldn't allow it. All of my brothers were able to go to school, though. When I was little, my father thought that at least I should be able to read and write *han'gŭl*. So I was lucky enough to be taught how to read and write a bit here and there. Later, when I had children, I taught all of them how to read and write Korean, because although we live in Japan, we are Korean. I told them that they must at least learn how to read and write in Korean.

I didn't want to come to Japan. What fourteen-year-old would want to leave her parents to go away to a far-off land? I cried so much. The people at the factory told me just to bear it for a little while longer. You know the thread in the lightbulb? Well, I was at a factory that made these threads. So I did that work for about three years, then my cousin brought me to Nagoya where my brother was. In those times there were rickshaws where you would sit in the back and then a man would pull you from the front. When we got off the train we rode a rickshaw to my brother's house. I thought that my brother would send me back to my *kohyang*. But instead he told me to marry this man and that is how I ended up marrying my husband in January of my seventeenth year. Actually, in the *umryŏk* (lunar calendar) I wasn't even sixteen yet. My mother agreed to the marriage because she thought that if I were to marry in Korea, I would have to really suffer with so much work, as well as having to take care of many in-laws. I guess my mother was hoping that I would find a better situation by marrying in Japan. I soon had children after that. My husband was twenty-four years old when we married. My husband, he really liked women very much, so even before I married him, he went out with this woman and that woman. Well, he was so-so looking. *Ha, ha, ha . . .* (she laughs shyly). But I didn't know all of this, so that was how I ended up marrying him. I guess my brother didn't know either.

Wartime

It was in Nagoya that I got married, and I had three children there. When I was twenty years old I came to Kawasaki. In Kawasaki, even women could find enough work to pay for some of the food. So that is why we ended up leaving Nagoya for Kawasaki. In Kawasaki there was the *Nihon Kōkan* (Japan steel pipe company). It was said that the *Kōkan* company was one of the biggest and most famous in Japan. It was said that if this company were to go down, half of the people in Japan would starve. I remember hearing one of the very first explosions coming from the chimney of this company. When I went outside, it was just black dust everywhere from the ashes. The black smoke rising from the chimneys of the steel factory was like a gigantic cloud.

You know, during the war when they were dropping bombs—I think it happened first in Kawasaki near *Kōkan-dōri*, the street near where Pastor Yi lives. After the bomb was dropped there, everyone had to move near where that marketplace is now. Bombs were dropped here in Kawasaki, and near Tōkyō, and Kamata on a daily basis. On the road there were dead bodies all over the place. If I'd had only one child then I could have put the child on my back and escaped to a faraway place. But I had three children—my first daughter who went to North Korea, my son, and then my second daughter. I put one child on my back and took the other two in each hand, and then I went from one place to another escaping the bombings. But I was never able to go very far. But as the war progressed, there was no other way but to escape, and so that is how I ended up in Gunma prefecture. In Gunma, there was nothing but tall mountains one after another. There was absolutely nothing but little houses far apart here and there. There really was nothing. . . . I couldn't live there. . . . And because it was high up in the mountains, during the summer the sound of thunder would be more frightening than the sound of the bombings. At night because of the thunder it sounded as if the sky were cracking in pieces and the children couldn't sleep. I stayed there for only one year, and then I came back out to Kawasaki lugging the children and our belongings, because I couldn't stand that place any longer.

So we moved out to Hama-chō. As the war progressed, every day bombs were dropping all over the place and we heard stories of so many people getting killed. The *tonari-gumi-chō*,[3] the person who was in charge of my neighborhood, told me that I had to take the kids and escape to the countryside, because the bombings were getting more and more frequent and closer to Kawasaki. So we ended up in the countryside of Saitama. All of my family, relatives, friends, and neighbors escaped to the mountains of Saitama. It was deep in the countryside and there was no work and no food. So one day when I saw a farmer working busily in the fields, I asked him if he needed some help in exchange for food. I had small children, but the wife of the farmer offered to look after the baby while I went out to work in the fields in exchange for some vegetables. I didn't know anything. In Korea, I had never even touched a hoe or an axe. When I went to work in the fields, I had to pull weeds or help plow the fields, plant seeds and sometimes harvest, but I didn't know how to do anything. The owner of the farm taught me the difference between weeds and plants—what to pull out and what to leave alone, how to plant, how to plow. . . . So every day he taught me what to do, and the first two years were very hard. In the mountains there was no food and no work except for farming. And you know in Korea, in my day, women did a lot of work inside the house, but they were never sent out to the field to do farmwork. I heard that in the Chŏlla area and also up North, women even in my time worked in the fields almost the same as men. But where I was from in the Kyŏngsang-do area, daughters and daughters-in-law—women in general—were never sent out to the field to do farmwork. Then when I came to Japan and had to go out into the fields to work in order to eat, I didn't know plants from weeds. In the fields there were some turnips, but I thought they were weeds, so I went right down the line and pulled them all out. Then the farmer whom I was helping told me that they were edible and to leave them alone, and he showed me what to pull out.

The landowner came from a very wealthy family. I heard that his brother made a lot of money during those times when many Japanese people were living in Taiwan. That is how he came to have so much land and houses. He was so kind. He used to tell me to come and clean the chicken coop and then he would give me a basket full of eggs. He taught me everything I know about farming, and by helping him out on his farm, I was able to feed my children with potatoes, barley, corn, and such. That really helped, because otherwise there would have been no food.

It was the hardest when I was in the countryside—escaping the war and with nothing to eat. I don't remember a day that we managed to eat three decent meals. I went here and there, and during winter there was no work in the fields, and so I went up in the mountains to get wood for fire. Up in the mountains there was plenty of wood, but it was full of sharp thorns and splinters. Of course, if it were now there would be gloves, but back then I had to gather them with my bare hands. By the time I came down from the mountains, I would be scarred and scratched all over my hands, neck, and face. My hands would be sticky from the blood. People who owned plots of land, including small hills and mountains, were able to go and get good wood. But Koreans and poor Japanese people had to go up to the wild mountains for wood. Anyway, I would gather enough wood to cook with, for the bath, and to keep us warm until late spring.

While we were living in the country, the children's clothes were so old and worn that if I washed them once or twice, they would fall apart. So I went around the neighborhood and looked in the trash for pieces of cloth, red or white or any color, and I used them to mend the holes and the torn places. But still you could see the holes and the tears. The children sometimes would say, it's because their mother never went to school, that I didn't know whether one color matched with another . . . (she smiles). At that time it didn't matter whether or not the colors matched, just going around town looking for pieces of cloth in the trash was hard enough work as it was. When we left the countryside and came to the city of Saitama, I saved some money and bought the children some decent clothes that wouldn't come apart after a couple of washings . . . they were so happy. I was really glad to move to the city. In the city when I went to work in the factories, they paid me with cash, but working in the fields I was compensated with flour, barley, potatoes. Together with whatever we received on *paegŭp* of oat and wheat was how we were able to eat. But it tasted so bad, no person who wasn't unusually hungry would be able to eat it. The kids would just stare at it gloomily, and so I would try to add some taste to it by adding salt, and then boiling it for a long time like gruel, but the kids wouldn't be able to eat it. So I would go out and stand in line for some *udon* (noodles) and make it for them.

Making Alcohol

This is kind of embarrassing, but my husband was living with another woman, and he was not with me and my children. One of my neighbors, a landowner, saw how I was struggling so much with all of my children and with my husband always away. He said he couldn't bear to look at the state that we were in. One day he gave me a small scoop of white rice and a bit of yeast, and taught me how to make alcohol. I brewed the alcohol and the landowner was kind enough to send one of his young workers. That really helped me out, because in order to buy the yeast, I would have had to go far into the countryside, but with my children there was no way I could have gone. The worker sent by the landowner also helped me sift the alcohol and brew it. And this was how I was able to feed my children—with the money that I made from making illegal alcohol.

In order to make the alcohol, you put rice and yeast in a large barrel and pour about twelve buckets of water in it, and then slowly brew it over the fire. Then you take a small bowl and continue to pour water into the barrel and sift the top as it simmers. I made various degrees of alcohol. The strongest was potent enough to be set on fire, and then the third degree of the alcohol was the weakest. Back then there was no alcohol to be found even if you had the money to buy it. Also, because there was no work, especially for Korean men, they would go into the countryside to slaughter animals like cows and goats to sell them. In order for them to eat and live, they had to do practically anything. You know, Koreans who came to Japan somehow had to make a living. So they started slaughtering cows and goats for the first time. They didn't do work like that in Korea. After slaughtering, the head, feet, and intestines were discarded. So my husband would bring it home for free, or sometimes pay a little money for it. Then I would wash it really well, put it in a big pot, and boil it all day. I would season it and sell it to those people who would come to buy alcohol from me. They would tell me how tasty it was with the brew that I made. You know, in Korea, selling alcohol was considered one of the lowest jobs and you would never marry your daughter into a household like that. But during my time in Japan as the war went on, in order to eat, we had to do work like this.

So I made illegal alcohol for about ten years. And as the business started getting busier, I had some helpers. I gave them the order sheets and told them that after reading them, they should throw the paper away. I told them this all the time because in case of bad luck, if we got caught, that would certainly be the end of us. If you got caught you would not only go to jail, but also have to pay an enormous fine. Then one of the young helpers forgot to throw away the order sheet and got caught while he was making deliveries. Then, the police came to my house and brought the order sheet with its big order written on it.

We have been living in Kawasaki for about forty years now. And about ten years before moving from Saitama to Kawasaki, I got caught. The penalty came out to about 200,000-300,000 yen. No matter what I said in my poor Japanese, and even when I asked a person who spoke very good Japanese from the North Korean organization to speak with the officials, they said nothing could be done about it and that I had to pay the fine. One of my relatives who is now living in North Korea, he was quite smart because he graduated from college. So I talked to him about it. He told me to say exactly what he taught me. When I went to the police station, my husband and one of our friends came with me. They sat in the corner shaking. I told the officials that my husband was away from home quite often, and it was hard for me to make a living and feed my children because of lack of work. I said a person gave me the ingredients to make the alcohol and to sell it to him to make a little bit of money to feed my children. I told them that I would never do it again. Then they questioned my husband. I sent one of my relatives who spoke really good Japanese to speak to the officials as well, but nothing worked. I ended up going to court.

It's quite a funny thing, but my youngest daughter who was one or two years old at that time shrieked and cried so hard each time they called my name to stand up and come to the front of the court. They stalled a bit, letting my turn come up later, and allowed me to let the baby suckle on my breast for a little while, but no matter what I tried, she wouldn't stop wailing. So my turn came up three times, but the baby would cry so hard each time they called my name. Even when I think about it now, I think how strange that was. I think that my ancestors really must have been helping me out then. So the trial luckily ended without a clear conviction. Also somebody told me to try going to the welfare office, and when I did, they asked me how much my husband was making. I told them that he was hardly at home, and that I worked for a local landowner in exchange for some food but it wasn't enough. After that, luckily, the welfare office decided to give me a hundred yen a month. Back then a hundred yen was pretty big money. Can you believe it? I told them that I had absolutely no money, and I had no way of paying the penalty for selling the alcohol. So I guess they discussed it among themselves, and they went to talk to the officials at court. They decided to let me go if I promised that I would never do it again. I was so relieved. You know, after selling alcohol for ten years, there was nothing to show for it . . . no house, no belongings, nothing but the pain and heartache of having to be called to the police station countless times, being questioned, going to court, and having to deal with the trial. I decided to quit the business for good.

So somehow, here and there, I made ends meet, and finally we bought a small house near the station in Saitama City. It had one six-mat room and one three-mat room, adding up to about twenty-four square meters. At that time I had seven children, and altogether there were nine of us. I started working for a factory that made ice and then after that another factory making toys, and during spring and fall I used to work where they raised silkworms. That would bring pretty good money—about three hundred yen a day. Working for the factory, I made about a hundred yen per day. So after living in the countryside for ten years, I lived in the city in front of the station for another ten years. I lived in Saitama for twenty years altogether.

Repatriation

After the war ended everyone was going back to Korea. All of my relatives and friends, everyone decided to go. We were the only ones left. We wanted to go to Korea, but because we didn't have enough money for the fares, we ended up pushing back our repatriation until we were able to save more money. My younger sister, my nieces, and nephews, all went back to South Korea, and we were the only ones left here in Japan. My husband was living with a Japanese woman at that time. Well, he said he couldn't leave that woman, and he told me to take the kids and go back to Korea by myself. So I made up my mind and decided to go back with my relatives. I sent everything with my sister-in-law, and told her that we would follow as soon as we had enough money to buy the tickets for me and the children. Well, making enough money took more than a year, close to two years. Then one evening when I was squatting in front of the house cleaning, I saw a figure in the distance coming closer and closer. He looked quite familiar and in fact looked like one of my distant relatives who had gone back to Korea. I thought to myself, I must be seeing a ghost. *"Why would a person who had left for Korea come back to Japan?"* When he came closer, I recognized him and asked him why he had come back. He told me that the situation in Korea was so poor that in order to live he came back to Japan. He said that there was nothing to eat, and that people were pulling grass and weeds for food and eating bark off the trees up in the mountains. So my sister-in-law who left before me asked him if he were to arrive safely back in Japan, to come and warn me not to come back if I didn't want to die of starvation. Thankful for him coming all the way to find me, I made some gruel mixed with barley and gave it to him. My kids always complained about eating such food, but he was eating it so delightedly. He said that in Korea one wouldn't even be able to see such food. Then, a while later after the Korean War, everyone was talking about how wonderful North Korea was and many people decided to go there. I decided to go to North Korea as well. Then, one of my friends from my hometown warned me not to go, because again, there was nothing to eat but potatoes, fern weed, and corn. That friend warned me a number of times, so I decided once more to stay in Japan.

Work

I couldn't go to North or South Korea and I was getting so frustrated with living in Saitama because nothing good ever happened there. Then after living there for about twenty years, I heard rumors that there was a lot of work in the factories in Kawasaki. Many of the other Koreans who had also escaped into the countryside during the war decided to go to Kawasaki to find work. Soon almost all the Koreans left, and my family and I were practically the only ones left. I decided to come to Kawasaki by myself. Before, Kawasaki wasn't a place for people to live.[4] There used to be huge explosions and the sky would turn black, and then there would be black and brown ash rain. These explosions were from the chimney of the *Kōkan* factory. Even if I were to wipe all day, I couldn't get things cleaned, because of the ash in the air. When you did laundry and hung it out, by the time it was dry, you'd have to wash it again. The laundry would be covered with dust and smoke from the steel plant. Everyone's faces were covered with dust and ash. You would sweep and clean your house, but every day around twelve o'clock there would be a kind of explosion from the chimney of the steel factory and then reddish, brown, and black ash would fall. This would go on several times a day. Because of the smoke from the big chimney, even in the afternoon the sky would be a grayish black.

Well, from the *Kōkan* factory, there used to be a stream of waste such as scrap metal and steel. It was said that in Kawasaki, picking up this waste and selling it could bring in some money, and that is why I decided to come to Kawasaki. A person I knew said her husband had a small business selling steel and metal, and she told me that I could make a living here. So I came to Kawasaki and rented a room, and then I went back into the countryside to talk to my husband about moving to Kawasaki. But my husband didn't want to come. He said that in the countryside, although there was no work, at least the air was clean. But I told him that many people lived in Kawasaki, although it was quite dirty. I stayed in the countryside for a few days, and I thought long and hard about it. I decided that whether or not there was dust, smoke, or whatever, people were able to make a living there. Finally, I made a decision, and I packed—and this is no lie—two pairs of underwear, two shirts, two work pants, and I headed for Kawasaki, leaving the children with my husband. At that time I was forty-four years old. Then, this daughter here came to look for me in Kawasaki. I think she was about fifteen years old then. Before she came, her two younger sisters were already living with me. So she came after them to join me, leaving her father in the countryside. I had been planning to go back to get the children after things got a bit settled, but even before that, the children came to join me.

The two little ones, who were in elementary school then, had to fend for themselves, because their father was not around very often. I guess they thought of their mother, and so they all ended up coming to live with me before things even got settled down. I had to go on welfare so that at least I could afford to send the kids to school. I worked day and night, not even knowing when one day had ended and another begun. I got a job in a factory, as well as working for the city cleaning parks and roads, and picking up trash. The pay was not so good . . . about 360 yen a day. When I worked in the factory I was able to earn 400 yen per day. For the city job, I had to work really hard in order for the city office to hire me again, so I really tried my best. Unemployed women with children who had no money coming in and claimed abandonment by their husbands could apply for this city job.

One morning I was going to work at a factory, which was supposed to be a secret, and I told a neighboring woman that the city office would probably come by to check around the neighborhood about me that day. So the woman told me not to worry and to go on to work. Then my daughter—she was in third grade at the elementary school—came home early that day, when the people from the city office came to visit my house to see how I was living. So the neighborhood woman saw them coming and came over to the house. The inspectors told her that they wanted to talk to my daughter instead, and for her to leave. My little daughter, being too innocent to lie, told them everything—that her father was well and living in Saitama, and her brother had graduated from junior high school and was working at the electrical company, and that her elder sister was working at a *pachinko* parlor. She told them everything. . . . So when I went to the office the next day, they said it wasn't right for me to lie. I tried to tell them in my broken Japanese that my little girl didn't know what she was saying, and that in fact my husband no longer supported our family and we were in financial trouble, and that I was having a tough time supporting all of my children. I cried and begged that they didn't take away the city job. So finally they gave in and I was allowed to work for the city pulling weeds at parks, cleaning roads, picking up rocks, and sweeping gravel. I picked up trash for twenty-some years. My husband ended up coming to Kawasaki, too. He worked selling steel and metal, and my eldest son continued working for an electrical company. Well, the kids were growing older, and I soon had to think about saving enough money to marry off my son and daughters. . . .

Religion

Coming to Japan, and the fact that I survived . . . sometimes I really wonder how I made it. . . .Well, I guess you can say that I felt so frustrated that I was desperate to try anything. Of course, I had many worries. If I didn't have any worries I wouldn't have tried all the things that I did.

My family was not such a happy one. I tried all sorts of religions hoping that somehow the situation would get better. I used to go up to the mountains to pray, and then before that I was involved in *Sōka gakkai* for seventeen years. A Japanese neighbor told me about this religion. For seventeen years I believed in this religion. Seventeen years. . . . At that time I was quite involved and I think I was one of their best members. I went day and night to people's houses, telling them how wonderful this religion was, and if they wanted things to change for the better in their lives, then they should join. When I went from house to house trying to recruit members, some people threw a handful of salt on my head[5] or a bucket of water, and a few times people chased me and another member out of their house with a stick. We used to have to deal with this kind of opposition from people in the neighborhood, but the high officials in the religion told us not to give up and continue to go out to search for new recruits. I used to get letters of appreciation from the top heads of this sect saying what a faithful member I was.

When I first started believing in this religion, well, it was because of my eldest daughter. She was quite fragile and she had a kind of nasal disease. Because of that, when she slept, she couldn't breathe at all through her nose. One day my daughter was attending one of the usual services, and her friends from the sect took her up to a mountain. They got some sort of herbal grass and told her to stuff it up her nose when she slept. She did as they told her and prayed. Then she said one night when she blew her nose, it hurt so badly that it felt like her nose was broken. When she looked at her tissue paper, there was a nasal polyp the size of an eyeball. After that she was able to sleep without any breathing problems. She became much healthier, and seeing her like that encouraged me to become involved in the religion. My daughter got so much healthier than before, and she became one of the top persons in charge of the *Sōka gakkai* women's group. After that she got married and had a child of her own and moved to North Korea.

After I got involved in the religion, and when I wanted to pray, my husband would tell me to turn off the lights or whack me on the head telling me to shut up. But I still continued to believe. For this religion, you have to read the entire sutra. The kids were all going to school and they were quite busy. But I made them all perform the rituals every day before school, and make the offering to the small altar. You have to recite a sutra that goes "*Namu myōhō renge kyō.* . . ."[6] In the evening you have to sit and read it for two hours and your legs get numb. The children and I, we all participated.

Well, I didn't know how to read and so the leaders told me just to turn the rosary in my hand, and so I would just sit and turn the rosary. Then the leader of the prayer told me that since my children go to a Japanese school, I should have them at least teach me some *hiragana* so that I could be able to read and recite the Sutra. I asked my daughter who now lives in North Korea to teach me and write some of the words in *hiragana* so that I could read it. And my son taught me some words as well. So the things that I could read I would recite, but the words that I couldn't read, I somehow bypassed, and that is how I learned to recite the prayer. I was very busy always, but I had to read the verses for at least two hours at a time. . . .

The *Sōka gakkai* is a kind of Buddhist sect, *Nichiren-shū*, and there are temples where you actually go to worship. It is Buddhism, but you don't believe in any other gods except that one god, so it is a bit different. Near Mt. Fuji in Shizuoka, there are many temples, and actually I believe the headquarters is located at Mt. Fuji. When you go up to the temple, there is a box with a lid, and when you look inside, they say you can see the face of *Nichiren*. They don't show it to ordinary people; they only show it to believers. The face of the founder of the religion can be seen inside. And one time they said they would show us his tooth, and so I went and saw it inside a bottle. My daughter who went to North Korea saw it several times, and she told me a lot about it. Now the *Sōka gakkai* has really become quite big.

To tell you the reason why I quit this religion. . . . well, the person who held the highest position of the sect had twelve children. They used to live in Kawasaki and it was said that they used to be so poor, but somehow he came to obtain such a high position in the sect. One day he happened to come to Saitama when

I was living there, and there were many people at that particular meeting. Well, during his speech he said he wondered why more Japanese people didn't get involved in this wonderful religion. Then he pointed his finger at me and said, "*Even that sort of being could learn to believe in this great religion . . .*"—I was shocked. Slowly I became disgusted by what he said. You know, when I really think about it, maybe I was being really narrow-minded, but I had faithfully believed in this religion for seventeen years. And when that top person had been running for that position, I had worked day and night for votes to get him elected. I went from person to person asking for support and I got him at least fifty votes. They even sent me about twenty letters of commendation. But on that day when he pointed his finger at me and said that if even "that thing"—a Korean—could come to know of this religion, he wondered why so many Japanese still have not come to know of it. . . . I had always believed them when they said that there was no difference between a Korean and a Japanese and that we are all equal according to this religion. I couldn't believe what he was saying. My mind and faith turned drastically after that day. That is how I came to quit this religion for good.

Then after that, when I came to Kawasaki, there was a person I knew who used to go up to Mt. Takao[7] near Tōkyō and pray up there. I went with a *mudang* who lived in the neighborhood. This person said that good things had happened to her since she started going up to the mountain to pray. So then, because of the situation with my family, I thought I wanted to give this a try as well. Well, the mountain is the god. There are other gods you pray to of course, and also you pray to your ancestors. Around one o'clock in the morning you go underneath the waterfall, and then afterward you go all over the mountain and light candles and burn incense and pray. You bring out all of your worries and frustrations and then pray to the mountain god[8] to make all situations better for everyone in the family. So I did this for thirteen years. Mt. Takao was very far from where we were living. It is on the opposite side of Tōkyō. Sometimes I used to go once a month and sometimes once a week, and sometimes even though it was so far, I went twice a week. I would go after I finished a long day at work. But before I went, I would get some alcohol and various food items to dedicate to the mountain god. I would carry all of that in a big sack on my back and go to the faraway mountain.

From Kawasaki to Mt. Takao I would take the train and get off at the station in Takao, then I would have to walk three hours one way up the mountain path. Back then, the mountain path was pretty rough and the big load on my back was so heavy. Sometimes I would fall over, and with the heavy weight on my shoulders, I could barely get back up. At home we also had a *butsudan*, a huge Buddhist altar that was built into a corner of the room. I asked a relative who went back and forth from Korea to buy all sorts of special dishes, verse texts, and such, to place on top of the altar. I also had another set that I would leave up on the mountain altar at Takao. So at that time, whether I was at the mountain or at home in front of my altar, I prayed constantly. Even though I went so faithfully, still there were so many unhappy things going on in my family. Then one day my son said, "*Mother, for the sake of our family, you work day and night and go to that faraway mountain to be pounded by that cold waterfall. . . . I heard of another religion that is said to be the best. Why don't you try going to church.*"

By that time I had already tried so many things . . . I had just about given up. I didn't want to be fooled by another religion again. But my son continued to ask me to go, and finally I gave in and went for the first time with him, and I took along one of my daughters. When we went to the church, it was a Japanese church—Jehovah's Witness. We didn't even know the difference back then between Jehovah's Witness and Christian churches. You know, I never went to school, and I never learned how to read Japanese, so I just tried to listen to the sermons. I asked them if they had a Korean Bible, but they said they didn't. I think we went there twice. Then a Korean coworker of mine who attended this Christian church in Kawasaki said that she would bring me to her church. In the meantime, one of my relatives started attending the sister church in Tōkyō asked me to come with her. So I went with her one day. I went there twice, and I listened to the sermon. But I also continued to pray at my Buddhist altar at home.

Well, one day I came back home from working, and my husband and my son were laughing and smiling to themselves. I asked them what they were laughing at. My son asked me if I had noticed something missing from the room. I told him that I didn't notice anything missing. He told me to look behind me. It was gone!!! The altar was gone. I was so shocked. "*K'ŭn il la ta, mo k'ŭn il la ta!!!—We are doomed, we are doomed!!!*" I thought to myself, this is it. . . . I went up to the mountains for thirteen years and then tried my best to please the gods, and ancestors. . . . But now this was the end of it all. You know, during those times of prayer in the mountains, whether I was sitting or lying down, I was able to see my ancestors as clear as day. It got to a point that even at home when I would be praying, I could see them all. I could see all the *hotoke-sama* right before my eyes. Sometimes I could even hear their voices. In the dark of the evening, I would take off all of my clothes, wash my whole body with salt, and then shower underneath the waterfall. The water is so, so very cold. Sometimes your body feels like it's going to crack into thousands of pieces, but after a while you get used to the feeling. On some nights I would go underneath the waterfall five or six times. After I came out, my legs would be bright red from the water stream hitting harshly against them. Then after I washed myself like that, I had to go throughout the mountain to pray in various corners in the still of the night when even the sparrows were sleeping. There would be absolutely nothing awake up there in the mountains, and I would go from corner to corner lighting the candles. I could see and hear my ancestors say in such a sympathetic voice . . . "*You are suffering so much in this dark, cold place.*" I could see them and hear them so clearly—my mother and father and some of the other people who have already passed away. . . . It sounds unbelievable, but I could see them so clearly. After you light all the candles, the area glows in the candlelight. When the flames go out, I would go and light them again, over and over. Up in the mountains there was absolutely no one. . . . As I went around to light the candles, some of the ancestors would talk to me, and some would just look on.

That day, I came home to find that my son had torn down the altar. I was in such a shock. I thought that I should rebuild it right away. Also I would have to call a *mudang* to perform a *kŭs*,[9] to somehow make amends with the ancestors for my son's foolish action. I thought I would have to do a *kŭs* in the mountains as well, and everything would cost more than hundred thousand yen. But where was I to get money like that? I was so crushed, and I felt hopeless. I thought that everything would be doomed and all of my efforts—thirteen years of making amends with my ancestors—had gone to waste. There was nothing, nowhere else for me to turn.

By this time I had already attended church twice because of my son's pleading. . . . I thought I had nothing else to hang on to now but the church and God. The strange thing was, my son had urged me to go to church, and in so doing, even destroyed the altar at home, but he himself wouldn't go to church. I pleaded with him and I said, "*Since you have broken down the altar and have angered the ancestors, you should at least come to church and stand in front of God and plead with Him to help you.*" But my son didn't listen. Then about a couple of months later, I was sitting in church one Sunday when the pastor ran up to me and said, "*Something terrible has happened! There has just been news that your son might be dead!*" The pastor said that while my son was working, he fell from a building, and he was taken to the hospital soaked in blood. When I rushed to the hospital, they had taken off all of his clothes. The thick blanket that they used to cover him was soaked in blood. My chest was about to burst because I was feeling so hopeless. All I could do was just pray and pray. "*Don't kill him, don't let him die. At the least let him live, at the least let him live. . . .*" Then suddenly from my own mouth, a voice came out saying, "*You begged that his life will be saved, so his life is saved, but his head won't be normal.*" . . . Well, I guess it has turned out just like that.

Well, you know that I live together with my son. And since his accident, he hasn't been the same. He married several times, but none of the marriages worked out, and I guess he feels angry about many things. Recently he has been attending church and he has gotten a lot better. But often he just yells out things, ridiculous things, just to pick a fight or get somebody bothered. So I leave the house early in the morning and take my *obento* (lunchbox) and don't come back home until later in the evening. Well, I've been going to this place in the city. It's mostly people my age, but you know, there are some young people too, mostly housewives. It's a place where they teach you all sorts of things about how to keep yourself healthy. They tell you what kinds of products are good for your body and what kind of things you should avoid. It's quite interesting. I went there once just to see what they had to say, but since then, I've been going there every day to listen to all kinds of information. It's quite fascinating all the things that you can learn. There I meet some of my friends—people my age. We talk about what we learned and also about our families and problems and such.

You know, all of my sons have died and the one son who has survived has gotten into this situation. Actually, I gave birth to three sons, but below my third daughter I had another son in my stomach . . . seven months . . . and I lost him.

So the one son whose life I held onto has turned out like this, and so my family is . . . I can't say we are happy. . . . Sometimes, I think that we have faced some of the worst situations, and are merely surviving. . . . I can't describe it in words.

Children

I actually had four children before my first daughter but I lost all of them. They died of fever. . . . You know, I was too young to have children. I was what, seventeen? It's too young to have a child. You don't know what to do with them. The elders used to say that when cats are in heat they disturb the neighborhood with their noise, but when women have children they should give birth quietly without anyone knowing. They said that children are made in secret, and when a woman makes all kinds of noise during labor, she is thought to be loose in her behavior. So you give birth quietly, and then cut the umbilical cord yourself, and then bathe the baby and wrap it up. After the babies were born, they were fine until they were three or four weeks old. . . .

That is why, I think now and I thought then, whether it was because I had my children when I was too young and I didn't know how to take care of them properly, or whether it was just bad luck. Well . . . *ha, ha* . . . (she laughs softly). I guess it all worked out according to what God planned. I thought back then that if I were to have a daughter, I would not allow her to marry until she was at least twenty years old. You know, in the old days they would forcibly marry off daughters who were only sixteen or seventeen years old. And young girls didn't know anything. Well, even if you were married at that young age, I guess you are somehow taught certain things before you marry, but I left my parents' side and came to Japan when I was fourteen years old. Right after I came, I began working for the factory, and then soon afterward, I got married, so even more, I didn't know anything.

After I got married, some of my husband's relatives said that I didn't know how to cook, or even make rice, and when I gave birth to children, I couldn't even raise them properly before they ended up dying. That was what some people used to say behind my back and sometimes right in front of my face, but . . . I guess, I just didn't know. That's the reason why I really thought in my heart that when I have a daughter, I would not allow her to marry until she became at least twenty years old. I thought that at twenty, she would perhaps understand the meaning of love between a husband and wife, and know a little something about children. Forcing someone who is too young to marry before they even know anything, well, I guess the final result is for the parents and siblings to see her tears and hear her crying. . . .

If my first son were alive, he would be about sixty-four by now. Between him and me, there was only seventeen years difference. And then I had another son and I took that son to Korea to show my parents. He was one year younger than the first one. He died in Korea. Then there was another one and if he were alive, he would be fifty-nine years old now. And then when I got pregnant again,

I went back to Korea to really try to take care of myself so that I could have the baby safely. I also went to see a fortune-teller. She said, *"If it is a son, it will die again, so even if you have a daughter, take extra care to raise her very carefully."* So when I heard this I really tried very hard. If my daughter wasn't feeling well even just a little bit, I would run to the Buddhist temple to pray, or call the *mudang* to conduct a purifying ceremony, or take her to all sorts of doctors.

You know, Koreans are not so pleased when they have a daughter, right? If a woman has a son, then everyone praises the household's good fortune and says that it will be a rich household, because they now have a son, and he will take care of all the ancestor worship ceremonies. But for me, I lost four sons, and then finally when I had another child, it was a daughter, and even then she was so weak and always so very sickly. For three years after her birth, it was like walking on thin ice. Whatever she ate, everything would come right back up through her mouth, and if not, from her behind—everything that I was just barely able to feed her. Her stomach was so thin, and her skin so transparent that it was almost like I could see right through her. She was so small and thin, and frail, just like a little tiny monkey. For just about three years, she was barely holding on to her life. When she cried, she didn't have enough strength to actually cry, but let out just a tiny whimper. I felt so sorry for her, and so wherever I went, I carried her on my back. One time when I went over to my friend's house she said, *"You know I feel so bad about telling you this, but you should leave that strange-looking child of yours at home instead of taking her out. It's really kind of disgusting to have to look at her."* Can you believe that? And several times one of my relatives came over to my house and said that she came over to see if the baby had died, because she didn't hear it cry for a few days. Because of that child, I have gone to temples, *Sōka gakkai*, shamans, mountains . . . everything . . . anything to keep her alive.

Then one of my husband's relatives suggested that I should get up at dawn and go to the *"Inari"* god, the "Rice god" at this particular shrine. At that time I was about twenty. She said I should go there when there was absolutely no one on the streets and pray. I had to walk about two-and-a-half hours, and then give some offerings, and pray that my Miyoko would somehow be saved. I was ready to try anything. . . . About two weeks after I went, can you believe it, my daughter said to me, *"Mommy, I'm hungry."* I was so shocked that I let out a big gasp. That was the first time I ever heard her say that she was hungry. Up until then I almost had to force her to eat in order to keep her alive. At that time there was hardly anything to eat in the house except some barley. So I took a bit of the barley and boiled it for a long time and then I added a little soy sauce. Well, she ate everything, the whole bowl. I was so happy, I didn't know what to do! I rushed over to the Chinese herbal medicine store right next door. I told the doctor, *"My daughter Miyoko, since the day she was born, she has never said that she was hungry. But today, for the first time ever, she told me she was hungry, and finished a whole bowl of gruel all by herself."* The doctor gave me some ginseng roots,[10] and told me to boil it for a long time and then mix it with the barley and feed it to her. I took the *ginseng* root and did as he told me and again she finished everything. Then her stomach got so bloated, and she had a bout of diarrhea, and after that . . . shall I say she was finished being sick. Because of that child, and everything else in my family, I went to temples and mountains and tried everything so faithfully.

Daughter in North Korea

With my son's situation and my daughter also in this state—there was absolutely nothing that could be done. There was no one to discuss these things with, no one to help my family and me. That was how my daughter here and I began attending church. Since that time we have been continuously attending. After we started coming to church, we changed over to the *Mindan* organization.[11] But my first daughter and her family live in North Korea. For a while people were talking about how wonderful North Korea was. You know, almost everyone who went to North Korea from Japan was originally from South Korea. After the war, everyone was carrying on about how wonderful a place North Korea was, that's why so many people moved there.

Before, I could send her things, and also write letters. But do you remember that time when North Korea had that heavy rainfall and everything was washed away? Since then, there was no contact. She got married here in Japan, and she had two sons and three daughters, and they all went there except for the youngest son who stayed in Japan. Her youngest son is about thirty-one years old now. Well, if I were to have really tried to get in touch with her, I'm sure I could have, but we changed over to *Mindan*. Two of my daughters are still involved in the *Chongryun* organization. And you know, the *Chongryun* schools send their children to North Korea for a class trip and my third daughter's second son is a teacher at a North Korean school in Chiba Prefecture. That child went to North Korea and met with his aunt—my daughter. You know, when they had that flooding, I was so worried about my daughter that I went to the organization and asked them about her. They said that where she was living wasn't very affected by the flood and that she was all right. I hear that rice doesn't grow there. They can only farm things like corn and millet. That is all that the land can produce. But I was told that where she lived was fine. I don't know if they say the truth.

Before, I used to think about going to see my daughter in North Korea. Most of my relatives were able to come and go to the North. But when the parents go to the North and see their children, if they slip and say that living in Japan is good, then I heard that after the parents leave, the children end up in a faraway place where people have nothing to survive on. Then I heard that they tell their families that they died. This kind of thing happened to some of my relatives. I heard this from someone who went to visit his younger brother in North Korea. The older one needed to go to the toilet, and the younger brother also went with him. When they went outside, there was a person who was watching them. The older brother did something with his hands that might have looked like a hand signal, and later he learned that they placed the younger brother to that faraway place. Several households of my relatives were sent away like that. They even sent friends of my relatives and anyone affiliated with them. I heard that there is nothing but sand in that place. There is no water. It's a sand pit with no trees, no farmland, and nothing else. . . . You know, an old woman like me— just because I want to see my daughter, I go there, and I might say something foolish. That is the reason why although I wanted to see my daughter so badly, I couldn't go. I can't even talk about it. What the government might do. . . .You know, even when you are sleeping, they have listening devices in the room and outside of the home. And even if you go to the bathroom they follow you.

Before, I used to send all sorts of clothing to my daughter. I would send this and that, thinking that my grandchildren could wear all of the clothes that I sent. So I tried to pack all sorts of things as much as possible and send it off. But I found out that they couldn't even wear one piece of clothing that I sent to them. I heard from my grandson that when times were hard, my daughter used to take the clothing into the country and exchange several pieces of clothing for two eggs. Just two eggs. . . . That was how my daughter was living at one point. So when I hear people here in Japan say that something doesn't taste good and they don't want to eat it, well I think about my daughter, and I think people have it too good here. I heard that there, it would be so cold in the winter that even the snot from your nose would freeze in winter. And even then my daughter used to go to the frozen river to do the laundry, and fetch water in the cold in order to make her food. The year before last I met my grandson, and that was when he told me about all of this. He said that just recently they finally installed running water.

So I thought that instead of spending that money to visit my daughter, I wanted to send it to her. But I heard that the government would keep it and my daughter would never know. So I went to a place where for an extra fee they would make sure that the money would end up in my daughter's hands. But still the government held on to that money and was giving it to her in small amounts each month. I was so frustrated. Several times my grandsons were going on their class trip with their schools to the North. I asked them to meet with their aunt if possible and just hand her the money, but when they went and asked to meet with her, they were told that they would work on it. But each time they had to return to Japan without being able to meet with her. So when one of my grand- sons who is a teacher at the school went, he was allowed to meet with her and was able to hand her some money. He took them to a *yakiniku* restaurant and told them to eat. They said they were full and that they didn't really need all that much, but when he ordered a lot and then went to the restroom, they had practi- cally finished everything by the time he came back. . . . *Ha, ha, ha.* . . . So, that is how they live. . . . *Ahh* . . . it can't be put into words . . . their suffering . . . (she sighs heavily and then pauses).

Three years ago I received a letter from my grandson in North Korea that she died. They said that she died of an illness, and there was nothing that could have been done to help her. Well, that's what they tell me. . . . Just before she died, she wrote asking me to send some money for her daughter's wedding. So without letting any of my other kids here know, I sent her as much as I could. The kids here used to get angry with me for sending her too much money. They said I could never be certain whether the money actually got to her.

In the letter my grandson said that on the day of the wedding party she just collapsed and died. I am told that she had been suffering from a stomach ailment. But who knows. In that terrible country there are no such hospital facilities like here in Japan. I am certain that if she were to have been here, she wouldn't have died so young. She was only sixty-three. When I received that letter, everything went pitch black, I couldn't even see right before my eyes. Awhile later, I was just burning up inside. My insides were on fire.

Recently, my son-in-law wrote a letter saying that he was sorry for all that has happened. This was the third letter, but I haven't answered back yet. Every time I think of him, I just feel burned up inside. *Ano baka!* (That idiot!) They would have been doing just fine here in Japan if it wasn't for him wanting to go to that country so badly. They could have still had their *pachinko* parlor in Niigata and had a good enough life. But like so many others they were fooled into thinking that life would be beautiful and prosperous in North Korea. But what did they find? A life of poverty. My daughter had to work in fields and do all sorts of manual labor. Whatever the government told her to do, she had to do. She worked like that with hardly anything to eat.

It just burns me up inside. . . . All these people in these *Chongryun* schools and offices sent many people there, telling lies about how wonderful it was. And so sometimes I look at the North Korean school near where I live and I think, "*Those robbers, they haven't even been to North Korea and they lured people into going there saying how wonderful a place it is. They sent back all those people and they themselves have remained behind in prosperous Japan!*"

For so long I thought I would never be able to see my daughter, no matter how much I wanted to, because I didn't want her to get placed in that terrible place. But now for sure there is no way I could ever see her again. . . .

Chongryun and *Mindan*

When we were in the countryside of Saitama for twenty years, I didn't know anything about *Mindan* and *Chongryun*. But after we came out to Kawasaki I was a bit more aware of such things. Sometimes, I heard people say things like *Mindan* and *Chongryun*. . . . But you know, not being educated, I didn't know anything. One time I asked one of my friends, "*Well, how does a Chongryun person look, and how does a Mindan person look?*" *Ha, ha, ha.* . . . The way everyone was carrying on about it, I really thought that there was a big physical difference. *Ha, ha.* . . . Afterward, I told my friend, "*Koreans of Chongryun and Koreans of Mindan are all our people, so why do they keep talking about them like they were from different places?*" *Ha, ha.* . . . Anyway, somehow I got involved with the *Chongryun* organization. I worked during the afternoon, but in the evenings I participated in demonstrations for *Chongryun*. Sometimes, my husband would say, "*Hey, why are you running around so much? Don't go out!*" But I still went. Of course, now I can't move around as much as before. We demonstrated so that Koreans who wished to go to North Korea would be allowed to do so. The demonstrations took place in the afternoons and evenings, and even in the unbearable summer heat, we walked all the way to Yokohama from Kawasaki. We demonstrated all the way there and finally came back to Kawasaki to demonstrate in front of the city office. I was so thirsty. This was in August, and I thought if I could have even a little ice cube or something to suck on, or just a sip of water. . . .

So we demonstrated walking around like that, and that was how Koreans were able to go back to North Korea. From that time on, Kawasaki became the center. Every time there was something that needed to be done, people would say we should demonstrate—for people to be able to visit North Korea, and for people with North Korean citizenship to be able to visit their hometowns in South Korea and so on. This all got started by people demonstrating in Kawasaki. Rain, wind, or snow, we would just do what we were told if we were given the order by the top person. My husband used to say that I was like a horse—I would work so much and then still participate in all the demonstrations. I worked during the afternoon and then after I came back I did my rituals for *Sōka gakkai*. Then when that was over, I went to help with the demonstrations. After I quit the *Sōka gakkai*, I went to the mountains once a week, and sometimes stayed overnight. You know, I was never sick. I never went to the doctor or the dentist. I always wondered why some people would go to the hospital or lie down with a cold. When my daughters caught colds, I would just tell them to eat some hot soup and put some spicy kimchi inside. So my children would say that I would tell them to eat kimchi for any ailments. *Ha, ha, ha.* . . .

Reflection

"*Chinpun kanpun, wake mo wakaranai hanashi wakarimasu ka?*—Can you understand all the gibberish that I'm talking?" . . . You know, we Koreans, when we raise our daughters, we are quite strict in their upbringing. When they go to their husband's house, they have to take care of not only their husband, but also their in-laws. So even when daughters are living with their own parents, they are raised severely. When I was growing up, my grandmother—my mother's mother—was quite terrifying. My mother used to tell us childhood stories all the time. She was one of three siblings. One day my grandmother told her daughter to bring a bowl of rice. And you know, Koreans eat their rice in steel bowls. Well, my mother dropped the rice bowl. Then my grandmother chased my mother out of the house and outside there was snow up to your knees, because it was *tongchi sŏttal* (eleventh lunar month). She was made to stand outside of the house in the middle of the courtyard until evening. So she cried and carried on, but she was told to stand out there. And by the evening, she said, her legs were frozen stiff to a point where she couldn't even bend them. In the evening when my grandfather came back home, he asked her why she was outside crying. She couldn't talk because her lips were trembling so much. My grandfather carried her back inside the house and her body was ice cold, and she had started to get frostbite. While she was getting warmed up, it was so painful that she couldn't stop crying. My mother used to tell me that story all the time. . . .

When Koreans in the old days had a daughter, they said it was better to raise her severely so that when she married and went off to another household, it became more comfortable than her own *ch'inchŏng*. You are told that once you leave, you can never come back. I once saw a girl in our neighborhood, a young girl who returned to her parents' house. Well, her parents refused to let her stay and so she had to go back to her husband's home crying all the way. I too once attempted to leave my husband, because I couldn't stand it anymore. That was when I went back to Korea. I told my parents that I did not intend to go back to Japan. My parents said that in our family there was not one woman who got married and then came back to her *ch'inchŏng*. They ordered me to go back to Japan. So that was the reason why I came back.

Sixty-two years after my parents sent me back to Japan, I went again to Korea. I went with two of my daughters. For a long time I couldn't go back to Korea because of my daughter in North Korea. I was afraid that it might affect her in some way to have relatives who went back and forth between Japan and South Korea. Now, whatever you do is fine, but before it was not like that. So I couldn't go back even when there was news that my mother was about to pass away. Finally, I went and visited my mother's grave. I thought I had better go while I could still move around by myself freely. So after we changed over to *Mindan*, the three of us went to Korea and visited my mother's grave. So after sixty-two years I went back to my birthplace. . . . You know, when I went to go see the grave site of my mother and sat in front of it and called out to her, I couldn't stop the tears. . . . I just couldn't stop the tears. When I called out to my mother, I just couldn't stop the tears from flowing. My daughters were consoling me and trying to stop me from crying—saying that it was enough—but somehow I just couldn't stop. When I called out "*Ŏmŏni*"—the tears . . . I just couldn't stop. . . .

My husband passed away when he was eighty-six years old. When I think about it now, my children, all seven of them—although we have suffered—I made sure that they were raised well so that people wouldn't be able to point fingers at them. Even though my husband was away for a long time, still I endured so that he would come back—hoping that our family would remain together and that we could all live together. To remain together . . . I think that is happiness. When you compare us to a rich family, we might look like the poorest of the poor. . . . But I feel that there are all sorts of human beings. . . . I think we are now—even like this—I can say that I am happy—the way things are now. My daughters' families are not rich, but they don't have to go and borrow from others or hold their hands out in need. And somehow they are with their husbands and continuing to live their lives. I think that is happiness. Since becoming a Christian, I come to a warm church like this and whether there is rain or snow, I can sit in a good place and listen to all kinds of good words. Within this comfort, the heavy burden always weighing on my mind has slowly started to disappear. The kind of life that I had then and the kind of life that I have lived until now, there are no words to describe it. . . . All I can say is that now I feel . . . happy . . . satisfied.

Notes

1. On the new year of the lunar calendar, Koreans who are affiliated with the Buddhist faith visit the temple or the fortune-teller for a reading of the upcoming year, using one's year, day, and time of birth.

2. Koreans wanting to travel abroad were required to submit to the police a written declaration stating purpose and destination of their intended travel. If the application was approved, a *ryokō shōmeisho* (Certificate of Travel) was issued, to be presented by the traveler at the port of departure. See Weiner (1989: 56).

3. *Tonari-gumi* is a local level neighborhood association. Weiner (1994: 588) writes that there were more than one million by the spring of 1941.

4. By 1938, Kawasaki was the largest industrial complex in Japan. The presence of the steel pipe company *Nihon Kōkan* as well as *Keihin* Petrochemical Complex and other factories took a toll on the atmosphere and living environment in this working class community. However, in the 1970s, through the efforts of the "Green Belt Project" to separate industry from human inhabitation, noticeable improvement in the level of pollution and environmental living standards has been achieved. See DeVos and Chung (1981: 228-231).

5. In Japan, as in many cultures, salt is believed to ward off evil spirits.

6. This expression invokes the Lotus Sutra.

7. In the Kantō region, the mountain most commonly visited by the practitioners of shamanistic faith is Mt. Takao, about two hours by train west of downtown Tōkyō.

8. On a scroll commonly seen in shaman's chambers, the mountain god or *Yama no kami*, represented as a Confucian bureaucrat, is seated at the foot of a twisted red pine amid mountain boulders and beside a waterfall with a tiger, his messenger and servant. See Hardacre (1984: 17).

9. An exorcism ritual to appease the spirits of ancestors and gods. The *mudang* serves as an intermediary between the world of the living and the spirit's world. See Harvey (1979) and Kendall (1985, 1988).

10. Ginseng roots are the most common and popular form of Korean herbal medicine.

11. Almost all of the *zainichi* Korean Christians are either apolitical or belong to the *Mindan* organization. They find that they cannot reconcile the North Korean ideology, according to which the late leader Kim Il-Sung is deemed almost a demi-god, with their Christian beliefs. Also at this time, in order to travel back and forth between Japan and their hometowns in South Korea, Koreans who did not have Japanese citizenship and a passport had to go through the *Mindan* association for their travel visa. Currently, although with special permission Koreans affiliated with the North can gain travel visas to South Korea, the political restrictions concerning travel to the South are still quite severe.

Part IV
Growing Up in Japan

Chapter 9

We Koreans Have Come a Long Way

Pak Hui-Sun (Uehara Tamae)

Pak Hui-Sun is an energetic member of the Ōsaka Korean Christian Women's Group. She cherishes a sense of independence and believes that the best thing for herself and her children is to be healthy as long as possible.

Hui-Sun's situation is a bit different from most of the women that I have interviewed. She laughed and told me the story of her son and daughter-in-law who insisted on living with her and her husband. Hui-Sun said that when her youngest son was going to marry his wife, he told her that one of the most important factors was that she was willing to take care of his parents. Her daughter-in-law agreed that it was also something that she wanted to do. However, Hui-Sun and her husband told their son and daughter-in-law to live by themselves for at least one year during which if they still insisted on living together they were welcome to move in. She laughed and said that exactly after one year the couple moved in and ever since then they have been living together in one household. She said at this moment she doesn't know who is taking care of whom, because most of the time she is helping with raising their children as well as sometimes with cooking and the laundry. Hui-Sun said although there is much work, now when she is in the position to help them is better than the other way around, when she may have to become fully dependent upon them.

Hui-Sun feels that now that she has raised all of her children to the best of her ability and no longer has to work the kind of hours that she once did in order to make ends meet, she wants to spend her time taking care of herself, doing various church work, and being with good friends.

It seems that the Koreans who emigrated to America were fairly well-off in Korea, and also were better educated. But the Korean people who came to Japan had a different background. Many people didn't want to come to Japan, but after their land was taken away during the colonial period there was no way out. Also, many were brought by force to become laborers.

Once when I visited Korea, a person whom I knew spoke well of Koreans in America but thought little of us Koreans in Japan. So I told him that before he makes judgments, he should know something about the different histories of Koreans in America and those in Japan. I told him off like that. Really, those who went to America didn't experience the kind of prejudice that we in Japan have experienced. I guess, when you think about it, there really was no need for Koreans in America to encounter such prejudice, because many of them had money after selling their property in Korea. I'm sure they also had some education, so they were able to learn English without too much trouble. But us first generations here, especially those who are even older than me—I guess people like my mother—we didn't know West from East. We didn't know the letters of either language. Can you imagine the kind of frustration that we must have gone through in our everyday life?

People of my generation, when I was a Miss, weren't allowed to speak Korean freely. We were told to speak in Japanese. At home we could wear Korean clothes, but when we went to work or stepped outside, we were told not to wear Korean clothes. We didn't have freedom to do what we wanted to.[1] All such things are forms of prejudice. So when our children visit Korea, people there say that they don't even know the language of our *kohyang*. But the children are not at fault. When we were little and came to Japan, we didn't know how to speak Japanese and we spoke in Korean. But after living here for about ten years, we slowly started to forget our Korean, and spoke Japanese naturally. So even when I got married and had children, most of the time we spoke Japanese.

I have four sons. My oldest child understands a little bit of Korean, but if he is asked to speak, he cannot. Although he knows how to read Korean letters, still he does not know the meaning. Even my daughters-in-law—at church, although they sing the hymns in Korean, they neither know the meaning of the words, nor understand what they are singing. There are many frustrating things like that.

My name is Pak Hui-Sun. I have a Japanese name—Uehara Tamae. When I was young, I used it for everything, but that is also a funny story. My oldest son doesn't care whether or not we use our Korean or Japanese names, but my youngest is different. Maybe it was because he grew up in Ōsaka. He was raised here and went to school here. At church, he was involved with the youth group, and one day, he suddenly said that he was going to use his Korean name.[2] He was in junior high school. He said that he didn't need a Japanese last name. He wanted to be called by his Korean name, "Kim." Then, when he was attending a technical school, one of his teachers called him aside. "*Kin-kun,*[3] *if you go out into the society and use your Korean name, there will be times when you will run into problems. Right now at school you can use your Korean name, but on your graduation certificate, do you want me to write your Japanese name?*"

Then, my son said, *"Well, if I run into problems, and people don't like me because I am Korean, then I don't want to deal with that kind of person."* He later married a woman from Kyōto who also thought like him and wanted to use her Korean name—Yi Kyong-Ja. Whenever she goes somewhere and they pronounce her name in the Japanese pronunciation, "Ri Kyoko," she makes a point telling them to read it in the Korean reading.[4] So I told her that she shouldn't make such a big deal about it. But she says that you have to tell them at least once how to say it in the Korean reading, otherwise they would continue pronouncing it in Japanese.

Before my youngest son decided to use his Korean name, we mostly used our Japanese name. We are called "Uehara." This is my husband's Japanese surname. We Koreans here in Japan had to take on Japanese surnames. People used to make up their own Japanese names as they liked. They would choose one name and then change it soon afterward. So one person sometimes had three or four different last names. It seems that during the war if people refused to adopt Japanese names, they were denied food rations. Often, people would decide what names they would use in Japanese society after consulting with the elders of the family. My first name "Tamae" was given to me by my father, and my surname before getting married was "Asamitsu.' I was born in 1927, on January 2, in Kyŏngsangbuk-do. I came to Japan when I was twelve years old.

Family

When I was a child in Korea, on very rare occasions I saw buses, but I never rode in one. I remember as a little girl running along the road to see a bus passing by far in the distance. As for a *yŏlch'a* (train), I saw one for the first time in my life when we came to the city on the way to the port from which we took the boat to Japan.

In Korea, we lived in Chunjŭk-do, in a small village right in the center between Ch'ungch'ŏng-do, Chŏlla-do, and Kyŏngsang-do. It was deep in the countryside, far in the mountains. After my father left alone for Japan, my family moved to a small town called Mosan. My father had already been living in Japan for ten years. He wanted nothing to do with farming, and I guess my grandfather considered him a *pulhyoja* (unfilial son). He didn't care for sticking around in the mountains and loved to travel here and there. From the time he was young, and even after he married and had us children, he was hardly ever at home. He probably has been to every city in Korea and even traveled up North to what is now North Korea. I remember that he once brought back a painted picture of a city that he visited. My grandfather—angry at my father's behavior—pretended to be uninterested. But when my father was away, he would bring it out to show us and tell us that my father traveled to all of these places. He never threw the picture away and always kept it very nicely.

When I was—let's see—four years old, and my younger sister was a year and a few months old, my father came to Japan, without having said anything about it to my grandparents or to his own wife. He told his younger brother that he was leaving for Japan and would be back after seeing a bit of the country. Nowadays you have passports, but in the old days, you had to have a *shōmeisho* (certificate). The Japanese could come and go between Korea and Japan freely, but to enter Japan, Koreans had to show proof that they had a good reason for coming. They needed a permit and a boat ticket. But my father had neither. So when his friend got all of his papers ready—can you believe it, he took his friend's entry permit and came to Japan. Then for ten years he never returned to Korea. For ten years, he said, he traveled all over Japan and saw everything. Of course, he never sent any money to his *kohyang*. We were lucky if he sent a letter or two a year. Other people went to Japan to earn money, and they did all sorts of manual labor in order to send money back home. But not my father. My grandfather had a letter sent saying that he wanted to at least see my father's face before he died, which he said would be soon. But my father was quite clever. He asked one of the people he knew from his hometown who had recently come to Japan. And that person told him that my grandfather was still very healthy. So my father, relieved to hear this news, didn't go. Then, true to his words, my grandfather did get ill and passed away. My father came a week after he passed away for the *chesa*. He said that he couldn't live in Korea and was going to take all of us back to Japan, and that was how we came here.

My mother really suffered a lot. For ten years she took care of her father-in-law and mother-in-law by herself. She was also raising the three of us, me, my older brother, and younger sister. When my grandfather passed away, it made my father come back to Korea, and we soon followed him to Japan. If all of this didn't happen, we probably would be living in that mountain village to this day. All of my relatives now live in Taegu. In a way, maybe it was a good thing that we ended up in Japan, especially during the Korean War. But at the same time, I think about all the *kosaeng* that we women had to endure during the war here in Japan. I'm not sure which would have been worse. After the war, and after Korean independence, my parents went back to Korea—even my father. But by that time I was married, and my husband and his family were not planning on going back to Korea. During those times, my *ch'inchŏng* had such a hard time back in Korea that I was really glad that we stayed. But later when things started to improve, I thought it would have been better in the long run if we had gone back along with my *ch'inchŏng*. As my father said, *kosaeng* or not, it is better to live in one's own country. Right before he left, he said that the Japanese government brought us to Japan by force, but when they didn't need us anymore they would chase us back to our country. He said it was better to leave on one's own two feet than be chased out. And that was how he left.

Childhood

When I was little, in Korea, my grandfather was very strict, and I was not allowed to attend school. He believed that a girl didn't need to be educated, but a boy had to have an education in order to go out into society. My father and his brother attended a *sŏtang*, where they learned Chinese characters. There were three books that had to be mastered. Afterward, they enrolled in a regular school in town, in the second and third grades of elementary school. But it seemed that they were behind the other children. So they didn't want to go back to school. My grandfather went as far as hiring a private teacher to teach them at home for three years. The teacher lived in our home. My grandfather was very keen on getting his sons educated, but my aunt received no education.

When I was seven years old, a night school was opened in our neighborhood for people who didn't have a chance to go to school. There were rooms on both sides of the house, and there was a hall in the middle separating the two rooms. One side was for the boys and the other for the girls. The night school was right next to my house. If you climbed the wall you could see right in and hear the children reciting their lessons. I wanted to go there so badly. One day, my grandfather went out for the evening. My cousin, who was two years younger, and I decided to visit the night school. My uncle found out about our plan, but surprisingly instead of scolding us, he brought out rough *washi* (paper), folded it into equal sizes and wrote the Korean alphabet "*ga, gya, gu. . . .*" It was a chart with all the letters on it, and he made one for me and one for my cousin. My cousin Chun-Yŏng and I would practice memorizing the chart. So on days when my grandfather wasn't at home, we went to the night school. It was so much fun. We had a tiny stub of a pencil, and we would shave the lead ourselves. It was so much fun.

One night we rushed and ate dinner and tried to go to school before my grandfather came back. But just as we stepped out of the front gate, we ran right into our grandfather. "*Where are you two going in the middle of the night!*" he yelled. When I think about it now, of course I should have just lied, but I guess not being able to tell a lie is what makes you a child. "*Grandfather, at that house, they started a night school, and uncle told us that we could go. He bought us this little notebook, and he attached this pencil with the string, see?*" Aigu. . . . My grandfather looked so shocked. He ordered us to come inside that instant. He grabbed and pulled my cousin and me to the corner, grasped his walking stick firmly in hand and started beating my legs with it. "*You both are girls! What do you mean attending night school?! Girls should stay home quietly and learn how to sew and make decent rice! That is what you are supposed to be doing and none of this night school stuff. You don't need to learn any of that!*" He hit me so hard so many times with his walking stick that I felt the warm trickle of urine running down my leg. Even now when I tell you about it, I feel the sting on my legs. *Ha, ha, ha. . . .* I could never forget that time. . . . When my cousin saw me getting beaten, she ran away to her house. *Ha, ha, ha. . . .* I was crying, yelling, and screaming, and my grandmother and mother came running out to see what was going on. Even the neighborhood women came to see what was going on. My grandfather ordered me into his room. He told me to take the chart and every page in the notebook and tear it up with my own hands. So I tore it all up. I didn't care about the notebook so much, but I really loved that chart with the alphabet. I still remember how hard it was for me to tear that chart to pieces. After I tore everything up, he grabbed the pieces and burned it in the little urn filled with coal and ashes used to warm up the room.

After that, I didn't dare try studying again. Four years later my grandfather fell ill and passed away. I was eleven years old. When I was twelve, I came to Japan. So I came without knowing how to read Korean or Japanese. I didn't know anything about the happenings of the world while growing up and living in the countryside. My mother was the same way. But my brother, since he was a boy, was able to go to school several villages away. There was three years difference in age between us. At his school, many of the lessons were conducted in Japanese. So even after we came to Shimonoseki and he attended Japanese elementary school, he didn't fall behind the other students. Although they didn't teach you Japanese in the Korean style *sŏtang*, at regular schools you learned Japanese, since Korea was under Japanese rule. My brother was quite smart. He took care of everything, all the reading, writing, and talking with officials. My father had already gone back to Japan and my mother had to stay behind in order to make arrangements for the land and the house. My grandmother refused to come, because she said she heard that in Japan everyone slept on tatami (straw mats), and that when you die your body is cremated. . . . *Ha, ha.* . . . She said, "*How can an old woman live in a country like that.*" She went to live with my uncle—my father's younger brother. So my mother, brother, younger sister, and I came to Japan to join our father.

Coming to Japan

From my village to get to the city we rode in what we call a taxi nowadays. It was a car that was high up, not as high as a bus. It was an old, old, black car that ran very slow. When we got to the city, my mother said, "*I'm going to buy the train ticket with your brother, so you stay here with your sister, and don't go anywhere. If anyone comes and talks to you, don't answer. We'll be right back.*" So I did as she said and stood right where I was supposed to, holding my sister's hand and staring at our sacks. I was waiting for what seemed like a long time, every moment thinking that my mother would be coming. Then, from behind me, I heard a noise "*Pah, pah, pah . . . !!!!!*" It sounded just like a wild pig! Then all of a sudden I heard a loud scream—"*Kyaaaaaaaaaaaa!*" I quickly looked back and saw black smoke. I heard the screaming again. Well, the screech of what sounded like some animal screaming in death just gave me a scare of a lifetime. I was terrified. I thought never mind the sacks, and I took my sister's hand and ran screaming in the direction my mother had gone to buy our tickets. My mother and brother had already bought the tickets and were just coming back around from the other end. The sacks were right where my mother had left them, but neither I nor my sister were anywhere to be seen. She panicked, afraid that someone had taken us. She and my brother were about to go and search for us, but just then she heard my sister and I crying. We were shaking like leaves. . . . *Ha, ha, ha.* . . . What we thought was a wild animal was in fact a train. That was the first time I saw a train in my life. I was so relieved to see my mother running toward us, and I thought now everything will be okay. "*Ŏmma!!!!!*" I cried out. She rushed over to us. "*Did somebody say something to you?*" I was crying and I could barely get the words out. "*I don't know. But there's something black and terrible, shooting out black smoke and screaming out like a dying pig!*" My brother started laughing. "*Ŏmŏni must not have told you about the train.*" . . . *Ha, ha, ha.* . . . When I remember those times, I can't help but think how deprived us kids were, brought up in the mountains.

In Shimonoseki, there were about ten to fifteen households of people from our *kohyang*, and about three households were actually related to ours. So it was like one group. My father got everything prepared for us to live in Shimonoseki as soon as we arrived. In Shimonoseki at that time there were many Koreans. The people who had relatives elsewhere would take the train from there to Tō-kyō, Ōsaka, or out to the countryside. Back then, to go to Ōsaka by train took four days. When we were coming to Shimonoseki from Pusan, it took one night. We boarded the ship around six p.m. at night. It was I think about seven or eight p.m. that the ship left dock. Then, when we arrived in Shimonoseki, it was morning. The ship was called "*Goan maru.*" It was a huge ship that also transported Japanese soldiers to Manchuria and such places. At that time, there was a ship that sailed from Chejudo, and also there were ships that arrived in Niigata, or Yokohama. The ship that traveled between Shimonoseki and Pusan was the biggest, the "*Goan maru.*"

The Japanese words "*hai*" for "yes," and "*konnichi wa*" for "good afternoon," were the first words that I learned from my brother before coming to Japan. My brother said we would have to know these words when we went to Japan. So what he learned in school, he would come home and tell my sister and me. Well, I was looking forward to coming to Japan, because I thought that finally I would be able to study. In my neighborhood back in Mosan there were seven girls who used to play together. Three of them used to attend school. One girl had a brother in Pyongyang, and one day he came to get her, saying that he wanted her to receive an education. I was so envious of the fact that she was able to go north to Pyongyang so that she could study. There were two other girls who attended night school. I was very envious of them for going to school with their little notebooks and pencils.

So I thought that when I go to Japan, I too will be able to study. But when we came to Japan, I was already twelve years old and too old to attend an elementary school. Of course, I didn't know any Japanese. For the kids who were about five or six, there was a small class organized by Koreans. It was kind of like a *Mindan* office, and within this organization they taught the children basic Japanese. At that time there was a teacher from Chejudo and a teacher from Seoul. Although I was a bit older than the other kids, I attended those classes for one year, and I thought that soon I would be able to attend regular school. By that time I was already thirteen years old, and I didn't yet know enough to attend junior high school. So, unfortunately, I couldn't go to school. But each summer some Korean college students came back home to their homes in Shimonoseki and formed a night school so that children like me could study. For three years I studied in these night classes. One day, one of the young teachers was taken away by the police. They said it was because he was reading a book on communism. It seems that somebody had reported him. After that our group was forbidden to gather. You know, the Japanese government at that time was quite frightening when it came to the question of communism. Even though it was a small book, the *kenpeitai* (military police) came to take him away. I heard that once they took you, there was no way for you to get out of prison. You were locked up for a long time without a reason and just left there to rot.

Work

I don't know what it was, but every time I wanted to study, something bad like this happened. After the teacher was taken away, we were all crying, and hoping that we could get another teacher who could be as good as him. But not long afterward, Japan went to war. It was Shōwa 16 (1941). Then in Shōwa 20 (1945), on August 15, the war ended. When I was sixteen years old, I started working in a factory. I couldn't go to school anyway, and I thought that instead of staying at home doing nothing, I should help out with the daily expenses. In the beginning, I worked at a fish cannery. I got into that company through an introduction of a friend from the neighborhood. I hardly knew Japanese then, and I had no experience working. But that friend told me that the company hired other kids like me and offered to introduce me to the manager. So I went with her and got the job.

Several months later, one day, we were sitting to eat our lunch. We always got together and turned away from the others when we ate, because the Japanese workers would say, "Koreans stink of garlic." The workers, both men and women, would start to grumble even before we brought out our lunch boxes. So if the weather was warm, we went outside and ate our lunch. We would get the wooden crates in which the cans were shipped, and make a little table and put our lunch boxes up there. That day, after we all finished eating, I got up with my lunch box in hand, meaning to go back inside the factory, when I saw a Japanese worker sitting on the ground. I didn't know that he was drunk. I was just minding my own business and walking toward the back entrance, when he abruptly got up. He started yelling that I didn't say "excuse me" when I passed in front of him. He rushed over and slapped my face so hard that—I don't lie to you—I thought my eyes were on fire. The blow was hard enough to make me fall. I didn't even know why he slapped me. I was so shocked that I rushed back inside. But the thing was I had to pass by in front of him again in order to get to the work area. I was so terrified that I just huddled in the corner shaking. Then, some of the Japanese women who were sitting between the man and me must have told him not to get so upset because I was still quite young and didn't know my manners. They motioned for me to walk behind them in order to avoid passing in front of the man again.

In that factory, there was a young *ajŏssi* (young man) who had worked for that company for quite a while. The *ajŏssi* confronted that Japanese man. *"What gives you the right to hit that young girl? Why didn't you just caution her in words instead of slapping her like that? You either go and apologize to that girl or, if not, you tell me that you are sorry and I'll tell her that you apologized."* The drunk man yelled back at him. *"A Chōsen-jin shouldn't open his mouth!"* Then the two men got into a huge fight. I could never forget that *ajŏssi*'s name—"Chiba-*san*." Back then everyone used Japanese surnames. Well, anyway, I heard that the man went to Chiba-*san*'s room that night where he was sleeping, and threatened to kill him with the knife that he used to cut fish in the factory. Chiba-*san* lived in the worker's dormitory.

Well, that day when I went home, I told my mother what had happened, and my mother asked me if I had done something or said anything to offend the Japanese man. I told her that I didn't do anything wrong. I didn't step on his foot or even go over his legs. All I did was pass in front of him. I told my mother that I wasn't exactly sure what he was saying, but I heard him yell *"Chōsen-jin"* a couple of times, and then he rushed over and slapped my face. The side of my face was quite swollen, so my mother held a cold wet towel to it. Then, the friend who had introduced me to that factory came to our house on her way home. *"Hui-Sun, you must have gotten quite a shock today."* She said that she talked to Chiba-*san* and he told her that the Japanese man felt angry because I passed by in front of him, and since I'm just a *"Chōsen-jin no ko"* (a Korean child), I shouldn't be so cheeky as not to say "excuse me." The Japanese man said that Chiba-*san* was defending me because we were both *Chōsen-jin* and that he wanted to kill all Koreans. All I could think of was that I never wanted to run into that Japanese man again. I asked the friend to tell the manager that I quit. From that time on, every time I even passed by that factory, my legs shook. I heard later that Chiba-*san* couldn't bear to work for the factory after the incident, because the Japanese man gave him such a hard time. I heard that he ended up moving away in search of another job. I felt really bad about what happened to him. All I can do is feel grateful for what he did for me that day.

After I quit that canning company, I took another job. My mother was working at home, and whatever we sold from our farmland and other properties in Korea was pretty much used up. I was introduced to another factory. In that factory we bound pre-dried *udon* (noodles). It was quite far from my home, but I worked there for nearly two years. Then a factory making and packing cookies was built right near my house. The owner was a Japanese who was married to a German woman. I thought that this was a great chance for me to work closer to home and in a cookie factory. I went to the interview wearing the Korean dress that I usually wore at home. At that time Korean people, even though we were living in Japan, usually wore Korean dress. Some of the children of course at certain times wore kimono, but adults and especially older people wore the *chŏgori*. In the market Koreans used to sell *komushin* (rubber shoes) and all kinds of other wear. In Shimonoseki, I guess because it was close to Pusan, there were a lot of Korean things out in the market. So it was almost the same as being in Korea. I guess the only *kosaeng* was the fact that we had to speak a foreign language.

When I went to the *Morimata* cookie factory for the interview, the manager said that he would hire me, on condition that I not wear *chŏgori* to work. I agreed, because the factory was less than a ten-minute walk from my home. Before, I had to walk more than forty minutes each way to get to work. Also, the factory smelled so good, like cookies, and as a young girl, I guess it seemed the best place to work. At that time, even if we had the money, we couldn't go out and buy cookies freely. Back then, Japan was at war so there were no luxury items to buy, and also we were constantly reminded that whether we were hungry or not we had to withstand it for the sake of the country. At the cookie factory, all the cookies that we packaged were sent to the battlefield. I guess even though it was a privately run factory, the owner couldn't sell to any other place, but set a standard price for the government to buy and ship the cookies to the soldiers. At that time, there wasn't yet bombing going on in Japan, but soldiers were being shipped out to places like the Philippines, Indonesia, and Manchuria. After a while, the war started coming as close as Okinawa. Then, we saw the B-29, the *kansaiki* (carrier-borne aircraft) and such planes starting to fly around. When that *kansaiki* came and shot its bullets, it was like rain or hail. It would just continue to shoot until it flew away and the ground would burst into flames.

Well, at the factory, they told me not to wear the *chŏgori*, and so I would only wear its black skirt, and instead of its white vest-blouse, wear a pullover that my mother got at a secondhand store. At the factory, I was the first and only Korean. Then after a while, about a dozen other Korean kids came to work and naturally we spoke to each other in Korean. We always had a morning meeting before we started work, and the manager always ended the meeting saying that our Japan was one Japan, and therefore we should speak our country's language and we should not speak other languages like Korean. But still, whenever we gathered, we spoke in Korean. A while later the manager went as far as putting up a sign with a small can attached to a bamboo pole that read, "ONE SEN FINE FOR SPEAKING KOREAN." Sometimes, we would each have to put in five or six sen a day.

At that time I was making eighty sen for a whole day's work. It wasn't even one yen. We didn't get Sundays off, just two days off a month, the first and the fifteenth. I would start work at seven in the morning and work until five in the evening. Back then, there was no such thing as an eight-hour workday. That didn't start till the Americans came in and the labor unions were organized. It was almost like slavery. Whatever the factory told you to do, you had to do it. Meanwhile, the war was getting more intense and the factory was slowing its production. Many people were laid off or moved to other factories, and there were only five of us left in our group. Maybe we Koreans don't always speak Japanese, but no matter what the Japanese people say about us, when it came to work we didn't lag behind. We all worked well. So we five Korean girls became a five-member team. But the Japanese workers expressed so much dislike toward us that one day we all decided to quit together. Although searching for work elsewhere would be troublesome, and of course in the beginning we wouldn't receive much salary, still, we decided that less money was better than having to deal with so much discrimination. The five of us used to say, *"When should we quit? When should we quit?"* We went on about this for months, and then finally we decided that all of us were going to quit at once right after we got paid. At that time it was about three years before the end of the war and Japan's surrender.

After quitting the cookie factory, we all got another factory job, this time making knitted work gloves for soldiers. We got in through the introduction of one of my friend's sisters. This factory paid us for the number of gloves that we produced, rather than an hourly wage. The factory was willing to hire all five of us, because at that time factories were short of hands with most men away fighting. So young women like us were welcomed. We worked in the new factory for about ten days. One day I returned home from work and my mother looked frightened and said that a postcard had come from the police station calling me in. I couldn't think of anything that I had done, and I thought that perhaps somebody had done something bad and used my name. That day I saw one of my friends from our five-member team and showed her the postcard. I told her that the police called me in to come in by 8:30 the next morning. Then, she said, *"Hey, did you get one of those cards? I got one, too."* All five of us had the same postcard from the police. None of us had any clue why. The postcards had nothing on them except our names and the order to appear at the police station. There was also a warning that if we didn't come by that time, they would come to our houses to get us. When I showed the postcard to my brother, he was very worried. He told me to think carefully whether there was something that I could have done to break the law, because when the police called you in, it was pretty serious. No matter how much I thought I had broken no law.

The next day, my friends and I went to the police station quite early and waited outside until a policeman told us to come inside. Soon we were all called and taken into separate rooms where we were questioned. I was so scared, I couldn't think straight. The policeman asked me why I quit the cookie factory. I didn't know what to say. I sat there without saying a word. He said that I would spend the night there and they wouldn't send me home until I answered all of his questions. So I said that from the beginning, the factory treated us Koreans badly and made us pay a penalty for speaking Korean. The work itself was fine, but the atmosphere created by the other Japanese workers was hard to bear. They would speak to each other, but as soon as we came near them they would stop talking and turn away. I told him that there were too many incidents for me to tell him everything. The policeman asked me if I was willing to go back to that factory. I told him that I was already working for another factory. The policeman said that because I have just started working for the glove factory, my level of production was slow. Also because we girls all quit at the same time—it would take time and money for the cookie factory to hire new workers and train them. He said that because of our selfishness, we were committing a disservice not only to the factory but also to the country during this time of war when factories were short of workers. He said that if we refused to go back to the factory, we would be sent away as part of the *teishintai* (military "volunteer" corps).

The *teishintai* was sending young girls abroad to Manchuria and elsewhere to help the soldiers with cooking, cleaning, and running errands, including taking ammunition to the front lines. I didn't know it then, but I realized later that *teishintai* was actually *ianfu* ("comfort women," the sexual slaves of the Japanese military).[5] We were only seventeen or eighteen years old. . . . We didn't know anything. Just hearing the word Manchuria and thinking that I would have to leave my mother and go off to a faraway country made me want to plead for my life, and I begged to be allowed to go back to the cookie factory. Afterward, I was sent out of the room, and I was able to join my friends. I was afraid of what my friends would think about my cowardice. I confessed and found out that they had said the same thing. Just thinking about having to go off to Manchuria made me burst into tears. All of my friends and I were grabbing each other and crying. The policeman told us to stop crying and that we would be able to go back home after the police chief spoke to us. We waited a long two hours, and the chief came and told us that he wanted to buy lunch for us. Back then there was no place to really eat but anyway he took us to this place where we had something like noodles with some vegetables. It was quite good. He told us that we had caused a great deal of trouble, but that we should rest for the day and from the next day go back to work at the cookie factory.

Can you believe that the factory went to the police about us like that? All we could think about was leaving our families and being shipped off to Manchuria. Going back to work for that factory seemed like a much better idea. I felt so grateful that they allowed us to go back and work there rather than sending us off as they said they would. So we went to the glove factory and explained everything. The manager said that it was too bad, because we had just started getting used to the work and would soon do as well as the other workers. He said at least for us to come in a few days to pick up our pay, but because we were so embarrassed about the whole situation, we never went back. But my friend's sister brought all of us our pay. We went back to the cookie factory and tried our best to put up with everything. But it really was hard to deal with the people and the atmosphere. A few months later one of my friends quit, because she was getting married. All of us decided to quit, but this time one at a time with several months in between. We gave excuses such as marriage, and having to help out other relatives, and we all quit. Toward the end of the war, with the military situation getting quite serious, we heard that a cookie factory was being built in Manchuria. The factory recruited people to go and work there. Three other Koreans decided to go. A while later, the factory in Japan closed down. After it was gone, my friends and I were so happy. We were feeling guilty, because four of us had lied and quit. Because of that, even if I had to pass in front of the factory, my heart would start pounding. I was afraid of what might happen if someone saw me and decided to report me to the police again.

Comfort Women

At that time I thought that *teishintai* was just a support group that helped out soldiers, but later I realized that it was young women who were forced to give their bodies to the soldiers. *Aigu!!!!* Can you believe that all I thought at that time was that I didn't want to leave my mother. . . . I could never have imagined that the *teishintai* meant helping out the soldiers by giving them my body. Can you believe that? It seems that these women who were serving as *ianfu* were about my age or maybe a year younger. After the war, about four or five years later, I remember there was a movie saying that some of the *teishintai* had become what we now call *ianfu*, but at that time they never mentioned the fact that they were mostly young Korean women.[6] All they said was that the soldiers sometimes, when they felt a tremendous amount of stress, couldn't fight effectively in the war, but when they were given women they could regain their strength and fight well. In the movie they showed a line of young women, and one woman would enter a room and it said that she would serve about three men. Then, when that group of men finished, the same women would serve another group. So this was what the movie called *teishintai*. I saw this movie in a Japanese theater. At that time it wasn't a secret, but I guess the only thing they held back was who they mostly sent—young Korean women—something we only found out recently. In the movie all of the women were wearing kimonos. The movie showed the soldiers looking so tired, but once they heard that the women were there, they became excited and looked as if they had renewed strength. It was a movie, so the scene was probably rehearsed. But anyway, after watching this movie, I really thought that men are so dirty. The women had no choice but to go. It seemed so terrible that the women didn't even have names and were called by number—number so-and-so to get into this or that room.

That the largest number of comfort women were Korean became known after a Japanese women's group brought this fact to public attention. They used the hall in the building right next door at the Korean Christian Center (KCC). They made this known several years ago, and they were having a gathering to discuss what we needed to do in order to compensate these women.[7] Attending these meetings, I found out that most of these women were Korean and some were Chinese, but there were hardly any Japanese women. Before the war, Japanese women were sold and bought and sent out to Asia. They were called "*ch'angnyŏ*" (prostitutes). The women dressed up and men went to visit them for a few hours and paid them for their services. So before, I thought that it was these women who were sent. I found out only later that it was Korean, Chinese, and Filipina women who were sent to these places and made to wear kimonos in order to do such work. They said that if they were to send Japanese women, they might end up serving their brothers or relatives. So that was the reason why we Korean and Chinese women who looked Japanese, were sent to places like Manchuria and Southeast Asia. When I heard about this from women activists who came to visit the KCC, it really made me feel angry. Several years ago, the first woman who came out in the open about her experience talked in an interview about those times. I thought to myself that if I hadn't been so lucky, that woman on TV could have been me. If I had refused to go back to work at that cookie factory, I could have very well been sent to these places to do those kind of things. I just couldn't believe it. . . .

During the war, if you were old enough to be in junior high school, you had to work in factories making all sorts of things in support of the war. Kids who were too young to work with complicated machinery were ordered to do simple things such as gluing things together or shaping screws with a *senban* (lathe). Such work was usually done by men, but when they were away at war, young women and children had to replace them. We Koreans were also trained to fight. My brother was called away for training. Those who were a year older than my brother didn't have to go to war. They were drafted as laborers. The men went to work wherever they were needed in support of the war. When the assignment came, you had to go. If you refused, they would come to take you away. So my brother was drafted to receive his training in the *heitai* (army).

Marriage

Well, I was reaching the age when I needed to think about marriage and my mother was quite worried about me marrying a good man who would treat me well. She wanted to make sure that I didn't marry an eldest son, because she knew from her own experience about the hardships of becoming the first daughter-in-law. So whenever there were offers for me, she always asked first if he was a first son, middle son, or the last son. She was determined to give me away to a really good partner, and so she was very choosy. But the war was getting more severe and most of the men were called away to fight. One day, a distant aunt came to our house and told my mother that there was a household that she knew in Hakata, Kyūshū, which was seeking out a daughter-in-law.

There were six siblings, three sons and three daughters, and the mother while giving birth to the last child had a partial stroke, and now could only speak very little and couldn't work. What was worse, the man was the first son. Although the situation was everything that my mother was against, with the war getting more serious and with no other prospects, I guess my mother was worried that I might not be able to marry at all if we waited too long. The only positive thing was that my future husband-to-be was twenty-three years old, which meant that he had just reached the age limit where he wouldn't be sent off to war. Let's see, I was born in 1927, and my brother was born in 1924, and luckily my husband was born in 1923. When they made the law to draft Koreans, it started with men who were born in 1924. So I guess my mother felt safe in the fact that I wouldn't lose my husband in the war like many women did at that time. Without even consulting me, she told my aunt that she was willing to give me away. That was when I was nineteen years old. The government was sending men off to *gunji kōba*, to places like Ōsaka and Hiroshima. You know the place where the atomic bomb was dropped? Right below that there was a city called

Hikari where there were many *gunji kōba*. We heard that men, young boys, and even girls who were of junior high school age were being sent for *chōyō* (conscription). We heard that the only way to get out of this was to be married. So back then a lot of women were married off to men who were more than ten years older than them. After meeting my future husband-to-be just once, I had to marry him in March. When I saw him for the first time, I thought he was quite okay. *Ha, ha, ha.* . . .

When I got married, my sisters-in-law were quite young. Two of them were going to school, and the youngest one was six years old. At that time I didn't work, because I was too busy looking after my big family. My mother-in-law was really a good person. I never received harsh words from her. She was so kind to the point that I thought when I myself have a daughter-in-law, I hoped that I could treat her as nicely as my mother-in-law treated me.

Repatriation

Well, I remember that when the war finally ended, all the Japanese were crying on the road, because they had lost, but we Koreans were so happy. My family and all of my neighbors were saying, "*Sara ta, sara ta . . .—We have been saved, we have been saved. . . .*" Our neighbors the Kobayashis were crying, because they had lost their son in the war. But in my family, we were so happy, especially my mother, because my brother was saved from going to the war. He had gotten basic training, but the war ended before he was sent off to the battlefield. She was so happy that she didn't know what to do. "*I never knew whether your brother would live or die, but now I feel that your brother has been given life again. There is nothing that I could feel happier about.*" I still remember when I first heard that the war had ended. My mother and I were riding the train to go to the countryside to buy some rice to sell in the black market. Sitting in the train, we heard that the war had ended and Japan had lost.

I remember that in the middle of August when the war had just ended, there were no ships going out, but by September the ships were running again. Many of the Koreans who were living in Shimonoseki, and others in the countryside, left everything they had or took whatever they could in sacks. My father too was saying that eventually Koreans were going to be chased out of Japan anyway, so we might as well go on our own. That was why my *ch'inchŏng* left Japan to go back to Korea in November of that year. The government provided a ship to carry all the Koreans back to our country. If we applied, within three weeks we would be able to get the tickets to go on the ship. But for my husband and our family, there was my mother-in-law's condition, and also we didn't have enough money to buy the train tickets to take all of us to Shimonoseki from Fukuoka. There were nine of us, including me. We just didn't have the money on hand then. My father-in-law used to always say, if only we had enough money for the train ticket to get to Shimonoseki, all we would have had to do was get on that ship to get back to our own country. We didn't own anything there, but if we at least had the strength to dig the ground, then we wouldn't starve. My father-in-law felt really bad for me that my *ch'inchŏng* went back, but we couldn't. He promised that we would all work hard and save enough money to go by the following year. So I took his word for it. But you know, things are not as easy as that. As time passed, we heard all sorts of rumors from people who had gone to Korea but returned starving. They said there was no food, and that people would steal just about anything. We decided to take more time to consider whether we wanted to go back to Korea. Then while we were still trying to make up our minds, the Korean War started. After that we decided that it was best for us to stay put in Japan.

Reflection

In my life to make ends meet, I did everything you can think of. During the time when Japan was at war, tobacco was hard to find, and only a small amount of it was passed out in rations. So I got in contact with a couple who introduced me to a farmer in the country who was growing tobacco leaves. I would get some of the leaves from them, roll the leaves, cut them with a slicing machine, tie the ends, make a bundle of them, and take it to the black market to sell. I made good money from that. In the evening I worked in the docks where the fishing boats came in. I had to clean all the fish and put them in boxes to get ready for the morning market the next day. I worked until dawn, and then I went to another job from early afternoon. All the Japanese people were having a hard time, too. We all received rations from the government.

Many Japanese, in order to get some more money, took all of their old kimonos to the market and sold them. Then they had enough money to buy some white rice on the black market. Many women, who had lost their husbands in the war and had to support themselves and their children somehow, did such things. Well, my husband would take the kimonos that he bought in the market from these women for a very low price, and take them to the countryside and trade with the farmers for food. He also bought shoes, socks, and gloves and traded them. He was able to get all sorts of things like white rice and vegetables. That's how he started in the wholesale business. Then, after we came to Shimonoseki, my husband opened a small store in the countryside where he sold items that he had bought at low prices in the city.

After my second brother-in-law got married in Fukuoka, my husband, our children, and I moved back to Shimonoseki. In Shimonoseki, although there were big factories, they didn't usually hire Koreans. This was also true of schools. Back then even if you were really intelligent and wanted to enter one of the better schools, it was almost impossible. My youngest son wasn't such a good student, but my eldest son was quite smart and he wanted to try out for the best school. But he wasn't accepted. He was very disappointed and sad because he had done the best that he could, but because he was Korean, he was not accepted. At times like that I used to think that even if we would have been struck by thunder in Korea, we should have gone back to our own country. In Japan, even if a Korean graduated from a university, when the company did a background check and found out that they were Koreans, they were not hired. After coming to Ōsaka, we never experienced such things personally. But while we were living in Shimonoseki, I felt very sorry for my kids, because they had to go through such things so many times. Then, eventually we moved to Ōsaka, because we felt that it would be better for our children's future.

You know, when I was growing up in Shimonoseki, after eating kimchi we couldn't even go out of the house. The Japanese would say *"Chōsen-jin kusai— Koreans stink."* Although there were many Koreans in Shimonoseki, still the Japanese people would say such things. They said that they, the Japanese people, were too clean to eat something that smells as bad as garlic and kimchi. Now these days they say garlic is full of vitamins and kimchi is sold practically everywhere. But back then there was no such thing as a market that would sell kimchi and Korean food openly. If there were such places, they would only be drinking establishments where they sold the Korean liquor *makkŏlli*. Then, also there were *hanba* where Korean laborers slept and ate, and there you could find Korean food. But at that time there was no such thing as a Korean restaurant. Even if there had been, no one would have eaten there. Koreans didn't have money to spend in restaurants, first of all, and the Japanese people thought that it would make them smell like Koreans. Now things have changed. The Japanese have come to know the taste of Korean food and to know that garlic is good for you.

But over the years I came to realize that those Japanese people who are uneducated are the ones who go around calling us *"Chōsen-jin, Chōsen-jin."* I got into a big fight with a Japanese guy once, because I was sick and tired of him calling my family and me *"Chōsen-jin, Chōsen-jin."* I yelled back at him. *"Hey, do you think we Koreans wanted to come to Japan? You Japanese forced many of our people to come here to work to our bones!"* Ha, ha, ha. . . . When I think about those times, we Koreans have really come a long way. . . .

Notes

1. In 1939 the *"Kyōwa* Association" was organized under the direct supervision of the Ministry of the Interior with branches in each prefecture and smaller units in cities and towns. Its main purpose was to assimilate Koreans as well as to control subversive activities. The program encouraged changing of Korean names (*soshi kaimei*), the acquisition of Japanese language and culture, and Shintō worship. Membership was mandatory, and all Koreans were required to carry their membership card at all times. See Lee (1981f: 162).

2. Recently, for third and fourth generation Koreans, the need to discover their ethnic roots has encouraged them to go through the legal process of changing their Japanese names to their Korean names. Some who neither see themselves as purely Korean nor Japanese have kept the Japanese readings of their first names while keeping the Korean pronunciation of their last names.

3. "*Kun*" is a Japanese name-suffix for younger men, meaning "boy," "junior," or "Mr."

4. The Chinese characters used for the Korean names can be read in their Japanese pronunciation. For example, "Kim" is read in Japanese as "Kin," or "Pak" as "Boku."

5. A number of Korean women were drafted or kidnapped to serve in the "volunteer corps" (*teishintai*), becoming military comfort women (sex slaves) serving Japanese soldiers overseas in the years after 1937. An estimated ninety thousand women from Korea, Taiwan, China, the Philippines, Indonesia, and Malaysia were mobilized to serve Japanese soldiers stationed in China and Southeast Asia. Approximately 80 percent of these women are believed to have been Korean. See Tanaka (2002: 31).

6. I am not certain whether Hui-Sun was actually able to see this type of movie after the war, since the whole issue of comfort women did not come out in the open until more recent years, and it was not until August 1993 that the Japanese government admitted to having forced women of the occupied countries into army prostitution during World War II. I asked her again to verify this fact, but she was certain that it was only about four or five years after the war that she saw this movie.

7. The Japanese government has thus far refused formal apology and government compensation to the former comfort women. Instead it has tacitly admitted the justice of their suit by backing the establishment of a "private fund" to provide unofficial payments following the exposure of the issues by former Korean comfort women and those from many other East and Southeast Asian countries.

Chapter 10

A Life Worth Living Is a Life That Has Meaning

Pak Sun-Hui

Deacon Pak Sun-Hui is president of Japan's Korean Christian Women's group and director of an assisted-living home called "Rainbow House." This nursing home, built by the women's group, was initially established to assist elderly Koreans, including men, women, and couples. However, the facility is presently open to both Korean and Japanese elderly. The home is supported through private donations, as well as monthly fees paid by its residents.

In the "Rainbow House" each resident has a private room with a small kitchen unit and toilet. There is a large community-style bathing facility. One can either cook in one's own kitchen or take meals in the spacious dining hall downstairs. There is a twenty-four-hour emergency service that is activated by pushing a button and constant camera surveillance to monitor any accidents or injuries.

Sun-Hui emphasized that the facility's concept of "assisted living" is still in the introductory stages in Japan. She said there were numerous challenges in building this facility, and it is still overcoming obstacles. First, Koreans still harbor a negative image of having their parents live in a care-home and view it as an act of cruelty. Second, the ultramodern building and facilities as well as the number of professional staff who are trained in caring for the elderly raise the costs. Since many Koreans, especially women, are not eligible for old age or disability pensions,[1] *they cannot afford such a facility without assistance from their children.*

It is Sun-Hui's dream that through fund-raising efforts more Korean elderly will be able to afford the facility without the financial burden falling upon their children. She would like to see a home that gives the elderly independence and freedom to lead the remaining years of their lives.

A long time ago we used the name Niiyama, but now everything is according to my Korean name, Pak Sun-Hui. I am seventy-three years old. I was born in Chinju on September 6, 1926. I came here when I was thirteen and was educated in Japanese schools. I think I am close to being a second-generation immigrant. Usually people of the first generation were so busy making ends meet and raising their children that they really didn't have the time to study the language or the customs.

My mother was from Munsang, near Kyŏngsangnam-do. It was quite close to Chinju. My mother was known throughout the town for her beauty. On Sundays, when she left home to attend church, the young men from the village would wait outside and whistle and call out to her, *"Whee, whee! Kim Sun-Ju, you are as beautiful as a flower in full bloom!"*

My father and his family lived in Chinju. My grandfather was an herbal doctor and was quite learned. My grandfather came with us to Japan. He passed away here when he was eighty-five years old. My father followed a friend to Japan, because he heard that one could make a lot of money here. He came to Japan ahead of us and we followed a while later. My father was raised in a wealthy house, so he was very spoiled. If he were to have studied a little bit more, he could have lived quite well on his own, but he didn't want to continue. My mother didn't know her letters. She tried to teach herself to write her name— *Kim Sun Ju.* My mother wanted to study, but she was told that because she was a girl, there was no need for her to study. Her parents thought it more important to educate her two brothers.

Coming to Japan

When I came to Japan, I was thirteen years old. From Chinju, my grandfather, mother, sister, and I went to Pusan and from there we rode the boat to Shimonoseki. From Shimonoseki we came to Ōsaka because we had a relative living here. I completed elementary school in Korea and then I came to Japan. My grandfather, my father's father, allowed us to study even though we were girls. Back then, even in Korea, we had to learn Japanese as our national language, because it was still during the Japanese colonial days. In school, from Monday through Saturday, we studied in Japanese. The class called *"Chosŏn-eo"* (Korean language) was much shorter. We took this class only twice a week, as if it were a foreign language class. Even during breaks between classes the teachers tried to encourage the students to speak in Japanese. In class we also had to make up stories in Japanese, for example, talking about what I did yesterday, and presenting it in an interesting manner. This time was called "*O-hanashi no jikan*" (Conversation time). The elementary school that I attended in Korea was a Christian missionary school. Most of the teachers were Korean, but the conversation teacher was a woman from Japan. While in Korea, I learned enough Japanese to understand everything I heard and I was able to speak quite well.

But after coming to Japan, I realized that although I was able to speak well enough to communicate, I had an accent. You know the abacus? These days, young people use computers or calculators, but back then we had to use the abacus. Well, there was a calculation class during which students had to take turns standing in front of the class and call out the numbers. For example, "*san en nari, go en nari, kyū en nari—sum of one yen, of five yen, of nine yen. . . .*" One day I had to stand in front of the class and call it out. I think at that time, instead of saying "*kyū*," for the number nine, I was saying "*ku.*" In combination with "*en,*" I must have called out something like "*ku-jen nari. . . .*" Suddenly, all the students roared out laughing, "*wah, ha, ha.*" They said that my accent was too funny. Now I don't have a problem, but this was right after I came to Japan. Well, I didn't know what they were laughing at. I just wondered what was the matter with these fools! Later I realized it was because I had mispronounced the word. For the abacus, I received really good training in Korea, and so I was better and faster than the Japanese kids. Anyway, this was one of the unpleasant experiences I had with Japanese kids. But fortunately at my school, I didn't have many bad experiences just for being Korean.

Wartime

During the war we had to escape to Shimane prefecture to avoid the bombing. Afterward, along with some people from my parent's hometown, we came back to Ōsaka. Right after the war we were very poor. I badly wanted to go to school, but we couldn't afford it. We lived in a small tenement housing in the middle of a tiny back street. There was a school nearby and every morning the students would pass by wearing their school uniforms. I was so envious. I wanted to wear a uniform and carry a school bag and go to school, too, but there was no money. So I attended a small Christian night school for girls sponsored by the YWCA. I studied there for three years. It was in Ōgimachi, the *Ōgimachi yakan joshikō*. It was there that I met Ms. Inagaki, a Japanese woman who became my favorite teacher. She has passed away already. She was an old maid. I heard that there was someone whom she loved very much, but he died. After that she lived alone. She taught English, and she was such a wonderful teacher. Every day after her class, she went downstairs to the small chapel to pray. One day I sat behind her and watched. I saw a dim glow around the back of her head. At that moment I thought that one day when I finished school I would like to become a teacher like her. You could say that I admired her very much. I looked up to her, because she was so sympathetic, kind, and gentle. She was a really great teacher who cared about her students. At that time I really loved English. During English class I was so happy. I would study my hardest the night before in order to prepare for the class. Whenever the teacher asked a question, I instantly raised my hand to give the answer. I think Ms. Inagaki knew that I was trying my best.

After three years, I really wanted to continue my education. But at home my father said in his heavy Kyŏngsang-do dialect, *"There's no need for a girl to study further."* So I thought that I might have to give up on the idea of continuing my education. My older sister was already married by this time. Her husband is a doctor now, but back then he was still attending medical school, and my sister was having a hard time financially. In order to support her family, she started a small steel factory that pressed all kinds of metal and steel and recycled them to sell. It was quite a small factory, but it allowed her to send her husband to school. My sister really endured a lot of *kosaeng*. My mother as well, when she was younger, wanted to study very much. So when I wanted to continue my education, she and my older sister decided to give me the opportunity.

During the war, while I was attending night school, there were countless sirens to warn of the incoming B-29s that might drop bombs. While going to school we wore scraps of fabric as scarves and *monpe* (women's work pants) and also carried a backpack. Because we attended night school, many of us were sent to the factories to make parts and equipment for the war. We were part of a group that worked during the day in these factories and at night attended school. School started at around six p.m., but often the class was stopped, because of the *"kūshū keihō"* (air-raid alarm) siren warnings. When the siren went off, we had to run into the basement and were not allowed to come out until the siren stopped. But by then it would be nine o'clock already. Finally, three years passed and it was time for graduation. But most of the time was spent in the basement and we hadn't studied much. So when I took the entrance examination to one of the trade schools with English as my major, I wasn't prepared at all.

Going to School

With Ms. Inagaki, my favorite English teacher, we had finished the first book of English, but we were not able to go on to the second book. In order for me to take an English proficiency exam, what I had learned so far wasn't even close to being enough. So I tried to study at home. I would read an English textbook called *"Tsuda eigo tekusuto"* (Tsuda English Textbook) and translate what I could and then take it to school and show it to Ms. Inagaki. She would look at it for me after class. It was when Ms. Inagaki taught me during our private lessons that I really learned something. She looked over all the passages that I had translated. I think I was nineteen years old at that time. It was already a bit late to do this kind of studying. I took several years trying to finish school, going here and there during the war, and attending night school as I worked for an automobile company during the day. Although I didn't have much confidence, I decided to take the entrance examination for several universities. During the language test there was a foreign teacher and a Japanese teacher, and I was told to read a story. Afterward, they asked several questions in English. As the last question, I was asked who wrote the story that I had just read. I answered that I supposed the name on the bottom of the story was the name of the person who had written it. Well, somehow I passed the test. I was accepted by both Kōbe Women's College and Dōshisha College. Kōbe College was famous for having a lot of wealthy young women from very prominent families. It was also known to be a really good school. I wasn't sure which school I should choose, so I asked Ms. Inagaki which she thought was the better school. She said that for English, Kōbe Women's College would be better. So that is where I decided to go.

It was a beautiful campus on top of a hill with a wonderful view. There was a wide green lawn and all the *ojō-san* (young ladies), dressed in elegant and expensive clothes, would sit on the grass and chat with each other after class. Compared to their beautiful clothes, what I was wearing looked even older, more tattered and wrinkled. Every day I would have to hold my breath to squeeze myself into the train and try to study in that crowd on my way to school. I was trying to learn one more word, one more phrase, and do my best. I was living like that, but when I came to school, I would see these rich princesses who would lie on the grassy fields, relaxing as if they had not a worry in the world. I thought how foolish they looked. They looked like a bunch of cows, lying around the way they did. I thought that there was no way I could study with that kind of people and in such an atmosphere. They were so comfortable and wealthy, and life to them seemed unimportant. They weren't set on fire having to study in order to survive; they had no desire to excel. It was too different from the kind of life that I was used to.

Until then, I had been living somehow from one day to the next, and often my family and I had had to wonder where the next meal was coming from. Even getting into that school was something that was so far from what I had expected. When I was going to the night school, my friends and I always had to find a little time here and there in order to learn a few more things as we worked during the day. Even while riding the crowded trains, we didn't want to waste our time, and so we tried to read our texts in that crowd. After trying so hard, I finally passed the test to attend the school, but once I arrived I started feeling really discouraged.

I went to Ms. Inagaki and told her that I wanted to quit. At that moment Ms. Inagaki said, *"Boku-san (Japanese reading of Pak), you have until now had a very hard life. You have always had to run in order to catch up. So leading that kind of life, it is hard for you to be able to see and accept another lifestyle. But you should try to understand and learn from a different way of life from what you are used to."* So for four days she went with me to school and waited until I finished all of my classes and came back with me. She told me to look closely at the girls and try to learn their good points. She said that learning from them what I did not yet possess would make me better rounded in my way of being, thinking, and behaving. So she taught me like that. That is what she did for me.

She was such a wonderful teacher. Then, after I completed one year at the college, there was a new system implemented by MacArthur,[2] and colleges and universities were changed to a four-year program. For someone like me who could barely make the tuition payments, the new requirement was a great burden. But I heard at that time that at Dōshisha I would be able to finish within three years. I took the entrance exam again and passed. So finally I was able to graduate from Dōshisha.

During my third undergraduate year, I applied to the graduate school of psychology at Kansei Gakuin University. I took a test and entered the master's course. One of the requirements there was to work in a lab feeding animals such as cats and rats. We conducted tests in the laboratory and gave the data to the professors to put together and assess. But while I was working in the lab, I was constantly coughing. I thought it was a cold. I was taking some medicine, but it wouldn't get better. About a month later I went to the hospital, and when I took the X ray, it showed that I had very weak lungs. I had to take about a year off. Just then there was a new drug out on the market to treat tuberculosis. Without knowing it, I took too heavy a dose and it had some bad side effects on my liver. Because of my failing health, I couldn't finish my graduate course. I stayed at home for a while and tried to recover. Then, a while later, I decided to go to America for a visit. I went to California and I was offered a full scholarship. I was going to stay there, but. . . .

Family

My father was a man with a terrible temper. When he returned from work earlier than the scheduled time and dinner was not ready, he would get very upset. My mother would rush and try to kindle the fire in order to cook the rice. In those days there was no such thing as a gas stove. So she would rush around trying to get the fire started fast enough to cook the rice. Then finally, when everything was prepared and set, my father. . . . He would complain that the food was too hot. He was that kind of a man, so short-tempered and always wanting everything his way. He was raised with plenty. It seems that his father, at one point, owned a lot of land. After a good harvest their shed would be filled with rice and they could eat as much as they wanted, any time they felt hungry. Whatever he wanted, it always came to him easily. So he would explode when things didn't go his way, and the person who had to take all of this was my mother. When my mother cooked for him, if something didn't suit his mood, then no matter how boiling hot the soup was, he would turn over the table.

It was when I was sixteen years old. I still remember it clearly. One night my father came home drunk and he was like a wild man. He was beating my mother and started yelling out and throwing things all over the place. Because of all the noise and the beatings, the landlord threw us out of our house. There was my old grandfather, my mother, and I. At that time I was sixteen years old. . . . We had no place to go, so we had to sit all night at a nearby playground. It was in August. I still remember that there was a full moon. It was then that I decided that I would never marry.

You know, even when something was black and white, if my father said that black was white and white was black, no matter what, you had to agree. The fact that you have to obey your husband and accept such oppression just because you are a female. . . . I decided no way was I going to marry. In Korean families, there are many cases where the father would cause such trouble. We lived in a small neighborhood in Kashiwara, where most of the people were Korean. There was one family living right next to us, where the man often came home drunk. Well, all night long you could hear him beating someone and then all of a sudden the shattering of glass. Right then you would hear the wailing of five or six kids crying all at once. I felt so sorry for the children. I thought that I would like to one day become a teacher and a friend to such children.

While I was attending Dōshisha, I stayed in a dormitory. On Sundays I would return home. It was after the war, so we were living quite a poor life. My parents were making sticky candy that they sold. Whenever I came home, I saw my parents crouched in the small corner of the kitchen, rolling the melted brown sugar to make the candies. My father was still against the fact that I was attending school, saying that it wasn't right for a girl to have so much education. My mother and sister did their best to allow me to continue my studies. One Sunday I came home and I was helping my parents. While my mother was crouched over melting the sugar, she accidentally dropped something and my father got very angry. He whacked her on the side of her head. When I saw that, it was like seeing fire. I looked over at my mother's small figure. She was trying to compose herself after the blow. I stared at my father with so much hate, and I told him exactly what I thought. My father yelled at me for talking back to him. We got into a big fight. Every time I came home, my mother would scrounge up some money and try to stick an extra thousand yen or two into my pocket. Sometimes, she would ask my father to let her have a little more money to give to me on my way back to school. Then they would get into an argument. I knew that if she pushed further, she would get it badly from my father after I left. So I always insisted that there was no need for her to worry. My mother . . . she was like my own life. . . .

One day after a couple of months, when I came back from school, my mother's cheeks were bruised and swollen and continuously bleeding. I asked her what had happened. She said that there was heavy rain and flooding in the outhouse. In the old days the bathrooms were outside of the house and every once in a while a truck came to clean out the holes and suck up the waste. Because of the heavy rain and the flooding, the wooden hole in the outhouse crumbled, making a terrible mess. Well, my father was drunk and saw the mess and blamed my mother. So in a drunken stupor mixed with anger, he shoved my mother onto the street. She fell and scraped the whole side of her face.

When I saw the bloody marks on her face, I was sick to death. I couldn't take it any more. I went up to my father and demanded that he divorce my mother. I told him that I was planning to quit school and work full-time to support my mother and the family. I told him to divorce my mother and leave the house right away. Although my father was drunk at that time, he looked quite shocked. He yelled, "*What are you saying?!?*" As he grabbed a stick, I ran out of the house and went to my sister's house. That night was one of the worst nights of my life. I realized that because I said all those things to my father, in return my mother would end up getting it from him. I couldn't sleep the whole night. I was sick with worry that everything that he wanted to do to me, he was taking out on my mother—every word that I said.

Korean men . . . *aigu*. I grew up seeing this kind of thing all the time. So that is how I started thinking that Korean men were like "*yaman*" (savages). They were ignorant and their children had to pay for their behavior. When some of my friends got married, I thought to myself, "*There's another one in the grave. Why is she so happy about getting married? You pop out children and then torment each other to death.*"

When I was fifteen, my mother had another child. It was a daughter. But three months later the baby died. Well, my mother had such a hard time giving birth to the baby. . . . She went through so much *kosaeng* to give birth to the child. But when my father found out that it was a girl, he just yelled out to my grandfather, "*She had another girl!*" I really hated him at that moment. *Aigu*, I felt so angry. I thought, "*What does it matter whether it is a boy or girl. . . .*" Then, when I was sixteen years old, she had another baby, and that one was a boy. When my brother Dong-Il was born, my father was happy beyond words. For the first time he put some honey in hot water and handed the cup to my mother with both hands. I thought to myself how unfair it was. Just because she gave birth to a son. . . . *Aigu*, I really hated him then.

Later, I heard this story from my mother. My mother was praying to God, "*Oh, Lord, if you bless me with a son, then when he grows older, I will make sure that he spends his life serving you by becoming a minister. He will become your servant whom I will raise to serve to you.*" She said she prayed like that every day. Then Dong-Il was born. The boy was quite smart. He was such a good student. He got into a good high school, and after he graduated, he wanted to go to medical school. But my mother absolutely was against the idea, saying that she conceived him through a special prayer to God. She said she promised that she would make sure he became a minister of God. She begged my brother to take the test for theology school. She asked my sister and me to help him prepare for the test, to become a minister.

At that time, I was quite cynical. I was raised in a terribly violent environment, and I couldn't think the way my mother did. There was no way I could make sense out of sacrificing oneself for God. So I harshly told my mother, "*Omŏni, what are you saying? He is not stupid. He has many talents and he has a good head on his shoulders. Pastor . . . that's a way to a poor life—a life of poverty, all his life! It's enough that we had to live a life with nothing. Let him have a chance at success and a good, comfortable life!*"

My brother was all prepared to take his exams and he was set and ready to go to medical school, but my mother wouldn't bend. She said, "*No!*" and she meant it. My mother didn't know how to get around by train. She didn't know her letters, and there was no way that she would be able to go all the way to my brother's school. So I went against my mother and secretly had my brother take the test for medical school. As expected, he passed with high scores. My mother was in disbelief. My sister was on my side. She asked my mother to give up her idea and allow my brother to pursue dentistry so that he could have a chance at a good life. My mother was physically weak and always suffered from dizzy spells. There was no way that she could take the train to my brother's school to make him drop his courses and take the test for theology school. I was young and strong willed. When I took the future of my brother in my hands, there was no way my mother could win. So although she felt hurt and sad about the fact that she had to break her promise to God, there was nothing that she could do. My brother happily started attending the school of dentistry.

One day during the summer he was riding his scooter from Yamamoto going to Nara. He was going along the Kintetsu train line. There were no traffic signs on this road, and he smashed into the side of a train. He died on the spot. When I heard this news . . . I think it was nerves—the blood rushed from my head to my feet in a second. . . . That was the first time I have ever had that experience. I could literally feel the blood moving through me—flowing down, leaving me empty. . . . My mother's health was already quite fragile. She couldn't ride the train to verify the body, so I went instead.

The child was lying there. . . . Just lying there. . . . He was red and bruised from the impact of the hit. He lay so quietly. . . . I felt deaf. I couldn't hear a thing. My body was being split in two. I couldn't stand the fact that I was living. I yelled out, "*Dong-Il, ya! Nē-san wa tta!*[3] *Okinasai! Nan de omae ga soko ni nete iru no! Oki! Nani shiran kao shite irun-ne!—Dong-Il!* Your sis' is here! Get up! Why are you lying asleep over there! Get up! Why are you ignoring me!*" I hollered at the top of my lungs. I was dying inside. I was cursing at him and yelling at him to get up. . . . "*Please . . . ! Get up!*" But he was like a piece of wood. A piece of wood. . . . He was nineteen years old. He died the year he started school.

I went back home to my mother. She sat in her room quietly for a long time. Finally, she whispered, "*God has given me a son as a blessing. Just to have a chance at a good and comfortable life, being greedy, doing things according to his own desires. . . . God has taken away what he has given.*" From that time on she never talked about my brother. My mother was a very quiet, gentle, soft-spoken woman who never showed outwardly feelings of happiness or sadness. With such heartbreak, without dropping a tear. . . . She said those sentences and she endured. I was worried about her, and every night I spread out my blanket next to hers. I would fall asleep, but every night at, I don't know, one or two o'clock, she would sit straight up, then put her head on the floor and start whispering a fervent prayer until dawn. I would pretend to be asleep, but through half-closed eyes, I would watch her go through this ritual in the middle of the night. Maybe her chest was on fire. . . .

Some time after my brother died, I went to America. I think I must have been close to forty. There was a professor at California Baptist College who asked me to come and visit. I studied at that school for about a year. I was going to return to Japan, but for the following year I was able to get a full scholarship. Through this professor's recommendation, I was able to get this scholarship. I wanted to study to become a teacher. But one day I got a telegram saying that my mother was ill and that she was in the hospital. After my brother passed away, I was taking care of my parents until I got this opportunity to study in America. My sister was married with her own children. When I wrote a letter back home, I was told that there was no need for me to come back. But no matter which way I thought, I needed to be with my mother. I decided to come back to Japan, just to see with my own eyes that she was okay. As expected, my mother was very weak in health. So I decided to stay back for more than a few months. I told myself that once I saw her well enough to sit up, I would return to America to finish the rest of my studies. But things don't work out the way you plan them. One day, my mother was walking on a narrow road, on her way back from church when a car passed by quite fast, grazing her side. The impact on her weak body made her fall quite hard. Soon afterward she passed away. She was seventy years old. I think I must have been about fifty-five or fifty-six. When my mother died, my father sat there like a child and couldn't stop crying. I'm sure that there were many things he regretted. That was the first time I saw my father cry. He was holding on to her, unable to stop his sobbing. . . . I wanted to tell him, "*What's the use of you crying now?!*"

When I think about the past, I sometimes feel really lonely. My father knew the extent of my resentment toward him for the way he treated my mother all her life. I think my father thought that since my mother had passed away, there was no way I was going to stay with him. So he went to one of his relatives in Korea and talked to them about his own funeral after he died. It seems that he left them a lot of money to take care of everything. When I found out about this, I told my father, "*Abǒji, why did you do something like that? If you were going to pay somebody to take care of your funeral, why didn't you give the money to older sister who has until now gone through so much* kosaeng *to support us, instead of paying those people in Korea whom you can't even trust?*" He didn't say anything. I think he knew that what I said was true. My sister supported us throughout her life. In order to provide a way for us to make a living, when her steel-pressing business began to do quite well, she built a public bath that we could run. My sister really sacrificed a lot so that we all could have something to live on. She was going to put my brother through medical school as well as have me continue my studies. It seems that my sister thinks that I have sacrificed getting married and having my own life to take care of our parents. Although I have told her many times not to be foolish, it seems that she feels it her responsibility to take care of me. Even now she supports me. I am so happy that I have a sister like her. She is three years older. I want her to be healthy, and live a long, long time.

Before my mother died, she asked me to promise that I would take care of my father. I think she was worried that I would leave my father in his old age, because of my resentment toward him. Due to that promise, I did what she asked and took care of my father until he passed away. My father became much softer in his ways as he got older. Whenever I told him to do something, he did what I said.

Then one day, the new pastor at my parents' church wanted me to take on the position of deacon. It was the church that my mother had attended all her life in Japan. I told them that I was not ready to take on such a responsibility due to my weak faith and terrible temper. I refused the offer. But I lay awake all that night. My mother, who promised God that she would raise her son to be a minister, went against her promise because of me and my strong will. I had made her lose her son. I had stabbed a nail through her heart. *Ahhh!* I realized that the only way I could make up for what I did was to take on this responsibility and spend my lifetime doing God's work in my brother's place. Although I would not be an ordained minister, I would be doing my best to help those who are in need. I thought that this was the true meaning and purpose of my life. I was fifty-nine years old when I became a deacon.

Reflection

I'd thought I had it all planned. I was going to go to America, get my graduate degree, and become a teacher, then come back to Japan and follow a particular course. I think this is called a dream. . . . All of that was crushed. Human beings can easily fool themselves into thinking that they have the power to do everything and that all is under their control. For me, my dreams and the direction that I thought I was going to take all took a different course. If my brother hadn't died, he probably would have taken care of my mother and father, and I would have gone on my own path and direction. Thinking that life was under my own control, I went here and there trying to make plans and make things happen.

But to be honest, I never considered taking care of my parents to be a burden. My mother's life was like my own. My mother loved me so much and I always knew that. She was always covering for me this way and that, protecting me from this side and that side. I thought that if I ever married, I would take my mother with me. When people used to say that I was an old maid and that my mother should tell me to hurry up and get married, or arrange a marriage, she never said a word. My mother never told me to marry early or pressured me to hurry. I think after her own marriage, she could not tell me that getting married was the best thing. I knew that she thought marriage was not everything.

Of course, I think that it is really good to have someone next to you with whom you can make important decisions, but ultimately, when you think about it, you alone are the person who has to make the final decision. I think to be married or to have someone has its pluses and minuses. I don't think much of those people who wait for their husbands to get back home at night just so they can make a decision about something.

Before, I used to think that all Korean men were like my father and those who used to live in our neighborhood. But you come to live your life and you meet this person and that person. You come to realize that there are some Korean men who are well educated and are quite good to their wives. I think in the old days, most of our fathers were involved in manual labor. I think because they had to experience prejudice from the Japanese society, and felt frustrated and angry about their lives and poor standard of living, they came home and took it out on their families. That is why many Korean men would come home drunk and beat their wives and kids. This was the sole image embedded in my mind. Sometimes, when I saw a man holding his child's hand and the child skipping along so happily next to his or her father, I used to be so shocked that there could be a family like that. All I have ever known of my father was to fear him. I could never imagine myself holding my father's hand. The way we were educated at home is so different from the way children are educated now. When I was young, whenever I said something, my father would yell, "*A girl shouldn't let her mouth run like that!*" I think that was the reason why I started to feel like marriage was the end and it equaled a life in hell. I thought that until the day you die you have to do everything for your husband and his family. I thought your only meaning in life was being a slave and having his children.

But there was a teacher, a Korean man, whom I thought was such a gentlemen and so very intelligent. He was educated and wasn't like any man that I was used to seeing. I thought he was one of the best men that I have ever met. But there's no need to talk about those things. *Ha, ha, ha. . . .* These are all things of the past. Of course, I, myself, am lacking in so many ways, but also, I was never able to meet someone whom I thought I wanted to depend on. But more than anything, there are so many things that are lacking in me. I think I was not able to meet anyone who could close his eyes to all of my faults. *Ha, Ha. . . .* Perhaps it was already something that was planned, a way that my life was supposed to be led.

Well, there are times now when I think that it would be nice to have had a child or two. When I was younger, I thought I didn't have a need for a child. And now that I am older, to want a child just so that I could be taken care of certainly is not right. These days, it is no longer an age in which children take care of their parents. Rather when people come to that point in life where they are no longer able to fully take care of themselves, there are facilities like the "Rainbow."[4] One can lead the remaining years of one's life with independence and, even more importantly, with integrity. But sometimes, when I really think about it, it wouldn't have been so bad to at least have a daughter. Not so that she can take care of me, but so that there might be someone to talk about everything with. A daughter who is very close to me. . . .

I think a life worth living is a life that has meaning. . . . It is a life that directs one's abilities and talents to helping those who are in need. I think that when one nears the end of a life and looks back on the road that has been taken, to feel satisfaction in a life lived well has the greatest meaning of all.

Notes

1. In 1982, the Japanese government revised the National Pension Law, removing the "nationality clause." Before this amendment was made, only Japanese were allowed to pay into the pension fund and become eligible to receive national pension. However, even after the changes were made, many first-generation Koreans were exempt from entitlement. The amendment stated that foreigners who were born before January 1, 1926, were unqualified to receive the national pension. See *Japan Times* (1996: 3). In addition, most of the women worked within the home or in minor part-time jobs, or had illegal sources of income through black market activities, which, for certain, would not have qualified them for any governmental or company benefits.

2. Douglas MacArthur (1880-1964), United States general and supreme commander of the allied forces in the southwest Pacific during World War II and of the UN forces in Korea 1950-1951.

3. *Nē-san* is Japanese, a shortened form of *onē-san* or older sister. *Wa tta* is Korean for "came."

4. Sun-Hui is the director of an assisted-living facility called "Rainbow House." The Korean Christian Women's group who wanted to provide a care facility for Korean senior citizens built this facility in Ōsaka. Presently, it is open to both Korean and Japanese elderly residents.

Photos II:
Present Portraits

Tokumoto Hiroko

Kōda Sumi

Pak Sam-Yang

Tanaka Kimiko

Kang Yang-Ok

Yasuda Kimiko

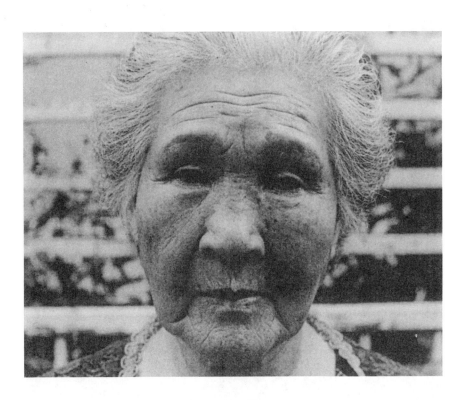

Sŏ Meng-Sun

Pak Hui-Sun

Pak Sun-Hui

Glossary

Abŏji: (Kor) father

Aga: (Kor) diminutive for baby, daughter, daughter-in-law

Agi: (Kor) baby

Ajŏssi: (Kor) a middle-aged gentleman; uncle

Akasshi: (Kor) young miss; young lady

Akogarete ita: (Jp) to long for (yearn after, admire, be attracted by) something

A-p'yŏn: (Kor) opium

Asa: (Jp) flax, linen, hemp

Awabi: (Jp) abalone

Barakku: (Jp) metal scrap housing barracks in makeshift squatter communities

Boku: (Jp) Japanese reading for the Korean name Pak

Burakumin: (Jp) lit. "hamlet people"; descendants of a feudal outcast group

Butsudan: (Jp) a Buddhist household altar, mainly used for praying to one's ancestors. Laid out on top is an array of fruits, raw rice, and water in silver bowls, candlesticks, incense urn, and other adornments

Ch'ama: (Kor) to endure, forebear, put up with

Changgun-nim: (Kor) honorific reference to a general, a title used for Kim Il-Sung, lit. "Dear General"

Ch'angnyŏ: (Kor) a licensed prostitute

Chesa: (Kor) mourning ritual for deceased ancestors. Various foods are arranged on a table following strict guidelines. All participants line up before the ritual table in order of age and status and follow ritual sequences of offering drinks and food to the spirits

Ch'inchŏng: (Kor) natal household; a woman's parents' home, her maiden home

Chŏgori: (Kor) short for *ch'ima chŏgori*, a traditional Korean

177

linen wear

Chojik: (Kor) organization

Ch'ŏltto-tari: (Kor) railway bridge

Chongryun: (Kor) (*Ch'ongryŏn* would be the correct transliteration in the McCune-Reischauer System, however, the former is used as their official spelling) short for *Chaeilbon Chosŏnnin Ch'ongryŏn haphoe* (General Federation of Korean Residents in Japan), created in May 1955. This organization pledged allegiance to North Korea and initially aimed at achieving reunification of Korea as well as protecting the rights of Koreans in Japan. It created its own ethnic education system and a nationwide organizational network

Chŏnjaeng: (Kor) war

Ch'ŏnja-mun: (Kor) [-**moji** (Jp)] "Classic of Thousand Characters" arranged in a long poem. The early sixth-century work appealed to neo-Confucians and became popular as school primer during the Chosŏn period

Ch'ŏp: (Kor) second wife, concubine, mistress

Choryŏn: (Kor) short for *Cheil Chosŏnnin Ryŏngmeng* (League of the Korean Residents in Japan) dominated the Korean community in Japan until forced by the government to disband in September 1949, accused of being a terrorist organization

Chōsen gakkō: (Jp) North Korean ethnic school

Chōsen-jin: (Jp) Korean; North Korean nationality; sometimes used derogatorily. Japan referred to Korea as *Chōsen* during the colonial period

Chosŏn: (Kor) name for the Yi clan Dynasty (1392-1910), the longest-lived imperial dynasty in Korea, until the establishment of the Republic of Korea (*Taehan Min-guk*, abbr. *Han'guk,* South Korea) in 1948 and the Democratic People's Republic of Korea, North Korea. The North continues to refer to its country as *Chosŏn.* Japan refers to it as *Kita-Chōsen*

Chosŏn-eo: (Kor) Korean language

Chosŏn-saram: (Kor) Koreans, Korean people

Chōyō: (Jp) drafting, requisition (workers, etc.)

Chungjong: (Kor) King (r: 1506-1544). He intensified royal adherence to Confucian etiquette and neo-Confucian theory, setting a precedent for the *yangban* class

Doburoku: (Jp) unrefined alcohol

Gaman: (Jp) patience, endurance, perseverance, self-denial

Genshi bakudan: (Jp) atomic bomb

Geta: (Jp) Japanese wooden clogs

Gunji kōba: (Jp) war plant

Gunji kōjō: (Jp) war plant

Halmang: (Kor coll.) Chejudo dialect for grandmother

Halmashi: (Kor coll.) granny

Hanba: (Jp) boarding houses for laborers

Hanbok: (Kor) Korean dress

Han'guk: (Kor) Republic of Korea (short for Taehan Min'guk); established on August 15, 1948, and formally acknowledged by the UN General Assembly and the world in December 1948

Han'gŭl: (Kor) Korean writing system, established by King Sejong in 1444

Hanko: (Jp) signature seal

Hanŭnim: (Kor) God

Harabang: (Kor coll.) Chejudo dialect for grandfather

Heitai: (Jp) soldier, army troops

Hiragana: (Jp) the normal (cursive) Japanese syllabary used mostly for inflected word endings, particles, etc.

Hotoke-sama: (Jp) a Buddha or the spirit of a deceased person

Hwangap: (Kor) sixtieth birthday, celebrated with a feast prepared by the children to commemorate the elder's longevity. Derives its special importance from the Chinese calendar, where the years are divided into a combination of ten calendar signs and twelve zodiacal "animal" signs. After sixty years one therefore has lived through every possible combination of this cycle

Hwat'u: (Kor) "flower contest" playing cards introduced from Japan in the nineteenth century. A pack has forty-eight colorful cards in twelve suits

Ianfu: (Jp) army prostitute, "comfort women," the sexual slaves of the Japanese military

Inari: (Jp) the Shintō deity of harvest and rice, usually represented by a fox as his messenger

Izakaya: (Jp) a traditional Japanese-style bar serving food and drinks

Jo-Chongryun: (Kor) women's group of the *Chongryun* organization

Juku: (Jp) a cram or prep school

Kāchan: (Jp) mother, "mom"

Kanji: (Jp) Chinese (Sino-Japanese) character

Kansaiki: (Jp) a carrier-borne aircraft

Katakana: (Jp) Japanese (square form) syllabary, mostly used to transcribe foreign words or for emphasis (like italics in alphabetical writing)

Kazoe-doshi: (Jp) "counted year," the traditional manner of reckoning one's age where newborns are considered a year old, and adding one year to the current age at New Year's

Kenpeitai: (Jp) regiment of military policemen

Kimchi: (Kor) pickled vegetable seasoned with garlic, red pepper, and ginger; Korea's national dish

Kimigayo-maru: (Jp) name of a ferry that connected Cheju Island with Ōsaka

Kisaeng: (Kor) a courtesan-entertainer; professional girls trained in music, dance, poetry, and conversation

Kohyang: (Kor) place of birth, hometown (province or village)

Kōji: (Jp) malt, leaven, yeast

Kokumin chōyō rei: (Jp) The National Manpower Mobilization Act (Imperial Edict No. 451 of July 8, 1939) facilitated the recruitment of Koreans to fill the labor shortage in Japan

Kokusaika: (Jp) internationalization

Kome: (Jp) (uncooked) rice

Komushin: (Kor) rubber shoes

Konban wa: (Jp) Good evening

Kongju: (Kor) princess

Konnichi wa: (Jp) Good afternoon

Kosaeng: (Kor) a hard life, privation, distress, adversity, hardships, suffering, toil, labor, pain. Written with the Chinese characters *ko* 苦 "bitter" and *saeng* 生 "life." The word's earliest attestation seems to come from the Buddhist text *Yompul pokwon mun* (1776)

Kotatsu: (Jp) a portable, low table with a heating lamp attached underneath and covered by a large quilt; used in winter to warm one's legs and lower body

Kŭn-abŏji: (Kor) the oldest paternal uncle. Traditionally, father's eldest brother is called "elder father" rather than uncle, since in absence of an elder, he assumes the senior position of the family

K'ŭn-nom: (Kor coll.) "big catch"

Kŭn-tŭl: (Kor coll.) gangster

Kurō: (Jp) troubles, hardships

Kŭs: (Jp) an elaborate exorcism ritual (usually in twelve stages) in an attempt to appease and make amends with the ancestors, gods, and spirits, in which the *mudang* (shaman) serves as an intermediary between the world of the living and the spirit's world

Kūshū: (Jp) air raid

Kūshū keihō: (Jp) air raid alarm

Kyohoe: (Kor) church

Kyōsei renkō: (Jp) "forced migration" to Japan for worker supply

Kyōsei rōdō: (Jp) forced labor

Makkŏlli: (Kor) Korean rice liquor

Mayak: (Kor) narcotics or drugs

Mikuk-nom tŭl: (Kor) derogatory word for Americans

Mindan: (Jp) short for *Cheilbon Taehan Min'guk Mindan* (The Korean Resident Association in Japan), organized on October 3, 1946, a year after *Choryŏn*, by anticommunists. Their primary interest was to promote the well-being of Korean residents

Minsei: (Jp) people's welfare or livelihood

Miso: (Jp) bean paste

Mizu-shōbai: (Jp) the "water trade," entertainment and night life businesses such as pubs, bars, or clubs

Monpe: (Jp) women's work pants

Mudang: (Kor) shaman, sorceress, a spirit medium

Muk: (Kor) jelly-like bean curd

Muljil: (Kor Cheju-do coll.) diving

Mushira: (Kor coll.) frightening, disgusting

Naishoku: (Jp) work received from factories to do at home. Women usually did such things as sewing for factories in order to earn extra wages

Namu myōhō renge-kyō: (Jp) "Glory to the Sutra of the Lotus of the Wonderful Dharma," an invocation mainly used in Nichiren-Buddhism

Na-no-hana: (jp) rape flowers

Nichiren-shū: (Jp) a Buddhist sect founded by the monk Nichiren (1222-1282) in 1253. Its doctrine is that of the Lotus Sutra "*Myōhō renge-kyō*," which contains the last instructions of Buddha

Nihon Kōkan: (Jp) Japan steel pipe company located in Kawasaki City

Nihon Seitetsu: (Jp) Japan iron and steel manufacture, formed in 1934 by fusing five smaller companies, which split after the war into Yahata-steel, Fuji-steel, etc. In 1970 the two aforementioned companies fused again to form *Shin-* ("new") *Nihon Seitetsu*

Nonbē: (Jp) heavy drinker, tippler

Nuka: (Jp) rice bran

Nukeru: (Jp) to fall or come out

Obā-chan: (Jp) grandmother, "granny"

O-bento: (Jp) box lunch

O-bon: (Jp) Buddhist festival (lantern fest) in midsummer for worshipping the souls of one's ancestors; the Buddhist All Souls' Day

Oe-halmang: (Kor coll.) Cheju-do dialect for maternal grandmother

Oe-harabang: (Kor coll.) Cheju-do dialect for maternal grandfather

Oeka: (Kor) mother's natal/maiden household

Oenom: (Kor) derogatory word for Japanese

Ojō-san: (Jp) young lady, honorific appellation for the daughter of someone else

Oku-san: (Jp) "Madam," a married lady, honorific appellation for the wife of someone else

Ŏmma: (Kor) mommy

Ŏmŏni: (Kor) mother

Onē-san: (Jp) older sister, Miss

Onī-san: (Jp) older brother

Ossan: (Jp) older man (derogative)

O-tsukare: (Jp) short for "*o-tsu-kare-sama desu*," "you are working hard." Often used among coworkers and acquaintances as greeting

Pachinko: (Jp) pinball machine/game

Paegŭp: (Kor) distribution, supply, rationing

Paeknyŏn tŭl: (Kor Cheju-do dial.) derogative for the Japanese

P'alcha: (Kor) destiny, fate, one's lot (lit. "eight characters"). It refers to the signs of the Chinese cyclical calendar that (written in pairs of two) form binomial designations for the year, month, day, and hour of birth of a person, which are supposed to have influence on one's fortune

Panjil panjil: (Kor) sleek, smooth, shiny

Pich'ang: (Kor) jackknife

Pin-dae: (Kor) bedbug

Pottaegi: (Kor coll.) Cheju-do dialect for sack

Pulhyoja: (Kor) an unfilial, impious child

Ryŏngmeng: (Kor) see *Choryŏn*

Samshin halmŏni: (Kor) domestic deity "old lady Samshin" embodies the spirits of fertility and protects children

Sanba: (Jp) midwife

Sat'uli: (Kor) dialect

Sazae: (Jp) turban shells

Senban: (Jp) a lathe

Sensō: (Jp) war

Sentō: (Jp) a public bathhouse

Shibori: (Jp) a small, wet towel (often hot) used to wipe one's hands before meals

Shika: (Kor) husband's household

Shinpang: (Kor) spirit chamber, shaman

Shokuminchi: (Jp) "colony," in this context often specifically meaning Korea under Japanese colonization (1910-1945)

Shōmeisho: (Jp) identification certificate, ID card or letter

Shōwa: (Jp) era name of Emperor Hirohito's reign (1926-1989)

Sōka gakkai: (Jp) "Society for the Creation of Values"; a Buddhist lay organization rooted in Nichiren-Buddhism and affiliated with the political party *Kōmeito*

Sokai: (Jp) evacuation, dispersal (e.g., during a war)

Sŏpsŏp'he: (Kor) (to be) sad, sorry, disappointed; regrettable

Sōshi kaimei: (Jp) "family name change." Based on a revision of the Korean civil law in November 1939, Koreans had to adopt a Japanese family name as well as

Japanese-sounding first name

Sŏtang: (Kor) private schools for primary education consisting of Chinese classics; a venue where boys of *yangban* class were prepared for the government service examination

Ssuk: (Kor) sagebrush

Sumi-komi: (Jp) a live-in facility with board and lodging at or near the working place

Taishō: (Jp) era name of Emperor Yoshihito's reign (1912-1926)

Tatami: (Jp) straw mats, used as floor coverings

Teishintai: (Jp) "volunteer corps," including military comfort women (sex slaves) serving Japanese soldiers overseas

Tōfu: (Jp) bean curd

Tojang: (Kor) signature seal

Tonari-gumi-chō: (Jp) head of a local level neighborhood association. These ten-household associations operated as self-monitoring agencies responsible to the central government. They were responsible for the distribution of rations, civil defense, circulation of official literature, and the identification of dissidents and spies

Tongchi sŏttal: (Kor) eleventh lunar month

Tongsŏ: (Kor) Husband's brother's wife

Tsuruhashi: (Jp) A district in Ōsaka famous for selling Korean food and items, with a large Korean population

Udon: (Jp) thick wheat noodles

Ŭm-ryŏk: (Kor) lunar calendar

Uri hakkyo: (Kor) "our school"

Uri saram: (Kor) "our people" (i.e., Koreans)

Wara-zōri: (Jp) straw sandals

Washi: (Jp) Japanese long-fibered paper with high rag content

Won: (Kor) Korean monetary unit

Yagakkō: (Jp) an evening school, a night school

Yakiniku: (Jp) "grilled meat"; Korean-style barbecue that has gained enormous popularity as one of the first "ethnic" food trends in Japan

Yakuza: (Jp) a gangster or hoodlum, general term for Japanese organized crime syndicates

Yaman: (Kor) savage, barbarous

Yami-bune: (Jp) illegal boat

Yangban: (Kor) a lineage-based aristocratic elite that prided themselves with being exemplars of Confucian social virtues. Members of this privileged noble class were educated in the Chinese classics and eligible to sit for the civil service examination as well as hold high public offices

Yangryŏk: (Kor) solar calendar

Yangt'ae: (Kor) the brim of a traditional black top hat, worn in former times by Korean men

Yen: (Jp) Japanese monetary unit

Yi Dynasty: (Kor) other name for Chosŏn Dynasty (1392-1910), the longest-lived imperial dynasty in Korea. During this period neo-Confucian ideology enforced by the dominant aristocratic *yangban* class promulgated strict political and social principles within society

Yŏlch'a: (Kor) train

Yukata: (Jp) light summer kimono

Yukchi: (Kor) mainland, land

Zainichi: (Jp) lit. "residing in Japan"; used with the intent to specify the type of foreigner living in Japan. When used as a stand-alone term it usually refers to prewar immigrant Koreans and their descendants who have been living in Japan since then

Zōri: (Jp) Japanese straw sandals

References

Amato, Joseph A. 1990. *Victims and Values: A History and a Theory of Suffering.* New York: Greenwood Press.

Antze, Paul, and Michael Lambek, eds. 1996. *Tense Past: Cultural Essays in Trauma and Memory.* New York: Routledge.

Aptheker, Bettina. 1989. *Tapestries of Life: Women's Work, Women's Consciousness, and the Meaning of Daily Experience.* Amherst: University of Massachusetts Press.

Berger, Peter L., and Thomas Luckmann. 1991. *The Social Construction of Reality: A Treatise in the Sociology of Knowledge.* [1966] London: Penguin.

Bertaux, Daniel, ed. 1981. *Biography and Society: The Life History Approach in the Social Sciences.* Beverly Hills, Calif.: Sage Publications.

Billson, Janet Mancini. 1995. *Keepers of the Culture: The Power of Tradition in Women's Lives.* New York: Lexington Books.

Burgos-Debray, Elisabeth. 1984. *I, Rigoberta Menchú, an Indian Woman in Guatemala.* London: Verso.

Burr, Vivien. 1995. *An Introduction to Social Constructionism.* London: Routledge.

Buruma, Ian. 1984a. "A Love-Hate Fuse Smolders beneath Japan's Korea Boom." *Far Eastern Economic Review* (29 November 1984): 51.

———. 1984b. "The Pride and Prejudice Sapping Roots Old and New." *Far Eastern Economic Review* (29 November 1984): 52-53.

Cha, Jae-Ho, Bom-Mo Chung, and Sung-Jin Lee. 1977. "Boy Preference Reflected in Korean Folklore." Pp. 113-126 in *Virtues in Conflict: Tradition and the Korean Woman Today*, edited by Sandra Mattielli. Seoul: Royal Asiatic Society Korea Branch, Samhwa Publ.

Chai, Alice, Y. 1996. "Picture Brides: Feminist Analysis of Life Histories of Hawaii's Early Immigrant Women from Japan, Okinawa, and Korea." *Asian Journal of Women's Studies* 2 (1996): 38-69.

Cho, Haejoang. 1983. "The Autonomous Women: Divers on Cheju Island." Pp. 81-96 in *Korean Women: View from the Inner Room*, edited by Laurel Kendall and Mark Peterson. New Haven, Conn.: East Rock Press.

Choi, Chungmoo, ed. 1997. *Positions Special Issue: The Comfort Women: Colonialism, War, and Sex.* Durham, N. C.: Duke University Press.

Chōsen-jōsei to rentai suru Niigata fujin no kai hen. 1982. *Niigata no Chōsen-jin ŏmŏnitachi* (Niigata's Korean Mothers). Niigata: Fujin no kai.

Clifford, James, and George Marcus, eds. 1986. *Writing Culture: The Poetics and Politics of Ethnography.* Berkeley: University of California Press.

Clifford, Mark. 1991. "Rusting Links: Support for Pro-North Korean Wanes." *Far Eastern Economic Review* (21 February 1991): 20.

Collins, Alan F., et al. 1993. *Theories of Memory.* Hillsdale, N. J.: Lawrence Erlbaum Associates.

Connerton, Paul. 1989. *How Societies Remember.* Cambridge: Cambridge University Press.

Conway, Martin A. 1990. *Autobiographical Memory: An Introduction.* Philadelphia: Open University Press.

Crapanzano, Vincent. 1986. "Hermes's Dilemma." Pp. 51-76 in *Writing Culture: The Poetics and Politics of Ethnography,* edited by James Clifford and George Marcus. Berkeley: University of California Press.

Cruikshank, Julie. 1990. *Life Lived Like a Story: Life Stories of Three Yukon Native Elders.* Lincoln: University of Nebraska Press.

Cumings, Bruce. 1981. *The Origins of the Korean War: Liberation and the Emergence of Separate Regimes, 1945-1947.* Princeton, N. J.: Princeton University Press.

Das, Veena. 1997. "Language and Body: Transactions in the Construction of Pain." Pp. 67-92 in *Social Suffering,* edited by Arthur Kleinman, Veena Das, and Margaret Lock. Berkeley: University of California Press.

Deuchler, Martina. 1977. "The Tradition: Women during the Yi Dynasty." Pp. 1-48 in *Virtues in Conflict: Tradition and the Korean Woman Today,* edited by Sandra Mattielli. Seoul: Royal Asiatic Society Korea Branch, Samhwa Publ.

———. 1983. Preface. Pp. 1-4 in *Korean Women: View from the Inner Room,* edited by Laurel Kendall and Mark Peterson. New Haven, Conn.: East Rock Press.

DeVos, George, and Changsoo Lee. 1981. "The Colonial Experience, 1910-1945." Pp. 31-57 in *Koreans in Japan: Ethnic Conflict and Accommodation,* edited by Changsoo Lee and George DeVos. Berkeley: University of California Press.

DeVos, George, and Daekyun Chung. 1981. "Community Life in a Korean Ghetto." Pp. 225-251 in *Koreans in Japan: Ethnic Conflict and Accommodation,* edited by Changsoo Lee and George DeVos. Berkeley: University of California Press.

DeVos, George, and Hiroshi Wagatsuma. 1972. *Japan's Invisible Race: Caste in Culture and Personality.* [rev. ed.] Berkeley: University of California Press.

Frankl, Victor Emil. 1963. *Man's Search for Meaning: An Introduction to Logotherapy.* New York: Pocket Books.

Fukuoka, Yasunori. 1993. *Zainichi Kankoku-/Chōsen-jin: wakai sedai no aidentiti* (Korean Residents in Japan: The Younger Generation's Identity). Tōkyō: Chūō-kōron sha.

———. 2000. *Lives of Young Koreans in Japan.* Melbourne: Trans Pacific Press.

Hardacre, Helen. 1984. *The Religion of Japan's Korean Minority: The Preservation of Ethic Identity.* Berkeley: University of California.

Harvey, Youngsook Kim. 1979. *Six Korean Women: The Socialization of Shamans.* St. Paul: West Publishing.

Hayashi, Eidai. 1989. *Kesareta chōsenjin kyōseirenkō no kiroku* (The Obliterated Record of the Forced Recruitment of Koreans). Tōkyō: Akashi-shoten.

✗―――. 1991. *Shōgen: Karafuto chōsenjin gyakusatsu jiken* (Testimonies: Massacre of Koreans in Sakhalin). Nagoya: Fūbaisha.

✗―――. 1994. *Chizu ni nai arirantōge: Kyōseirenkō no ashiato o tadoru tabi* (The Arirang Hill That Cannot Be Found in the Map: Pilgrimage to Follow the Route of the Forced Recruitment). Tōkyō: Akashi-shoten.

✗ Hayes, Carol. 2000. "Cultural Identity in the Work of Yi Yang-ji." Pp. 119-139 in *Koreans in Japan: Critical Voices from the Margin,* edited by Sonia Ryang. London: Routledge.

✗ Hicks, George. 1997. *Japan's Hidden Apartheid: The Korean Minority and the Japanese.* Aldershot, UK: Ashgate.

Honda, Katsuichi. 1981. *Chūgoku no tabi* (A Journey to China). Tōkyō: Asahishinbunsha.

―――. 1993. *Ainu minzoku* (The Ainu Nation). Tōkyō: Asahishinbunsha.

―――. 1999. *Nanjing Massacre: A Japanese Journalist Confronts Japan's National Shame.* Armonk, N.Y.: M.E. Sharpe.

Honda, Yasuharu. 1992. *Watashi-tachi no ŏmŏni* (Our Mothers). Tōkyō: Shinchō sha.

Hurh, Won Moo, and Kwang Chung Kim. 1984. *Korean Immigrants in America: A Structural Analysis of Ethnic Confinement and Adhesive Adaptation.* Rutherford, N. J.: Fairleigh Dickinson University Press.

✗ Inokuchi, Hiromitsu. 2000. "Korean Ethnic Schools in Occupied Japan, 1945-1952." Pp. 140-156 in *Koreans in Japan: Critical Voices from the Margin,* edited by Sonia Ryang. London: Routledge.

Izumi, Seiichi. 1966. *Seishūtō (Chejudo).* Tōkyō: University of Tōkyō Publication Association.

Janelli, Roger L., and Dawnhee Yim Janelli. 1982. *Ancestor Worship and Korean Society.* Stanford, Calif.: Stanford University Press.

Japan Times. 1993. "Japan and Korea: Looking to the Future," 28 November 1993.

―――. 1996. "Give National Pensions to Koreans, Lawyers Say," 28 February 1996.

Kashiwazaki, Chikako. 2000. "The Politics of Legal Status: The Equation of Nationality with Ethnonational Identity." Pp. 13-31 in *Koreans in Japan: Critical Voices from the Margin,* edited by Sonia Ryang. London: Routledge.

Kendall, Laurel. 1985. *Shamans, Housewives, and Other Restless Spirits: Women in Korean Ritual Life.* Honolulu: University of Hawaii Press.

―――. 1988. *The Life and Hard Times of a Korean Shaman: Of Tales and the Telling of Tales.* Honolulu: University of Hawaii Press.

―――. 1996. *Getting Married in Korea: Of Gender, Morality, and Modernity.* Berkeley: University of California Press.

Kendall, Laurel, and Griffin Dix, eds. 1987. *Religion and Ritual in Korean Society.* Berkeley: University of California.

Kendall, Laurel, and Mark Peterson, eds. 1983. *Korean Women: View from the Inner Room.* New Haven, Conn.: East Rock Press.

―――. 1983a. "Introduction: 'Traditional Korean Women'―A Reconsideration." Pp. 5-22 in *Korean Women: View from the Inner Room,* edited by Laurel Kendall and Mark Peterson. New Haven, Conn.: East Rock Press.

Kim, Bu-ja, et al. 1995. *Motto shiritai "ianfu" mondai: Sei to minzoku no shiten kara* (We'd Like to Know More About the "Comfort Women" Issue: Seen from Gender and Nation). Tōkyō: Akashi-shoten.

✗ Kim, Chanjŏn. 1997. *Zainichi Korian hyakunen-shi* (100-Years History of the Korean Residents in Japan). Tōkyō: Sangokan.

✗ Kim, Chanjŏn, and Senki Hŏ. 1977. *Kaze no dōkoku: Zainichi Chōsen-jin jokō no seikatsu to rekishi* (Wailing Wind: Lives and Histories of Korean Female Factory

Workers Residing in Japan). Tōkyō: Tabata shōten.

Kim, Yŏng-dal. 1996. "Hoshō: Kaisetsu to tōkei no hosoku (A Supplement with Additional Explanation and Statistics)." Pp. 149-183 in Morita Yoshio, *Sūji ga kataru zainichi kankoku chōsenjin no rekishi* (History of Koreans in Japan Seen from Statistics). Tōkyō: Akashi-shoten.

Kim, Yung-Chung, ed. and trans. 1977. *Women of Korea: A History from Ancient Times to 1945.* Seoul: Ewha Woman's University Press.

Kleinman, Arthur, and Joan Kleinman. 1997. "The Appeal of Experience; The Dismay of Images: Cultural Appropriations of Suffering in Our Times." Pp. 1-24 in *Social Suffering*, edited by Arthur Kleinman, Veena Das, and Margaret Lock. Berkeley: University of California Press.

Kleinman, Arthur, Veena Das, and Margaret Lock, ed. 1997. *Social Suffering.* Berkeley: University of California Press.

Koshiro, Yukiko. 1999. *Transpacific Racism and the US Occupation of Japan.* New York: Columbia University Press.

Krause, Corinne Azen. 1991. *Grandmothers, Mothers, and Daughters: Oral History of Three Generations of Ethnic American Women.* Boston: Twayne Publishers.

Kurahashi, Masanao. 1994. *Jūgun ianfu mondai no rekishiteki kenkyū* (A Historical Study of the Military Comfort Women Issue). Tōkyō: Kyōei-shobō.

Lee, Changsoo. 1981a. "The Period of Repatriation, 1945-1949." Pp. 58-72 in *Koreans in Japan: Ethnic Conflict and Accommodation*, edited by Changsoo Lee and George DeVos. Berkeley: University of California Press.

———. 1981b. "Koreans under SCAP: An Era of Unrest and Repression." Pp. 73-90 in *Koreans in Japan: Ethnic Conflict and Accommodation*, edited by Changsoo Lee and George DeVos. Berkeley: University of California Press.

———. 1981c. "The Politics of Repatriation." Pp. 91-109 in *Koreans in Japan: Ethnic Conflict and Accommodation*, edited by Changsoo Lee and George DeVos. Berkeley: University of California Press.

———. 1981d. "Organizational Division and Conflict: Ch'ongnyŏn and Mindan." Pp. 110-130 in *Koreans in Japan: Ethnic Conflict and Accommodation*, edited by Changsoo Lee and George DeVos. Berkeley: University of California Press.

———. 1981e. "The Legal Status of Koreans in Japan." Pp. 133-158 in *Koreans in Japan: Ethnic Conflict and Accommodation*, edited by Changsoo Lee and George DeVos. Berkeley: University of California Press.

———. 1981f. "Ethnic Education and National Politics." Pp. 159-181 in *Koreans in Japan: Ethnic Conflict and Accommodation*, edited by Changsoo Lee and George DeVos. Berkeley: University of California Press.

Lee, Changsoo, and George DeVos, eds. 1981. *Koreans in Japan: Ethnic Conflict and Accommodation.* Berkeley: University of California Press.

Lee, Hwain Chang. 1994. *Confucius, Christ and Co-partnership: Competing Liturgies for the Soul of Korean American Women.* Lanham, Md.: University Press of America.

Lee, Ki-baik. 1984. *A New History of Korea* [trans. by Edward W. Wagner with Edward J. Shultz]. Cambridge, Mass.: Harvard University Press; Seoul: Ilchokak.

Lie, John. 2000. "Imaginary Homeland and Diasporic Realization: *Kikan Sanzenri, 1975-1981*," *Korean and Korean American Studies Bulletin* 11, no. 1 (2000): 11-26.

Maanen, John van. 1988. *Tales of the Field: On Writing Ethnography.* Chicago: University of Chicago Press.

Maher, John C., and Gaynor MacDonald, eds. 1995. *Diversity in Japanese Culture and Language.* London: Kegan Paul International.

Mattielli, Sandra, ed. 1977. *Virtues in Conflict: Tradition and the Korean Woman Today*. Seoul: Royal Asiatic Society Korea Branch, Samhwa Publ.

McCormack, Gravan, ed., and Kang Ok Su, trans. 1981. *Twice Victims: Koreans at Hiroshima*. [n. p.]: The Korean Peace Committee in Japan.

Mintz, Sidney. 1974. *Worker in the Cane: A Puerto Rican Life History*. New York: Norton.

Morita, Yoshio. 1996. *Sūji ga kataru zainichi kankoku chōsenjin no rekishi* (History of Koreans in Japan Seen from Statistics). Tōkyō: Akashi-shoten.

Mukuge no kai hen. 1972. *Shinse tāryon: Zainichi Chōsen josei no hansei* (Lamentation: Half a Lifetime of a Korean Woman Residing in Japan). Tōkyō: Tōto-shobō.

Nishino, Rumiko. 1992. *Jūgun ianfu: Moto heishi-tachi no shōgen* (Military Comfort Women: Testimonies of Former Soldiers). Tōkyō: Akashi-shoten.

Oguri, Keitaro. 1990. "Resident Koreans Are Native Speakers Too." *Japan Quarterly* 37, no. 4 (October-December 1990): 424-431.

Okely, Judith, and Helen Calloway, eds. 1992. *Anthropology and Autobiography*. London: Routledge.

Ōsaka-shi gaikoku-jin kyōiku kenkyū kyōkai. 1992. *Fureai no machi Ōsaka: zainichi gaikoku-jin to tomo ni ikiru* (Ōsaka, a City of Contact: Living Together with Foreign Residents in Japan). Ōsaka: Ōsaka-shi jinken keihatsu suishin kyōgikai.

Pak, Kyŏng-sik. 1965. *Chōsenjin kyōseirenkō no kiroku* (The Record of the Forced Recruitment of Koreans). Tōkyō: Miraisha.

——. 1992. *Zainichi chōsenjin, kyōseirenkō, minzokumondai* (Koreans in Japan, Forced Recruitment, National Problem). Tōkyō: San'ichi-shobō.

Pak, Kyŏng-sik, Shōji Yamada, and T'ae-ho Yang, eds. 1993. *Chōsenjin kyōseirenkō ronbunshūsei* (Collected Essays on the Forced Recruitment of Koreans). Tōkyō: Akashi-shoten.

Pak, Su-nam. 1982. *Mō hitotsu no Hiroshima: Chōsenjin kankokujin hibakusha no shōgen* (Another Hiroshima: Testimonies of Korean A-bomb Victims). Tōkyō: Sarang-pang shuppanbu.

Personal Narratives Group, ed. 1989. *Interpreting Women's Lives: Feminist Theory and Personal Narratives*. Bloomington: Indiana University Press.

Peterson, Mark. 1983. "Women without Sons: A Measure of Social Change in Yi Dynasty Korea." Pp. 33-44 in *Korean Women: View from the Inner Room*, edited by Laurel Kendall and Mark Peterson. New Haven, Conn.: East Rock Press.

Research/Action Institute for Koreans in Japan. 1990. *Japan's Subtle Apartheid: The Korean Minority Now*. Tōkyō: RAIK.

Rhodes, Daisy Chun. 1998. *Passages to Paradise: Early Korean Immigrant Narratives from Hawaii*. Los Angeles: Keimyung University Press.

Ro, Seong-Og. 1996. *Mugunghwa: Mō hitotsu no josei no issei* (Rose of Sharon: The Life of One More Woman). [n. p.]: Yamanami kikaku.

Romero, Patricia, W., ed. 1988. *Life Histories of African Women*. London: Ashfield Press.

Ross, Bruce M. 1991. *Remembering the Personal Past: Descriptions of Autobiographical Memory*. New York: Oxford University Press.

Ryang, Sonia. 1997. *North Koreans in Japan: Language, Ideology, and Identity*. Boulder, Colo.: Westview Press.

——. 1998a. "Inscribed (Men's) Bodies, Silenced (Women's) Words: Rethinking Colonial Displacement of Koreans in Japan." *Bulletin of Concerned Asian Scholars* 30, no. 4 (October 1998): 3-15.

——. 1998b. "Nationalist Inclusion or Emancipatory Identity? North Korean Women in Japan." *Women's Studies International Forum* 21, no. 6 (1998): 581-597.

———, ed. 2000a. *Koreans in Japan: Critical Voices from the Margin*. London: Routledge.

———. 2000b. "The North Korean Homeland of Koreans in Japan." Pp. 32-54 in *Koreans in Japan: Critical Voices from the Margin*, edited by Sonia Ryang. London: Routledge.

———. 2001. "Ethnography of Self-Cultural Anthropology? Reflections on 'Writing About Ourselves,'" *Dialectical Anthropology* 25, nos. 3/4 (2001): 297-320.

———. 2003. "Impacts of the Abduction News on Chongryun Koreans." No. 3 in *Significance of Koizumi's Visit to North Korea*, Online Monograph Series edited by Yone Sugita. Tōkyō: Architect Press, <www.smallworld.co.jp>.

———. (in preparation). "On Diaspora and My Grandmother: A Note on Gender-Specific Experience of Homelessness among Koreans in Japan."

Shim, Jae Hoon. 1990. "Fingertip Diplomacy." *Far Eastern Economic Review* (17 May 1990): 15.

Shin, Gi-Wook, and Michael Robinson, eds. 1999. *Colonial Modernity in Korea*. Cambridge, Mass.: Harvard University Press.

Shostak, Marjory. 1981. *Nisa, the Life and Words of a !Kung Woman*. Cambridge, Mass.: Harvard University Press.

Shōya, Reiko, and Tōru Nakayama. 1997. *Kōrei zainichi Kankoku- Chōsen-jin: Ōsaka ni okeru "zainichi' no seikatsu-kōzō to Kōrei-fukushi no kadai* (Old-Age Korean Residents in Japan: The Subjects of Livelihood Structure and Old-Age Welfare for Foreign Residents in Ōsaka). Tōkyō: Ochanomizu shobō.

Song, Young I. 1996. *Battered Women in Korean Immigrant Families: The Silent Scream*. New York: Garland.

Sorensen, Clark. 1983. "Women, Men, Inside, Outside: The Division of Labor in Rural Central Korea." Pp. 63-80 in *Korean Women: View from the Inner Room*, edited by Laurel Kendall and Mark Peterson. New Haven, Conn.: East Rock Press.

Stoll, David. 1999. *Rigoberta Menchú and the Story of All Poor Guatemalans*. Boulder, Colo.: Westview Press.

Suh, Kyungsik. 2003. "Japan through the Eyes of a 'Quasi-Refugee,'" *Japan Focus*. <http://japanfocus.org/077.html>.

Suzuki, Yūko. 1993. *"Jūgun ianfu" mondai to seibōryoku* (The "Comfort Women" Issue and Sexual Violence). Tōkyō: Miraisha.

———. 1996. *"Ianfu" mondai to sengosekinin* (The "Comfort Women" Issue and War Responsibility). Tōkyō: Miraisha.

Takagi, Ken'ichi. 1987. *Machiwabiru harumoni-tachi: Saharin ni nokosareta kankokujin to rusu kazoku* (The Endlessly Waiting Grandmothers: The Koreans Left Behind in Sakhalin and Their Absent Families). Tōkyō: Nashinoki-sha.

———. 1990. *Saharin to nihon no sensōsekinin* (Sakhalin and Japan's War Responsibility). Tōkyō: Gaifūsha.

Tanaka, Yuki. 2002. *Japan's Comfort Women: Sexual Slavery and Prostitution During World War II and the US Occupation*. London : Routledge.

Tedeschi, Richard G., and Lawrence G. Calhoun. 1995. *Trauma and Transformation: Growing in the Aftermath of Suffering*. Thousand Oaks, Calif.: Sage Publications.

Thompson, Paul. 1988. *The Voice of the Past: Oral History*. (2d ed.) Oxford: Oxford University Press.

Tieszen, Helen Rose. 1977. "Korean Proverbs about Women." Pp. 49-66 in *Virtues in Conflict: Tradition and the Korean Woman Today*, edited by Sandra Mattielli. Seoul: Royal Asiatic Society Korea Branch, Samhwa Publ.

Tonkin, Elizabeth. 1992. *Narrating Our Pasts: The Social Construction of Oral History*.

Cambridge: Cambridge University Press.

Wagner, Edward. 1951. *The Korean Minority in Japan: 1904-1950.* New York: Institute of Pacific Relations.

Wagner-Martin, Linda. 1994. *Telling Women's Lives: The New Biography.* New Brunswick, N. J.: Rutgers University Press.

Weiner, Michael. 1989. *The Origins of the Korean Community in Japan, 1910-1923.* Atlantic Highlands, N.J.: Humanities Press.

———. 1994. *Race and Migration in Imperial Japan.* London: Routledge.

———. 1997. "The Representation of Absence and the Absence of Representation: Korean Victims of the Atomic Bomb." Pp. 79-107 in *Japan's Minorities: The Illusion of Homogeneity*, edited by Michael Weiner. London: Routledge.

Wender, Melissa. 2000. "Fleshly Inscriptions of History: Yi Yang-ji's *Koku*." *Korean and Korean American Studies Bulletin* 11, no. 1 (2000): 27-47.

Yamada, Meiko. 1991. *Ianfutachi no taiheiyōsensō* (The Pacific War of Comfort Women). Tōkyō: Kōjinsha.

Yamagiwa, Hiroshi. 1995. "Korean Residents See Unity Here as Common Goal: Unification, Unity Urged by the Protector of Compatriots' Remains." *Japan Times*, 8 November 1995.

———. 1996a. "More Playing the Name Game: Korean-Japanese Challenge Ethnic Exclusiveness." *Japan Times*, 28 February 1996.

———. 1996b. "Korean Schools Weigh Ethnic-Identity Cost." *Japan Times*, 20 November 1996.

———. 1996c. "Mindan, Chongryun Keep up Cold War." *Japan Times*, 22 November 1996.

Yang, Hyunah. 1998. "Re-membering the Korean Military Comfort Women: Nationalism, Sexuality, and Silencing." Pp. 123-139 in *Dangerous Women: Gender and Korean Nationalism*, edited by Elain H. Kim and Chungmoo Choi. Berkeley: University of California Press.

Yoon, Soon-Young. 1977. "Occupation, Male Housekeeper: Male-Female Roles on Cheju Island." Pp. 191-207 in *Virtues in Conflict: Tradition and the Korean Woman Today*, edited by Sandra Mattielli. Seoul: Royal Asiatic Society Korea Branch, Samhwa Publ.

Yoshida, Reiji. 1993. "Korea Town Plan Pushed: Kawasaki Group Work to Build Youth Awareness." *Japan Times*, 4 December 1993.

Yoshitome, Roju. 1980. *Aigo! Murŭl tarla! Hiroshima, Nagasaki hibaku chōsenjin no 35-nen* (Give Me Water, Please! 35 Years of Korean A-bomb Victims in Hiroshima and Nagasaki). Tōkyō: Nigatsu-sha.

Young, Allan. 1997. "Suffering and the Origins of Traumatic Memory." Pp. 245-260 in *Social Suffering*, edited by Arthur Kleinman, Veena Das, and Margaret Lock. Berkeley: University of California Press.

Yu, Eui Young, and Earl H. Phillips, eds. 1987. *Korean Women in Transition: At Home and Abroad.* Los Angeles: Center for Korean-American and Korean Studies, California State University.

Yun, Jŏng-Ok, et al. 1992. *Chōsenjin josei ga mita "ianfu mondai"* (The "Comfort Women" Issue Seen by Korean Women). Tōkyō: Sanichi-shobō.

Index

About the Author

Jackie J. Kim received a B.A. in journalism from the University of Hawaii. After living in Niigata, a northern prefecture in Japan, for three years through the JET Program, she completed an M.A. in Asian Studies at the Institute for Comparative Culture of Sophia University in Tōkyō, Japan. She also was a visiting researcher for two years at the University of Tōkyō and did fieldwork in an ethnic Korean community in Yanji, a city near the North Korean border in Jilin province, China.

Currently, she is an advocate for a nonprofit organization, helping immigrant women better adjust to their new environment through education and assistance as well as implementing awareness of social aid and resources in resisting domestic violence.

She is now writing her second book, titled *Songs of Redemption*, which traces the history of the women in her family during the period of Christian missionaries in Korea in the late nineteenth century, the Japanese colonial experience, the Korean War, and the subsequent immigration to the United States.